D1531404

INDIVIDUALS
IN
RELATIONSHIPS

UNDERSTANDING RELATIONSHIP PROCESSES

Series Editor
Steve Duck, *University of Iowa*

This series of books on the theme **Understanding Relationship Processes** provides a coherent and progressive review of current thinking in the field. Uniquely organized around the notion of relational competence, the six volumes constitute a contemporary, multidisciplinary handbook of relationship research for advanced students and professionals in psychology, sociology, communication, family studies, and education.

Volumes in the Series

EDITED BY
STEVE DUCK

INDIVIDUALS IN RELATIONSHIPS

UNDERSTANDING RELATIONSHIP PROCESSES SERIES
VOLUME 1

SAGE Publications
International Educational and Professional Publisher
Newbury Park   London   New Delhi

For information address:

 SAGE Publications, Inc.
2455 Teller Road
Newbury Park, California 91320

SAGE Publications Ltd.
6 Bonhill Street
London EC2A 4PU
United Kingdom

SAGE Publications India Pvt. Ltd.
M-32 Market
Greater Kailash I
New Delhi 110 048 India

Printed in the United States of America

Library of Congress Cataloging-in-Publication Data

Main entry under title:
  Individuals in relationships / [edited by] Steve Duck.
      p. cm. – (Understanding Relationship Processes Series: v. 1)
    Includes bibliographical references (pp. 207-233) and index.
    ISBN 0-8039-5156-6 (cloth)
    1. Interpersonal relations.   2. Interpersonal communication.
  I. Title.   II. Series.
  HM132.D8194   1993
  302–dc20   93-16819

93 94 95 96 10 9 8 7 6 5 4 3 2 1

Sage Production Editor: Diane S. Foster

Contents

Series Preface

This short series **Understanding Relationship Processes** attends to recent calls for an attention to process in relationships. A close look at the nature of processes in relationships will reveal that, over and above the importance of change, temporality, and an orientation to the future, beneath most process thinking on relationships lies the implicit notion of competent use of knowledge across time. For example, this assumption is true of many elements of the work on relationships, such as the (competent) transition to marriage, (skilled) conflict management, (appropriate) self-disclosure in relationship development, and (orderly) organization or (satisfactory) maintenance of relationships diachronically. The assumption also is contained in discussion of intimacy assessment of couple creation (by which authors evaluate the degrees of intimacy or progress that are adequate, allowable, suitable, or competent) and is latent in discussion of relationship breakdown where discussions treat breakdown as failure or incompetence, contrasted with skill or competence.

Such competence is evident in, and constrained by, a variety of levels of influence on behavior. In focusing on some of these topics, this series moves conceptually outward; that is, the series begins with the contributions of individuals and their developmental experiences to relationships, and moves toward the social context and interpersonal interaction. Individuals bring into relationships their individual characteristics and factors that reflect their point in the life cycle and their developmental achievements. Individuals are influenced by the social setting (situational, cultural, linguistic, and societal) in which the relationship takes place; they are constrained and influenced by the structural, transactional, behavioral, and communicative contexts for their relationships; and they sometimes conduct the relationships in dysfunctional environments or disrupted emotional contexts. The series takes the contextual themes in sequence and deals with the latest research and thinking that address these topics.

Accordingly, each volume focuses on a particular context or arena for relationship activity. The first three volumes of the series deal respectively with the following topics:

Individuals in Relationships. Volume 1 deals particularly with the ways internal or intrapersonal context is provided by structures of the mind or of knowledge that are prerequisite for success in relationships; however, rather than focusing on such things as if they were the end of the story, the chapters place such knowledge styles and structures in context by referring frequently to behavioral effects of such structures.

Learning About Relationships. Volume 2 covers especially the skills and experiences in childhood that lay the groundwork for competence as a properly functioning relater in adult life; the volume emphasizes the wide range of social sources from which development of competence is derived and the richness of the social sources from which developing minds acquire their sense of relationship competence.

Social Contexts and Relationships. Volume 3 focuses especially on the social structural constraints within which relationships are located and the ways the two partners must negotiate and deal with the dialectical and interior pressures created by such contexts. Other volumes in the series deal with the dynamics of relational transactions, overlooked elements of relating, and challenging contexts for relating.

STEVE DUCK

Volume Preface

This first volume in the Sage series **Understanding Relationship Process** begins with the individuals and the individual minds that come to any relationship. In this respect it launches itself from the older traditions in the field and uses them as a starting point; it looks at one mind in a social setting as it deals with social information rather than at two interacting and communicating individuals. However, authors were encouraged to go beyond such older traditions and to show how they relate to the newer developments in the field in terms of process thinking. Such an analytic focus is somewhat artificial even though much good work has been done on the mental structures that individuals bring to relationships. Nevertheless, by employing the notion of competence that lurks beneath any discussion of knowledge, this volume ties into the theme of the series and shows ways to make the individual level of analysis connect with the dyadic or relational level.

For two persons to interact competently with each other, they must each have an appropriate knowledge base both of "relationships" and of each other and also of appropriate ways to construe relationships. Such constructions, whether competent or not, affect the expectations and interaction patterns that the individuals bring to future relationships. For their interactions to succeed in laying the basis for a relationship, the two partners individually must know something about interaction, the rules to be followed, the appropriate ways to develop intimacy, the best means to interpret incoming social information, and strategies for tying it all together meaningfully. Thus, although this book starts the series with an individual focus, it is an important way to lead the series outward and upward to a dyadic level of analysis.

Accordingly this volume (closely tied to, and published with, Volume 2) deals with the mental structures that individuals bring to relationships, ranging from their thought processes and factors that influence those, to the ways they recall and remember relationship events or treat and manipulate relationally relevant information. Such factors include their individual cognitive abilities, the prototypes that they hold of relationships, the beliefs about relationships that individuals endorse, the everyday language structures that persons typically use in entering or conducting relationships, and the plans that they create to smooth the interactional path. The guiding questions for authors here were: What knowledge or information must a person have before relationships become a possibility? What schematic knowledge, strategic ability, planning, or interpretive skills are presumed when we begin to discuss the individual in relationship to others? Authors were asked to deal carefully with their own research area (but not only their own research) from this standpoint and to provide an integrated guide to the individual processes necessary to, and presumed in, discussions of relationships.

Peter Andersen leads off the book with a consideration of the schematic knowledge structures that individuals take with them into any dyadic relationship. His focus on *meaning* provides the launching pad for discussion of relationships as combined products and producers of interpersonal interaction and the cognition of interactants. By exploring several kinds of relational schemata (cultural, self, situation, state, interpersonal, and relational), Andersen demonstrates the diversity of ways people use to think about their relationships and the ways such thoughts drive action.

In some ways conceptually following from this approach, Charles Berger, in Chapter 2, considers the area of planning and illuminates the relation among individuals' plans and planning processes, dyadic communication activity, and the formation of relationships. This approach is based on the exploration of cognitive representations of desired end states for relationships and the mental representation of action sequences that may be used to achieve goals. Several important issues related to level of analysis are discussed in the chapter, but the emphasis is on the ways in which plans for action drive behavior.

In Chapter 3, James Honeycutt also notes the effects of individuals' cognition on behavior and then focuses specifically on the ways in which persons organize cognition about relational change, whether positive (growth) or negative (decline). Through an exploration of organization of cognition into memory organization packets (MOPs), Honeycutt casts light on a number of processes in relationships and reconceptualizes the nature of *phases* in relationships in a new and exciting way. In essence he argues that the phases of relationships are in the eye of the beholder rather than in the phenomena, and he uses this argument as an explanation for results that previously have puzzled students of phases in relationships.

Love is also in the eye (or heart) of the beholder according to some, yet in Chapter 4 Beverley Fehr argues convincingly that it is also in one's prototypes of the experience. She reviews work on the layperson's knowledge of categories for love and related concepts and provides a thorough review of a convincing program of research into the issues. She concludes that relational competence may depend, in part, on knowledge about the application of different methods of processing information and offers several new avenues for further work. Once again the emphasis is on exploration of the knowledge on which people base their actions and the ways in which such knowledge is used and organized.

In Chapter 5 Garth Fletcher and Julie Fitness note that laypersons share with social scientists a fascination for the phenomena of relationships and that in some very important ways they approach them similarly; that is, both categories of observer develop hypotheses to explain, predict, and control behavior and experience in relationships. The authors review research and develop a model to locate attributional processes within a social cognitive perspective that emphasizes the role of the layperson's theories of personal relationships. Use of such knowledge constructs is explored, and the authors conclude that the path ahead is best charted with theories that integrate attributional processes and structure into more general social cognitive models.

Going beyond individual explanation, in Chapter 6 Linda Acitelli compares that model and several others as she explores individuals' perceptions of themselves, their partners, and their relationships. She argues that interpersonal perceptions are the threads from which the fabric of shared reality is constructed in a relationship. In a meticulous discussion of the concept of *relationship awareness* and the comparison of several models for dealing with it, Acitelli relates relational thinking to concepts such as *relational talk, identity,* and *understanding.* This work is used to suggest ways of understanding the contribution of cognition to well-being in relationships.

In Chapter 7 Marcia Dixson and Steve Duck make a number of points about the parallel ways in which various disciplines create views of phenomena and come to share meaning in interpreting them. Using a system of analyzing symbols and explanation derived from rhetorical analysis, the authors explore the underlying structure to human efforts at comprehending one another, whether as partners or as members of the social scientific community. In this analysis the attribution of motivation and the explanation of behavior are illuminated by a consideration of the structure and use of explanatory language in everyday discourse.

Several themes in the chapters recur in the discussion and explicitly and implicitly weave themselves into the arguments of the authors to make the book a coherent contribution to the series. First, many authors refer to individual and personal meaning and its construction in relational activity. Second, the authors are uniformly concerned with the mental representation of the social and relational world and the ways in which this representation affects behavior in relationships or the presentation of relationship images in talk. Finally, most authors are concerned with the subtle effects of existing knowledge on the gathering and interpreting of new knowledge about partners and relationships. As such, these emphases take us back to personal meaning and to the view that the individual in relationships is largely a seeker after meaning and a constructor of it.

This book attempts to add to the understanding of the role of human cognition in relationship processes. However, it also seeks to place that understanding in the context of other work on other processes discussed in the series. We have some way to go before we can claim that we do understand relationship processes, but the paths will be laid out by strong reference to the individual's knowledge. It is for future volumes in the series to travel along these paths and indicate other important elements of the landscape.

STEVE DUCK

1

Cognitive Schemata in Personal Relationships

Peter A. Andersen

During the past decade, research on cognition has flourished. The demise of behaviorism, perhaps the academic equivalent of the breakup of the Soviet Union, has ushered in an era in which mind and meaning are central to the study of personal relationships. Though the mind never was completely banished from the study of personal relationships, increased focus on meaning, cognition, strategy, dialectic, and schemata are becoming increasingly central in relational research. In his recent keynote speech at the Third Conference of the International Network on Personal Relationships, Duck (1991) reiterated the need to study *meaning* as a central construct in relational research.

> In the area of relationships we can increase the explanation of the variance by attending more closely to the *personal* meanings that subjects attach to the signs and symbols that others also recognize, or in the dyadic meaning systems that persons create or negotiate in dyads . . . our goal as researchers should be to unpack two key factors: the reason why and the ways individuals develop

personal meaning systems; and the ways these are shared in relationships. (pp. 4-5)

Other researchers similarly have advocated a cognitively based
approach to relationship research. Wilmot and Baxter (1984)
stated: "Our assumption is that communicative behavior becomes meaningful only through the interpretive work of the
interactants. Such interpretive work does not occur in a cognitive vacuum but instead is embedded in a set of cognitions about
the social world" (p. 5). Montgomery (1988) argued that in interpersonal relationship research, "from a communication perspective partners are seen to interact with *multiple levels of meaning*"
(p. 235). Interpretation and attribution of relational behavior has
become a central focus of relationships research.

This focus on cognition and meaning raises important questions for relational researchers. What cognitive structures exist
for storage and processing of relationship meaning? How is
relational knowledge acquired? What forces change in relationships and the meanings they have for people? What other social
knowledge structures have an impact on our relationships and
on relational communication? Is there a dark side to relational
cognition?

One premise of this chapter needs to be established at the
outset: Relationships are the combined products and producers
of both the interpersonal interactions and the cognitive activity
of the interactants. Cappella (1988) maintained: "Experience
and common sense tell us that relationships are formed, maintained, and dissolved in interactions with partners. At the same
time interactions can reflect the kind of relationship that exists
between the partners" (p. 325). Moreover, cognition affects the
interpretation of relational behavior. Reis and Shaver (1988)
added: "Research indicates that expectations and schemas pro-
foundly influence interpretations of interaction partner's behavior" (p. 378). Mutually causal associations exist between our
cognitive schemata, our relational states, and our communication behavior. This chapter, therefore, will feature cognition
and the role it plays in personal relationships and relational
communication.

Relational Schemata

An important theoretical breakthrough in the past decade is the emerging construct of relational schemata. *Schemata* are knowledge structures that derive from prior experience and organize the processing of past and future information (Mandler, 1982; Smith, 1982). Schemata guide future behavior and create expectations, anticipatory assumptions, and contingency rules (Fiske, 1982; Smith, 1982). In short, schemata are memory structures that people rely on to summarize experience and guide future behavior.

Evidence for Relational Schemata

Of particular relevance to relationship researchers are relational schemata (Planalp, 1985; Wilmot & Baxter, 1984) that provide interactants with definitions and interpretations of interpersonal relationships. Planalp (1985) provided experimental evidence for the existence of a relational schema, at least on the power dimension. In her experiment, subjects recalled relationship-consistent conversations more frequently than relationship-inconsistent conversations, a result that implies the existence of schema-guided memory. One study demonstrated that relational partners possess complex interpretive cognitions (Owen, 1984) about their relationships. In an ethnographic study by Wilmot and Baxter (1984), participants were found to possess cognitive schemata that included two important elements. First, virtually all subjects were able to provide natural language labels that distinguished among personal relationships, a finding that suggests relational schemata are cognitively available. Although each person had a unique number of relationships and unique language labels for each, Wilmot and Baxter (1984) claimed that people typically distinguished among friendship prototypes on a closeness dimension (e.g., casual friends, good friends, and best friends; or superficial friends, friends, and close friends). Second, their respondents were able to generate criterial attributes that were common to and distinguished among their prototypic relationships. Common attributes of romantic and friendship prototypes included "trust, caring, ease in communication, general comfort and security in each other's presence, and openness" (p. 10). The fact that people can access relational information and label them suggests the existence of some sort of relational storage structure.

Some additional indirect evidence suggests the existence of relational schemata. Studies have shown that self-disclosure increases as relationships became more intimate (Altman & Taylor, 1973; Berg, 1984; Derlega, 1984; Hays, 1985), although because relational labels were provided by the researchers, the existence of behaviorally differentiated schemata must be inferred from the data. Similarly Guerrero and Andersen (1991) unobtrusively observed couples' tactile behavior and then asked them to select a relational label from a set of descriptors. As hypothesized, newly acquainted and married couples showed less touch than couples who were engaged or going steady, a finding that suggests couples' relational schemata were related to their tactile behavior.

The dearth of literature on relational schemata is surprising because most theories of relationship development (Altman & Taylor, 1973; Berger & Calabrese; 1975; Duck, 1988; Knapp, 1984) posit that communication and relational behavior change across stages of relationship. The subjects are alleged to have meaning for each stage that drives behavior, but the exact cognitive mechanism by which the relational stage information is stored is unspecified in these theories. It is suggested here that relational schemata organize relational behavior. Critics have raised two important questions about cognitive and relational schemata. First, does direct evidence for relational schemata exist; second, why are schemata the structures that store relational information? Relatively strong evidence suggests the existence of relational schemata (see Planalp, 1985, for more detail). As developed above, individuals not only behave consistently with the existence of cognitive schemata but also can differentiate among behaviors across relationship types and can articulate the cognitions they hold about their relationships. However, the term *relational schemata* should not be accorded privileged status. It is a useful label for relational cognitions, but terms such as *relational knowledge* or *relational expectancies* would do little violence to the substance of this argument. More research and conceptualization regarding these relational knowledge structures is warranted.

The Development of Relational Schemata

Crucial to the development of relational schemata is input in the form of relational knowledge. Research suggests that at least six influences on relational knowledge are important.

First, relational schemata may be derived from the norms of the culture. Family and kinship roles, for example, are defined by each culture, are labeled for cultural indoctrination or socialization, and are taught to the young in each culture in each era (Swerdlow, Bridenthal, Kelly, & Vine, 1981). Indeed family relations, because of their deep roots in cultural, religious, and moral values, are highly resistant to change, even in times of social upheaval. Nonkinship relations are more flexible; the term *friend*, for example, can cover a wide variety of relationships from casual acquaintances, through pals, to lovers. However, Contarello and Volpato (1991) have shown that for the past eight centuries, discussions of friendship in European literature have regarded intimacy, respect, mutual help, and confrontation to be central core components of friendship, a view suggesting a relatively stable conception of friendship in Western culture. Cohabiting couples use a variety of terms, such as *roommate, significant other, lover,* and *relational partner.* Even informal relationships have definitions that are meaningful to the relational participants. Participants provide relationships with meaning and labels that have relevance to other people in their culture (Hays, 1988; Wilmot & Baxter, 1984).

Second, the mass media provide a wealth of relationships to emulate and model. An abundance of mass media research has suggested that media–television in particular–provide prototypic family, sex-role, and relationship information that children imitate and incorporate into their cognitions and behavior through the modeling process (Gerbner, Gross, Morgan, & Signorielli, 1980; Reeves & Lometti, 1979; Roberts & Bacher, 1982). Media are both a reflection of and a role model for family relationships. Public awareness of the potential impact of television on personal relationships leads to annual controversies over the content of television shows. Young Doogie Howser's sexual encounter during one television season raised the ire of many parents who worried that their own children would imitate Doogie's behavior. Certainly television relationships have changed from the 1950s prototypes—*Father Knows Best* and *Leave It to Beaver*—that portrayed highly traditional, intact families.

Third, and perhaps most important, information from each individual's past relational encounters creates schemata for future relationships. Individuals generate relational expectations based on their cognitive appraisals of prior interactions (Chelune, Robison, & Kammar, 1984). Planalp (1985) suggested that communication messages are relationally adapted to the present relationship, based on knowledge of past interactions and schema-based anticipated interactions. It is necessary to recognize that relational schemata are not static entities; rather they are both quantitatively and qualitatively dynamic. The "friend" schema, for example, can be updated quantitatively as more information and attributes about friendship are acquired. Qualitatively, relational schemata may change as levels, types, or salience of relationships differentiate friendships into additional relational categories. Most importantly, humans are active cogitators who reflect on relational interactions and both alter and expand relational categories. Ongoing relationship information combines with information from the immediate communication situation to produce updated cognitive information that affects future relational interaction (King & Sereno, 1984).

Unfortunately some individuals who were intermittently reinforced in abusive or dysfunctional relationships create similar future relationships that may become equally dysfunctional. Intergenerational patterns of child abuse may result from dysfunctional parent-child schemata. Loving, bonded child-parent relationships, on the other hand, set the stage for functional, intimate, adult relationships.

Fourth, information from third parties may provide either general relational schemata or relationship-specific data. According to Harvey, Weber, and Orbuch (1990), interpersonal accounts about relationships are a common kind of communication. Both the creation and the reception of relational accounts produce schema development and alteration. "As an illustration, a person's account about a previous disappointment in love may embody plans for the future based on the schemata about self, simulations of future possibilities, and degrees of central processing of input (some being persuasion messages) from close others about the account" (Harvey et al., 1990, p. 113). In a study of events that increase relational uncertainty, Planalp, Rutherford, and Honeycutt (1988) reported that major relational events were discussed with someone other than the partner 75% of the time. People frequently talked to their own friends, and many talked to mutual friends. Such conversations are certain to alter relational perceptions and to provide considerable material for schema redefinition.

Fifth, individuals also acquire relational information by observing friends interact. Like the media, friends provide relationship prototypes to emulate or reject. Relationships are highly salient, and information from close friends provides us with powerful schemata. Even competing relationships shape and provide information for our relational schemata (Planalp & Honeycutt, 1985; Planalp et al., 1988). Discovering that your dating partner is dating someone else, for instance, may create both new schematic categories and update information for an existing schema.

Sixth, both theory and research suggest that schemata are developed, analyzed, and changed in the intervals between interactions. Unlike the relatively automatic, minimal, cognitive activity about the relationship that occurs during interaction, between-interactions participants retrospectively recollect experiences and relabel their relationships. Intimate experiences are recalled and redefined relationally, and conflicts are processed to shape relational schemata. Duck (1980) pointed out that "people's views of their emotions, plans and intentions often change with retrospection about interaction (hence the experience of regret, remorse, guilt, triumph, surprise, etc.)" (p. 118). Indeed cognitive demands are high during interaction, so conscious cognitions about relational definitions during an interaction are unlikely and even detrimental (Andersen, 1986).

It is after an interaction that schematic updates usually occur. Duck and Miell (1986) argued, "We suspect that retrospections about relationships are a major force in their shaping. Far from being pernicious or biased, such activity is essential to the creation of a relationship" (p. 142).

Reis and Shaver (1988) suggested that reconstructions of prior encounters determine whether partners will be open and responsive to future intimate interactions. Metts, Sprecher, and Cupach (1991) found that self-reported retrospective data may be the most valid data if the researcher is interested in "participants' attitudes, emotions, and perceptions of relationship qualities" (p. 164). It is outside of interaction that people can and do reflect about prior interaction and construct relational schemata.

The Dynamic Process of Relational Cognition

Relationships are dynamic entities destined to change with time, interaction episodes, and cognitive activity. Most recent conceptualizations of relationships recognize that they are non-linear, uncertain, and ever-changing. For this reason participants devote considerable cognitive energy to understanding their relationships and attempting to strategically control them (Duck & Miell, 1986). The presumption of many relational models that relationships are a series of plateaus (Knapp, 1984) or reach stable, intimate levels (Altman & Taylor, 1973) are not shared by most recent relational researchers. Some years ago a researcher (who will remain unnamed) presented a paper showing very low test-retest reliability coefficients for measures of relational attraction across just months of the relationship. His conclusion that reliability and validity problems existed with the attraction scales was, of course, erroneous. He had measured something much more interesting and had measured it well: He found that relationships change across relatively short time intervals. For most relationships the idea of a plateau or stage is at best a useful snapshot and at worst a destructive illusion.

Relationship members, as noted previously, try to put their relationships in static categories that have meaning for them. But recent research and conceptualization indicates that "relationship parties have a cognitive repository of relationship process knowledge in addition to their conceptions of various relationship types. Such process cognitions or schemata serve to frame any given communicative action" (Baxter, 1987a, p. 193).

Relational Dialectics

A primary reason that relationships are dynamic, nonlinear, and even turbulent is the nature of human dialectical cognition. In recent years Baxter has shown the importance of a dialectical perspective to understanding close relationships (Baxter, 1988, 1990). Relationships are rarely unequivocally perceived as positive and advantageous. With each relationship we simultaneously lose and gain freedom. In each relationship we become greater and lesser than we were prior to that relationship. We become greater because opportunities for dialogue, intimacy, cooperation, sexuality, disclosure, and reproduction exist in personal relationships. We become lesser because relationships take time, effort, and resources; they constrain our individuality and autonomy; and they create hazards and risks of various sorts. Logically these risks, of everything from sexually transmitted disease to the loss of a close friend, should inhibit relational development. The fact that most of us develop close relationships is a testament to our ability to rationalize these risks as well as our desire for closeness and intimacy.

Baxter's (1988) dialectical perspective suggests that dialectic models take a relationship-level perspective as opposed to individual perspectives, which have dominated the field of relationship research. However, it is these dialectical contradictions that are processed as part of the individual's relational schema and occur in parallel at the individual level. Baxter's (1988) concept of dialectical theory focuses attention on the situation and locates relational dialectics in the external actions and communication environment of relational interactants. Alternatively the perspective taken here is that relationship dialectics reflect cognitive ambivalence about personal relationships. Cognitive resolution of ambivalence is a fundamental part of human cognition and

neural structure (Stacks & Andersen, 1989). Out of ambivalent cognitions, coherent behavior will result unless a person behaves in a continually contradictory or even schizophrenic manner. Indeed Baxter (1988) suggested that cognitive, strategic behaviors are employed to manage and respond to dialectical contradiction.
     Duck (1990) contended:

> Individuals, dyads or relationships resolve their dilemmas and establish patterns of response or behavior over time as a consequence of resolving dialectic tensions. As thinkers, people are in constant dialog with themselves (and others) considering arguments and counter-arguments, proposing or speculating about one possible future as against another. (pp. 7-8)

Four fundamental relational dialectics have been discussed in the literature. The first dialectic, variously called autonomy/connection (Baxter, 1988), individualism/collectivism (Lustig & Andersen, 1990), freedom to be independent/freedom to be dependent (Rawlins, 1983), is the fundamental relational contradiction. This dialectic emerges as an important factor in cognitively defining a particular relationship. Baxter and Bullis (1986) found that the autonomy/connection dialectic was very real in partners' accounts of relationship turning points that led to relational exclusivity or disengagement. It is the autonomy/connection or affiliation/avoidance dimension that is the underlying basis of the major theoretical efforts explaining intimacy and immediacy increases (Andersen, 1985, 1989; Argyle & Dean, 1966; Burgoon, 1983; Cappella & Greene, 1982). Baxter (1990) empirically examined the autonomy/connection dialectic in a recent study and discovered it was present in 88% of individual relationships and particularly prevalent in moderate to long-term relationships. Relational partners coped with this contradiction through a strategy called *cyclical alternation,* in which couples get closer, then farther apart, then closer, in a cyclic fashion. Rarely was cyclical alternation reported as a conscious strategy. A second response was partner selection, a proactive strategy that legitimated one of the contrasts (e.g., "giving it a shot" despite autonomy needs).

Novelty and predictability constitute the second primary dialectic tension. Certainly an abundance of theory and research has shown that relationships, particularly in their early stages, are driven by a need to reduce uncertainty (Berger, 1988b; Berger & Bradac, 1982; Berger & Calabrese, 1975). But too much certainty can produce boredom, mundane interaction, and a lack of spontaneity and adventure. Berger (1988b) grants that "uncertainty and unpredictability can create excitement, something at least some persons wish they had more of in their close relationships" (p. 246). One study showed that the primary reason both men and women terminated their dating relationships was becoming bored with the relationship (Hill, Rubin, & Peplau, 1976). Livingston (1980) conceptualized love in close relationships as a process of uncertainty reduction, but he maintained that at the very moment obstacles to romantic love are removed, the love dissipates. As Sternberg (1987) maintained, "In order for love to thrive there has to be some mystery—some degree of doubt about what will happen when" (p. 132). Relationships are energized by cognitive uncertainty, a state that produces arousal and enhances feelings of emotion. But too much uncertainty is frightening, and too much spontaneity and arousal can easily become fear or stress. Cognitively and emotionally we walk a fine line in our relationships between stressful excitement and boring predictability.

Recently Baxter (1990) reported data showing that the novelty/predictability dialectic was represented cognitively in 79% of her subjects and that 83% of long-term relational partners reported struggling with this contradiction. Most relational participants used a segmentation strategy to cope with this contradiction, striving for relational stability on the one hand and interactional spontaneity on the other. Likewise, temporary separation ,which broke down routines, was another commonly used strategy.

A third dialectic that perplexes relationships is the risk/reward or skepticism/trust dimension. The aphorism "It is better to have loved and lost than never to have loved at all" reflects an optimistic view of this dialectic. Similarly the poet Gibran (1923) warned that when "Love beckons to you, follow him . . . for as love crowns you so shall he crucify you. Even as he is for your growth, so he is for your pruning" (p. 12). The fears of false love, hurt, and dashed hopes inhibit individuals from closer relationships even though the rewards of closeness, intimacy, and passion are substantial. To trust another is to make a relationship possible. Violations of trust cause rapid de-escalations of close relationships. Holmes and Rempel (1989) believe that "issues of trust have their origin in the dialectic between people's hopes and fears as close relationships develop" (p. 187). Feelings of dependency are essential but demonstrate a major risk of relational involvement. Trust of another individual has been shown to be essential to relational involvement and solidarity (Wheeless, 1978), while generalized trust is not positively related to relational attachment (Holmes & Rempel, 1989; Wheeless, 1978). Certainly, positive cognitive appraisals of trust are essential to relationship development. Indeed, communicators strategically and secretly test relationships to establish a baseline of trust, fidelity, and loyalty before increasing their intimacy (Baxter & Wilmot, 1984) as an alternative to open communication and disclosure with their partners. Secret tests include jealousy tests, fidelity tests, endurance tests, third party discussions, and trial intimacy escalations. The risk/reward dialectic is one force creating dynamism and even turbulence in close relationships.

A fourth dialectic that pervades personal relationships is the openness-closedness contradiction. Baxter (1988) cited considerable research suggesting that indirect communication is much more prevalent than open, honest disclosure. Indeed, the prescription to be open and disclosive once promulgated by communication researchers has been replaced with strategic and tactical advice that disclosure is not necessarily a formula for relational success. Nonetheless a degree of openness is essential to the development of a close and intimate relationship, and most evolving relationships show increases in disclosure at least during their early stages (Berg, 1984; Cline, 1989; Derlega, Wilson, & Chaiken, 1976). Cline (1989), however, demonstrated that disclosure is a strategic, cognitive, exchange behavior based on the value of disclosure intimacy and the value of the relational partners' power in the relationship. Global assessments of future gains primarily govern disclosure. Investigations showing that people strategically maintain and restore privacy (Burgoon, Parrott, et al., 1989) have corrected a bias toward emphasizing affiliation, inclusiveness, and intimacy in relationships. Recently the openness-closedness dialectic was examined empirically and was reported by 72% of the relational partners (Baxter, 1990). It was particularly prevalent in relatively new relationships. Couples coped with this dialectic primarily through openness on some safe topics while declaring other topics taboo. Because individuals consciously strive for both inaccessibility and affiliation and because partners may cycle through periods when they are on opposite poles of this dialectic, this additional dynamic quality produces periods of change in relationships. The poet Gibran (1923) invoked this dialectic when he advised the spouses, "Let there be space in your togetherness . . . for the pillars of the temple stand apart, and the oak tree and the cypress grow not in each other's shadow" (pp. 16–17).

The dialectics of relationships are cognitive processes that produce strategic, cognitive responses in close relationships. Partners in any relationship actively think about their partners and their relationships and make decisions to behave consistently with prototypic conceptions of ideal relationships in their personal lives. Sometimes, as Baxter (1988) maintained, individuals will strategically select actions that attempt consistently to move the relationship toward one pole of the dialectic contradiction. Other attempts to cope with relational dialectics involve cycling and recycling through phases representing opposite poles. Ambiguous or equivocal communication (Bavelas, Black, Chavel, & Mullett, 1990) is used to avoid commitment to one pole of the dialectic. These factors, as well as the fact that both relational partners may be employing different cognitive strategies, make relationships exciting and frustrating, but always dynamic.

Relational Trajectories

One useful, intriguing concept is that of the relational trajectory. Although little research has been conducted on such a con-

cept, it is appearing with increasing frequency in the relationships literature (Andersen, 1989; Baxter, 1987a; Berger & Roloff,
1982; Duck, 1985; Stephen, 1985). *Relational trajectories* are
conceptualized in this chapter as cognitive schemata incorporat-
ing relationship history, relationship state, and relationship future. The concept of *future trajectory* is an important one
because one's own behavior, as well as evaluation of one's
partner's behavior, is likely to be based on the anticipated
future trajectory of the relationship rather than its current state
(Andersen, 1989).

Clearly trajectory schemata exist and have an impact. It is
common to hear relationship accounts of a romance that is
"headed for marriage" or a relationship that is "going downhill
fast." Baxter (1987a) maintained:

> These relationship trajectory schemata allow the relationship par-
> ties to make sense of the sequence of episodes that occur when
> relationships are forming and breaking up. In the formative state
> of romantic relationship growth, for instance, the parties' growth
> trajectory schemata allow them to gauge whether the relationship
> is "on course," to predict which sort of events should occur next
> in the trajectory sequence, and to make retrospective sense of
> episodes. (p. 194)

Harvey, Agostinelli, and Weber (1989) argued that relational
accounts provide a schema that implies a future trajectory for a
relationship: "Just as accounts were suggested to be represented
as schematic knowledge, expectations can also be represented
schematically" (p. 49). Just as all stories have an ending, accounts of relationships lead to the question of what future a
person will share with close, intimate others. It is likely our
actions will be an attempt to write the final chapters in a
satisfying way.

Even infants seem to have relational trajectory schemata. Stern
(1980) maintained that infants form a representation of the
history of a relationship that affects the course of each new
interaction. He suggested that "each infant-caregiver pair can
develop an individual course for their own relationship, and . . .
the outcome of seemingly similar interactions can be quite

divergent for different pairs with different histories" (p. 106). It is early interaction, of course, that bonds infants to caregivers. A schematic representation of what the infant expects from each relationship is evident in individual episodes across years of a relationship. A game such as peekaboo capitalizes on the existence of an infant's interaction schema and expectations. The periodically disappearing parent violates normal conversational expectancies, creating concern that turns to glee at the parent's reappearance. Disappearing for longer periods creates uncertainty and negative affect and results in the separation anxiety display that often occurs even with an indirect cue such as the arrival of a baby-sitter.

Experimental evidence has shown that anticipated relational trajectories have an impact on judgments of conversations and projections for the relationship's future. Wilmot and Baxter (1983) gave subjects three conversations between romantic partners or friends who were described as either growing closer or growing apart. Conversations in relationships described as growing apart were perceived as less personalized, less honest, and less disclosive than the growth trajectory relationships. Growth trajectories should result in positive expectancies and interpretations of behavior.

All growth trajectories are not the same, however. Baxter (1987a) identified two types of romantic involvements: the friendship first trajectory and the whirlwind trajectory. The friendship first trajectory was reported more frequently and seemed to be the more desirable condition for a romantic relationship. It is likely that both the excitement and the uncertainty experienced in whirlwind, instant-intimacy relationships are due to the lack of a clear future relational trajectory. In the friendship first trajectory, a solid foundation is laid for the relationship that is perceived to decrease uncertainty and promote stability.

Finally it should be noted that trajectories affect behavior and behavior affects trajectories in mutually causal ways. Duck (1985) maintained that "thinking about relationships affects their trajectory at early formative stages . . . thoughts about partner, and information gathered about partner, are effected by relationships too" (p. 670). The process of thinking about relationships and the course of the relationship are simultaneously causal. Of course, even this statement is an oversimplification because relationships exist in the perceived behavior and the cognitive schemata of two individuals who are unlikely to agree about what they perceive, what they expect, and what they plan for the relationship's future.

Relationally Related Schemata

Obviously, humans think about many social stimuli other than their relationships. Some of these stimuli are organized systematically into cognitive schemata, and these schemata affect our personal relationships. Andersen (1985, 1989) proposed a cognitive valence theory that argues for six types of schemata that affect our relationships. Potential relationship partners do not communicate in a vacuum; they communicate while employing a cognitive repertoire of schemata and expectations about how they should communicate. Andersen (1989) argued that it is relatively easy to behave inappropriately in relationships by violating a partner's schemata for what constitutes appropriate relational behavior. The development of close personal relationships is a fragile process because violating any of a partner's cognitive schemata can have negative relational effects. Indeed, among our hundreds of acquaintances, most of us have relatively few individuals with whom we are relationally, sexually, or emotionally intimate. What sorts of schemata are relationally relevant? Andersen (1989) suggested that the following six schemata valence relational communication: culture, personality, situation, psychological or physical states, interpersonal valence, and the relational trajectory itself.

Cultural Schemata

One of the most powerful schemata is that of *culture*. From birth, culture shapes us and molds us. It provides us with a powerful schema for what constitutes appropriate interpersonal behavior. Andersen (1989) maintained that "culture is such a pervasive influence that it is often confused with human nature itself" (p. 13). Gudykunst and Kim (1984) contended that cultural beliefs or "postulates consist of ideas accepted as 'the way things are.' Postulates are thus assumptions, accepted without being questioned; they are 'the facts of life' " (p. 12). Cultural schemata for talk-turns, touch, smiling, distance, and a host of other communication behaviors are deeply ingrained. So deep are these cultural schemata that they are invisible to most members of a culture; indeed, they are part of us.

Interaction behavior of people from other cultures tends to be labeled as inappropriate, incompetent, gross, or insulting. Anecdotes of negative impressions that result from cultural differences abound in the literature of psychology, anthropology, and communication. Americans believe that Arabs stand too close. Swedes think the French use too much eye contact. North Americans dislike the smells of almost all cultures. The Japanese think Westerners talk too much. Unfortunately violations of cultural schemata produce negative attributions, and typically these follow the pattern of the fundamental attribution error. Cultural differences are attributed to deficiencies in the character or personality of the interactant. There is an increased tendency for the fundamental attribution error to occur during communication with people from other cultures than when communicating with one's own kind (Gudykunst & Kim, 1984). These attributions often hold that people from other cultures are pushy, aloof, unclean, too talkative, loud, sexually aggressive, or stupid, when in fact what is occurring is merely the enactment of different cultures.

These cultural schemata can get in the way of relational development. Moreover, these cultural differences need not be huge international differences. It has been shown that even among regions of the United States, norms are different for touch, verbal assertiveness, and openness (Andersen, Lustig, & Andersen, 1987, 1990).

Cultural differences affect all relationships but are magnified in close relationships. Cultural schemata are so habitual, overlearned, and automatic that cross-cultural intimacy behaviors are likely to violate one's cultural schemata in a variety of ways. Reactions to these violations are typically both negative and unconscious because people may not be able to put their finger on what is disturbing them. The kiss that did not happen, the touch that occurred too soon, and the disclosure that is much too intimate are labeled negatively due to intercultural misunderstandings. Only very sensitive communicators with great cultural sensitivity and considerable intercultural contact can avoid employing cultural schemata in a negative way.

Self-Schemata

Without a doubt, personality traits or schemata are the most prevalent type of schema in the human species. It is estimated that 20,000 trait terms are present in the English lexicon. As Andersen (1987) maintained: "Whether traits are called individual predispositions, person variables, individual differences, or personality variables, the focus on the individual communicator has generated a number of robust communication research programs. Attributing trait or dispositional qualities to individuals is a common endeavor in everyday conversation" (p. 48). Moreover, a disproportionate share of trait descriptors refer to relational behaviors such as sociability, dominance, shyness, aggressiveness, and dependency. "The fact that personality language is so heavily interpersonal underscores the importance of personality for social relationships" (Park & Waters, 1988, p. 163).

Personality data are the most accessible schemata to oneself. Andersen (1987) maintained: "Research has demonstrated that subjects are generally aware of their own characteristics both from self-observation and from feedback from others" (p. 56). Mabe and West (1982) conducted a meta-analytic study that showed a .63 correlation between trait self-reports and trait behavior when comparing themselves with other subjects. Moreover, even when self-information is not consciously accessible, it is likely that our personalities still have considerable effect on our interpersonal behavior.

Our own trait information is stored in *self-schemata*, knowledge structures about the self that organize and direct the processing of self-relevant information regarding an individual's social experiences (Markus, 1983). Markus stated:

The individual is thought to construct actively both generalizations and hypotheses about the self from ongoing life events (e.g., "I am independent," "I work well with people," "I am shy.") . . . In particular, these generalizations often involve the self-relevant responses of other people. Self-schemas develop around those aspects of the self that become personally significant in the course of our social interactions. (pp. 547-548)

Self-schemata are more than summary cognitions of one's prior behavior. They actively determine the future of one's social relationships. For instance, a person self-defined as "shy" or "apprehensive" will actively avoid social interaction. A person who is self-labeled as "adventurous" or "sensual" will be more inclined to accept sexual overtures from a relational partner.

Communication research has shown that personality traits and communication predispositions have substantial effects on people's relational behavior. Andersen and Coussoule (1980) found that high communication apprehensives are insensitive and oblivious to immediacy and intimacy cues from others. In fact, these individuals perceive averted gaze to be as intimate as continuous gaze. High communication apprehensives avert eye contact, cover their face, lean backward, block their body, and are nonimmediate and detached from others (Burgoon & Koper, 1984). Communication apprehensives are viewed as inhibited, unsociable, and unfriendly (Cheek & Buss, 1981), engage in less disclosure and elicit less self-disclosure from others (Miller, Berg, & Archer, 1983), and are less open and socially confirming than less apprehensive people (Lustig & Andersen, 1991).

A similar body of research has examined *touch avoidance,* an individual's attitude toward intimate touch. These individuals are less likely to touch and dislike it when others touch them (Andersen & Leibowitz, 1978). Sorensen (1979) reported that touch avoiders had significantly more negative attitudes toward an experimenter who touched them than one who did not touch them. Touch approachers, however, had more positive attitudes toward an experimenter who touched than one who did not touch. Touch avoiders also maintained much greater interpersonal distances during interaction (Andersen & Sull, 1985), and touch avoidance is negatively correlated with openness (Andersen, Lustig, & Andersen, 1987).

Similarly Eysenck (1967, 1982) found that extroverts tend to approach relationships and to label arousal positively, whereas introverts label arousal negatively. McAdams (1988) found that intimacy motivation predicts increased readiness for close relationships, thoughts about positive relationships, higher peer ratings, as well as more eye contact, smiling, and laughing. In sum, countless personality traits and self-schemata have dramatic effects on relational behavior.

Situation Schemata

Another class of schemata involves cognitions about the situation or context in which interactions occur. Andersen (1989) maintained: "It has become axiomatic that any human action cannot be interpreted and understood outside of its context. The term 'out of context' has become synonymous with being meaningless or misleading" (p. 27). For example, intimate touch and long stares might be entirely appropriate in one's bedroom but totally inappropriate at the office. Contextual and situational sensitivity are essential components of competent communication (Goffman, 1959; Spitzberg & Cupach, 1989). Indeed, Ginsburg (1988) maintained that all human action, including actions in relationships, depends in part on the context in which it occurs.

Situational schemata have been examined as a central part of research on social cognition (see Cody & McLaughlin, 1985; Hewes & Planalp, 1982). A *situational schema* is structured, intuitive knowledge about one's current context as an instance of a general class of similar contexts. During interaction, employing an implicit theory of what the interaction is "all about" and under what constraints it is taking place is essential for the interaction to be coherent, appropriate, and "in context." Likewise, situational knowledge enables individuals to enter or avoid situations selectively (Cody & McLaughlin, 1985). As we enter situations, we may find them entirely consistent with our situational schema; somewhat inconsistent, requiring a situational update and redefinition; or totally inconsistent, leading to confusion, disorientation, and even panic.

Situational schemata permit relational partners to perform appropriate, strategic, and competent relational communication behavior. Initiating intimacy in a public place may violate a partner's schema for such an interaction, as well as others in the social situation. Chelune et al. (1984) maintained that certain physical settings are more conducive to intimate interaction than others. Such settings are stored as situational schemata that individuals match with perceived situations during relational interaction. Mismatches are negatively valued, particularly if they deviate substantially from one's schema for a situation. Acitelli and Duck (1987) suggested that cognitive appraisals of the situation are critical to appropriate relational behavior. They maintained that "elements of intimacy are both dynamic and static, both personal and situational: The mediating factor is the perspective on it that is taken by the participants, particularly their judgments about the level of intimacy appropriate for a given situation or occasion" (p. 301). Situationally appropriate intimacy or immediacy behaviors enhance relational closeness. Situationally inappropriate immediacy behaviors are likely to have negative effects on relational closeness and satisfaction. Several models suggest that slight violations of intimate communication expectations can produce positive relational outcomes (Burgoon, 1983; Cappella & Greene, 1982). Andersen (1989) maintained that situational intimacy violations in the direction of the established relationship trajectory will be perceived positively and actually may enhance relational closeness. Thus, for example, sitting "too close" to one's partner at a party or kissing in public may have positive relational consequences if these behaviors are in the direction of the expected relational trajectory according to one's partner's relational schema. So situational schemata and relational schemata interact to produce relational change.

State Schemata

From moment to moment and day to day, people's schemata are dynamic. Our self-perceived psychological or physical state provides an additional schema for evaluating our relationships. *States* are an individual's transitory physical or emotional conditions. Individuals feel and can report these transitory states and can provide labels for them, such as grumpy, tired, unsociable, gregarious, hung over, excited, or happy. Despite widespread confusion in the literature of communication and psychology, states are not the same as situations. States are internal, and *state schemata* refer to such internal sensory conditions. Situations are external, and *situational schemata* refer to external environmental exigencies. Andersen (1988) pointed out that state is to situation as personality is to culture.

State schemata have an important effect on relational communication. Although communication behaviors such as intimate disclosure, eye contact, or touching typically are valenced positively in close relationships, such positive evaluations are dependent on an individual's state schemata. As Andersen (1985) suggested, "A fight with one's boss, a headache, a raise, a heavy workload or any number of temporary factors can cause immediacy behaviors to be valenced either more positively or more negatively" (p. 28). Similarly Badzinski (1986) observed: "Interactants' moods influence their judgments of the conversation and the qualities they attribute to their partners" (p. 6). Indeed, "reading" the psychological states of one's relational partner is essential to appropriate relational behavior.

Interpersonal Schemata

Interpersonal schemata are the knowledge structures we possess regarding other people's characteristics and our attitudes toward their relational characteristics. The content of these cognitive schemata is called *interpersonal valence* (Garrison, Sullivan, & Pate, 1976), a superordinate construct encompassing source credibility or ethos (K. Andersen & Clevenger, 1963), attraction (McCroskey & McCain, 1974), and homophily (Rogers & Shoemaker, 1971). Burgoon, Parrott, et al. (1989) called these features the "reward value" of a communicator because high status, credible, attractive, homophilous communicators are intrinsically rewarding. Obviously it is persons with high interpersonal valence with whom we establish and maintain close relationships.

Interpersonal schemata are not relational schemata. *Interpersonal schemata* involve our knowledge structures about characteristics of people and their positive or negative qualities. *Relational schemata* are our knowledge structures regarding types of relationships. Theories of relationships distinguish between people and relationships and how we think about them (Andersen, 1989; Burgoon, 1983). We might feel attracted to or impressed by a political figure or movie star with whom we have no relationship. This example employs interpersonal schemata even in the absence of any relational schemata (other than public figure/audience member). Indeed, Berger (1988b) argues that different schemata are employed to reduce uncertainty when he states, "Persons not only attempt to reduce their uncertainty about each other, they also try to reduce uncertainty about the future of their relationships" (p. 245).

Similarly, attribution theory has long held that explanations of others' behavior tend not to be attributed to the situation or the relationship but to qualities of the other person (Jones & Nisbett, 1971; Sillars, 1982). Likewise, research has shown that individuals have very well developed schemata for individuals and their personalities (Leone & Ensley, 1985; Tesser & Leone, 1977).

Current theories of relationship communication hold that well-developed interpersonal schemata exist and have powerful effects on how relational communication is perceived and valenced, as well as how the relationship progresses in the future (Andersen, 1985, 1989; Burgoon, 1983; Burgoon & Jones, 1976). Andersen (1989) called these factors "interpersonal valence" and argued that they are among the most central constructs in interpersonal communication research. "Valencing of the person is critical to our evaluation of any attempt on their part to increase intimacy" (p. 23). Attempts at increasing intimacy by a person with negative interpersonal valence, unlike a person with positive valence, will be evaluated negatively. Similarly a central construct in Burgoon's (1983) theory of expectancy violations is the construct of "reward valence." Low reward communicators should not violate expectancies, while high reward communicators benefit from such expectancy violations.

> In the case of a low reward communicator, it is predicted that the greater the deviation from the expected pattern, the greater the negative consequences. Thus, a high reward person may gain a more favorable image by engaging in a violation, whereas a low reward person will end up with an even more negative image. (Burgoon, Parrott, et al., 1989, p. 255)

Likewise, Reis and Shaver (1988) suggested that attitudes toward other interaction partners dramatically influence interpretations of their behavior.

Interpersonal schemata, like relational schemata, are developed, digested, altered, and analyzed in the intervals between interactions (Andersen, 1984; Duck & Sants, 1983). Although some cognitive work is done during interactions, the high cognitive demands of an interaction prevent too much cognitive work on one's schemata during interaction. Most scholars agree that actual interactions proceed much too swiftly for complex cognitive processes to occur during interaction (Cappella & Greene, 1982; Stern, 1980). During interaction, schemata are activated and behavior simply is compared with such schemata; the heavier schema formation and information updating functions are saved for times when cognitive loads are lesser than during interpersonal interactions.

Research on relational cognition suggests that thought and cognition in the absence of interaction or external information results in attitudinal and schematic alterations (Tesser, 1978). Indeed, cogitating or mulling tends to polarize such attitudes (Cloven & Roloff, 1991; Tesser & Leone, 1977). Evidently this polarization occurs both when reflecting positively about a person or negatively, as in the case of recalling and thinking about conflict.

Finally information about other people comes from third parties through gossip, conversation, and narratives. Friends make comments to us about other people, such as "What a nerd" or "He's charming," that enter our cognitive repertoire and are stored for future use. Andersen (1984) claimed that "people stereotype other individuals and reinforce those stereotypes with third party conversations and interpersonal accounts" (p. 11). The role of such interpersonal accounts in the formation of person perception schemata has been discussed extensively by Harvey et al. (1990). They suggested that "account gists" fill our memories and provide information for schematic analysis. Hewes, Graham, Doelger, and Pavitt (1985) reported results of two studies that showed people estimate that 30% of their information about friends, acquaintances, and other members of their social networks comes to them from third party interactions.

Although interpersonal schemata are distinctly different from relational schemata, interpersonal schemata affect our relationships at all stages of development. Planalp et al. (1988) discovered that substantial relational redefinitions occur when an individual "perceived a change in the other's personality, value system or characteristic way of behaving" (p. 528). Positive perceptions of another person's values, background, physical appearance, and communication style are the primary reasons why we initiate and maintain close relationships.

Relational Schemata

Recent research suggests that among the six schemata posited by Andersen (1985, 1989), relational schemata have the most substantial effect on excessive intimacy (Andersen, 1992). It even suggests that relational schemata are more important than the other five schemata (culture, personality, situation, state, and interpersonal valence) combined. In accounts of interpersonally intimate interactions, Andersen (1992) found that people overwhelmingly attributed the appropriateness of another individual's intimate behavior to the relationship, not to the other five factors. Typical statements describing excessive intimacy include: "My relationship with another woman made her behavior seem even more intimate and added to my discomfort"; "The relationship happened too quickly, destroying any chance of 'chemistry' between us"; "I don't like someone I barely know touching me"; and "I saw our relationship as one of friendship, nothing more." Overwhelmingly, relational inappropriateness, as opposed to the other aforementioned factors, was invoked by subjects to explain why they perceived certain communication as "too intimate." As Planalp (1985) put it, "People enter interactions with some sense of what communicative behaviors are appropriate for the type of relationship and the relationship they communicate" (p. 3). Current research suggests that individuals have well-developed relational schemata as well as a repertoire of behaviors that fit these schemata as relationally positive and appropriate or negative and inappropriate. Engaging in relationally "correct" behavior appears to be the sine qua non of interpersonal relationships.

Excess Cognition

In relationships, cognition is certainly ubiquitous, probably necessary, and usually beneficial. But there is a dark side to our thoughts about our relationships. In another context, Shakespeare's Caesar (Act 1, Scene 2) declared, "He thinks too much: Such men are dangerous." Is there a danger of excess cognition regarding our relationships? The probable answer is yes.

First, relational competence demands a relatively large proportion of mindlessness and spontaneity. Conscious mental activity may be necessary when individuals first learn something or in novel situations, but research is demonstrating that excessive consciousness leads to "self-consciousness," stilted behavior, and incompetent communication (Baars, 1983; Spitzberg & Cupach, 1984). Competent communication requires the formation of habits so that on-line cognitive activity can be saved for other necessary adaptations (Hample, 1984). Is conscious cognition typically beneficial to interpersonal communication? According to Andersen (1986), "the emerging answer is a tentative no. Economy in consciousness is essential to competence in communication" (p. 97).

Second, a body of knowledge is developing that warns of the dangerous nature of too much perceptiveness and thought. Several studies have reported that high levels of skill at decoding nonverbal communication might be relationally detrimental

(Rosenthal, Hall, DiMatteo, Rogers, & Archer, 1979). The studies show that people who are very good decoders of nonverbal communication have less satisfactory interpersonal relationships than their less skilled counterparts. Similarly, deception research suggests that many lies are collaborative and that relational partners profit little from their detection. Andersen (in press) maintained that "collusive lies are particularly common when the consequence of discovery is relational conflict or destruction" (p. 28).

Third, research indicates that high levels of rational thought may impede spontaneity and may lead to excessively predictable and obligatory patterns. These patterns result from the erroneous belief that only one type of response is appropriate. Such excessively compulsive desires to control relationships can lead to *schismogenesis,* a dysfunctional condition that results in overly rigidified role-oriented interaction (Bateson, 1972; Baxter, 1988). Although schismogenesis may result from a number of antecedent causes, a primary precursor is dwelling on appropriate relational behavior to the extent that patterns become calcified and any sense of spontaneity is lost. Arms races and interpersonal one-upmanship result from excessive dwelling on certainty and need for control. Rigid adherence to cognitive rules of interaction has been shown to lead to unwanted repetitive patterns (URP) in personal relationships (Cronen, Pearce, & Snavely, 1979).

Perhaps the most compelling finding regarding relational cognition is that it tends to magnify attitudes (Tesser, 1978). Cognition makes positive attitudes more positive and negative attitudes more negative. As Shakespeare's Hamlet (Act 2, Scene 2) stated, "For there is nothing either good nor bad, but thinking makes it so." Recent studies have verified that in negative relational circumstances, thinking or mulling exacerbates relational problems. Cloven and Roloff (1991) found that mulling about disputes increased both the perceived severity of conflicts and the likelihood that partners would blame each other. Cognitive activity also interacted with subsequent communication, such that negative, distributive communication magnified the negative consequences of mulling about conflict, but constructive, integrative communication attenuated the negative consequences of thought. Similarly Eloy, Guerrero, Andersen, & Spitzberg (1992) reported that cognitively experienced jealousy in romantic relationships reduced relational satisfaction among dating couples and reduced marital satisfaction among married couples. The authors suggested that dwelling on jealousy makes it more cognitively salient and leads to subsequent relational problems. Apparently, mulling about negative aspects of one's relationship is detrimental to the relationship. Ironically, this statement itself is a paradox because in totally dysfunctional relationships, thinking of alternatives or means of extraction may be the only escape from violence, abuse, or injury. However, dwelling on the negative aspects of generally positive relationships guarantees that they will become less positive. The ability to rationalize and forget a partner's flaws is an essential component of personal relationships.

Conclusion

The central thesis of this chapter is that human beings think about their relationships and that these thoughts drive their actions. Additionally it is not uncommon to discuss and share relational information with other people. Listen to what people discuss in the workplace, at the dinner table, in bars, and at the hair salon. Relationships with employers, children, lovers, and friends often dominate these conversations. It is as though virtually everyone is attempting to understand his or her relationship to others, to unlock the secrets of his or her personal relationships.

This chapter has attempted to provide students and relationships researchers with some insights into the roles that schemata play in our personal encounters, so a few salient insights are in order. First, relationships are more than behavior in another person's presence. Relationships are, to a large degree, states of mind. We collaboratively can think relationships into and out of existence. Because these relational cognitions exist for both partners and rarely match exactly, relationships are tricky, dynamic, and sometimes frustrating.

Retrospections play a large role in interactions. Note the subject of many of your thoughts when driving, walking, or trying to sleep; relationships are a common cognition. We dwell on relationships that might have been, conversations that we wish we could perform again and improve, and the relational implications of prior interactions.

Researchers should recognize also that some of our relational actions are strategic and tactical. Interactants plan encounters, script conversations, and attempt to control relational outcomes. Of course, we accomplish these objectives with varying degrees of success. This is not to say that we control all of our actions or even most of them. Relational behavior is *both* biological, determined, and mindless, *and* cognitive, strategic, and mindful.

Nor are cognitive schemata simple structures. A web of schemata regarding culture and personality, state and situation, self and others surrounds our relationships. Also each schema is contained with complex dialectics that simultaneously may provide centripetal and centrifugal forces in our relationships. The unraveling of the mysteries of the mind in our personal relationships promises to be one of the exciting adventures of the next century.

2

*Goals, Plans, and Mutual
Understanding
in Relationships*

Charles R. Berger

In an effort to provide a meta-theoretical frame for understanding the past 25 years of social and personal relationships research, Duck (1991) suggested that a useful point of departure would be to focus on the personal meanings that those involved in relationships create for themselves and the mutual understandings they negotiate with their relational partners. He concluded his ambitious meta-theoretical statement by asserting the following set of postulates:

> The world is in need of interpretation and meaning, individuals construct meanings for themselves, while partaking of the meaning already available through language; Pairs of individuals develop

AUTHOR'S NOTE: I express my appreciation to Leslie Baxter, Robert Bell, and Alan Sillars for their thoughtful comments on earlier versions of this chapter. In particular I thank Robert Bell for suggesting the Vulcans' mind fusion and mind meld capabilities as potential "ultimate" states of mutual understanding.

refined overlapping meaning systems; Symbolic union and sharing
of meanings underlies all aspects of relationships. (p. 29)

These assumptions suggest that to understand how relationships
work, researchers must first ascertain how individuals arrive at
interpretations of the world around them, including, of course,
other persons. They then must determine how multiple persons
develop interpretative systems that "overlap" in such a way that
they achieve a reasonable degree of mutual understanding. Presumably at least some degree of mutual understanding is a
necessary condition for carrying out relationships. Duck's two-
stage model for studying relationships implies that part of
understanding how persons develop mutually comprehensible
interpretations for each others' actions, as well as the symbols
used to define their relationships, rests on the ability of researchers to determine how individual interpretations evolve into
socially shared interpretations.

Considerable interest has been shown in the problem of how
persons achieve the level of intersubjectivity necessary to develop mutual understandings of the intentions underlying the
multitude of stimuli emitted by individuals during communication episodes (Green, 1989; Gurwitsch, 1974; Hewes & Planalp,
1987; Laing, Phillipson, & Lee, 1966; McLeod & Chaffee, 1972;
Reddy, 1979; Schutz, 1967; Schutz & Luckman, 1973; Sillars &
Scott, 1983). Reddy (1979) argued that the English language
itself, unfortunately, leads us to think about communication as
a process in which ideas or thoughts are transplanted from the
head of one individual to the head of another and that words are
the vessels that carry these thoughts and ideas. The pervasive
conduit metaphor, as Reddy (1979) termed it, is very misleading
as a heuristic for understanding how communication works. He
proposed the toolmaker's paradigm as an alternative view. Under
this paradigm, sentences, and the words of which they are
constructed, are viewed as very rough blueprints that are subject to a multitude of interpretations by individual receivers,
depending on a host of contextual and individual difference
factors. In contrast to the conduit metaphor, the toolmaker's
paradigm implies that successful communication is achieved

only after considerable effort because variable interpretations must be negotiated. In the context of personal relationships, nowhere is the plausibility of claims concerning the inherent difficulties involved in communication suggested by the toolmaker's paradigm more aptly demonstrated than in studies of marital communication. The degree of agreement between husbands and wives across a variety of issues, some of them highly sensitive, is sometimes so low that it has been suggested that in any given marriage there are really two marriages: her marriage and his marriage (Bernard, 1972; Fitzpatrick, 1987; Frank, Anderson, & Rubenstein, 1980; Sillars, Pike, Jones, & Murphy, 1984). Even more intriguing is the finding indicating that couples exhibiting a direct style of communication show no greater understanding of one another than do couples who display an evasive or nondisclosive communication style (Sillars et al., 1984; Zietlow, 1986).

The idea that persons attempt to "make sense" of their own and others' actions in order to achieve a stable, predictable view of the world so that they can exert some degree of control over events in that world is also a ubiquitous one in social psychological theorizing. Festinger's (1954) social comparison theory, Kelly's (1955) theory of personal constructs and its application to friendship development (Duck, 1973), Heider's (1958) naive analysis of action, White's (1959) competence motivation construct, Rotter (1965) and deCharm's (1968) locus of control research, various attribution models (Bem, 1972; Jones & Davis, 1965; Kelley, 1967) and their extensions to the broader phenomena of account making (Harvey et al., 1990), marital relationships (Bradbury & Fincham, 1990) and conflict (Sillars, 1981), work on learned helplessness (Seligman, 1975), and uncertainty reduction theory (Berger, 1979, 1987; Berger & Bradac, 1982; Berger & Calabrese, 1975) are all predicated on this set of fundamental assumptions. Consequently Duck's (1991) suggestion that relationships be studied as mutual efforts after meaning is a specific instance of a broader, more fundamental concern for how persons are able to communicate successfully in any context.

The perspective advanced in this chapter is based on the considerable work, which addresses the "how" of successful communication, that has been done in the area of planning by researchers from a wide array of disciplines. This chapter seeks to illuminate the relationships among individuals' plans and planning processes, dyadic communicative activity, and the formation of relationships. In the process of explicating linkages among these phenomena, the problem of the relationship of individual meanings to mutual understanding is addressed. It must be recognized from the outset, however, that a considerable proportion of the variance in mutual understanding may be accounted for simply by the fortuitous overlap of individual understandings rather than by some more complex process involving mutual negotiation of meanings. The fact that total strangers who share considerable background knowledge are able to interact with each other with relatively little evidence of miscommunication (Gumperz & Tannen, 1979) suggests that the notion of fortuitous overlap may have more explanatory power than first supposed. Whether the perspective advanced here produces the kinds of insights about relationships envisioned by Duck (1991) is, of course, a question that only time and research can answer.

Plans, Planning, and Social Interaction

A commonplace assumption in current thinking about natural language processing is that persons achieve understandings of the streams of actions emitted by others, including sequences of words, by making inferences about the goals that persons being observed are pursuing and the plans they are using to attain their goals (Allen & Perrault, 1980; Bruce & Newman, 1978; Carberry, 1990; Cohen & Perrault, 1979; Cohen, Morgan, & Pollack, 1990; Green, 1989; Hobbs & Evans, 1980; Schank & Abelson, 1977; Schmidt, 1976; Schmidt, Sridharan, & Goodson, 1978; Sidner, 1985; Wilensky, 1983). In other words, the meaning that is attributed to a sequence of actions, a sequence of words, or some combination of the two is at least partially determined by the goal-plan inferences made by the comprehender, as the following examples indicate.

(1) John kissed Mary passionately.

Although most adult users of the English language know what the act of two persons kissing passionately looks like, their interpretation of this act will vary substantially, depending on their knowledge of the goals and plans of the persons involved in the passionate kissing episode. Thus, for example, if (1) is embedded in the following goal and precondition statements, its interpretation is radically altered.

(2) John wanted to be rich. Mary was a millionairess. John kissed Mary passionately.

(3) John had been stranded alone on a desert island for a year. John kissed Mary passionately.

Asking why John kissed Mary passionately in (2) and (3) yields very different answers because John's goals in the two instances appear to be quite dissimilar. These interpretative differences would no doubt occur whether the passionate kiss was observed directly or the event was presented in written form as it was here, provided, of course, that in both instances the comprehender had access to the additional information presented in (2) and (3). Note also that in contrast to (2), (3) has no explicit statement of John's goal or goals. Given the precondition statement that John was deprived of all direct human contact for a year, although he may have had access to a radio, one plausibly might infer that John would have a particularly elevated need for such contact, but this is only an inference about John's goal. Nonetheless such inferences are necessary to fill in inevitable gaps in both direct experience of event sequences and their symbolic representations in narrative texts. Such inferences enable comprehenders to experience discrete and perhaps somewhat chaotic action sequences as continuous, meaningful streams of purposive action.

Although *goals* are cognitive representations of desired end states that persons seek to attain, *plans* are mental representations of action sequences that may be used to achieve goals (Berger, 1988a, in press; Galambos, Abelson, & Black, 1986; Schank & Abelson, 1977; Wilensky, 1983). Plans generally are conceived of as hierarchically organized and relatively flexible cognitive structures that allow for multiple paths to the same goal; thus one would not speak of *the* plan to get from San Francisco to New York City, as if there were only one way to accomplish this goal. In (2) John's passionate kissing may be understood to be part of a plan to gain access to Mary's money; that is, John becomes involved with Mary romantically and gains access to her fortune. By contrast, John's passionate kissing in (3) may be an action sequence that is part of a larger plan to induce Mary to have a sexual encounter with him. Although sexual activity could occur in (2), in John's view it would be a by-product of his get-rich plan—unless, of course, he had the twin goals of attaining a more affluent life-style and satisfying his sexual desires.

Examples like those previously outlined seem to make the case for the claim that knowledge of goals and plans guides interpretation processes. Unfortunately, however, "for example" is not proof. Beyond such examples, several studies (Abbott & Black, 1986; Black & Bower, 1979, 1980; Cahill & Mitchell, 1987; Lichtenstein & Brewer, 1980; Seifert, Robertson, & Black, 1985) provide evidence that supports the following postulate:

Postulate 1: Event knowledge is organized in long-term
    memory partially in terms of goals and plans.

Black and Bower (1980) and Lichtenstein and Brewer (1980) both found that abstractions of event sequences that were higher in plan hierarchies were better recalled than more concrete, particularistic representations lower in hierarchies. Abbott and Black (1986) reported that the conditional probability of recall was higher for sentences organized in a source-goal-plan (SGP) format than for sentences related simply by concept repetition (Kintsch & vanDijk, 1978; vanDijk & Kintsch, 1983). Studies like these provide some evidence for the psychological validity of such constructs as goal and plan.

Although there are almost always multiple interpretations for a given sequence of actions, the important point is that inferences based on knowledge of the goals that social actors pursue and the plans they use to attain them are vital to the interpretation of action sequences. In Green's (1989) terms, "Understanding a speaker's intention in saying what she said the way she said it amounts to inferring the speaker's plan, in all of its hierarchical glory, although there is room for considerable latitude regarding details" (p. 14). Because reasonably intelligible communication involves mutual assessments of intent, in order for such communication to occur, interactants must develop relatively plausible mental representations of each other's goals and plans; otherwise, they may find themselves to be mutually unintelligible. Much of the time, the development of these mental models of others' plans takes place outside of conscious awareness; however, as the examples demonstrate, such models are absolutely necessary for the development of plausible interpretations of action sequences, including those that we as social actors produce.

Up to this point, the focus has been on the role played by plans in understanding the actions of others; however, plans also play a potentially important role in the production of human action, including speech (Berger & Bell, 1988; Berger, Karol, & Jordan, 1989; Brand, 1984; Bratman, 1987, 1990; Greene, 1984; Hjelmquist, in press; Hjelmquist & Gidlund, 1984; Levelt, 1989; Miller, Galanter, & Pribram, 1960; Pavitt, 1991; Sacerdoti, 1977; Waldron, 1990; Wilensky, 1983). This role is summarized in the following postulate:

Postulate 2: Plans guide goal-directed action.

Brand (1984) emphasizes that plans guide rather than energize human action; although Bratman (1987, 1990) suggests that plans involve future commitments to action. In addition, it is important to distinguish between plans and planning. Given a goal or a set of goals, *planning* involves cognitive assessments of the situation, the mental linking of relevant actions to determine a path or paths to the goal, and perhaps a mental simulation of the plan to determine whether it might work or must be debugged before its implementation. The outcome of this planning process is a plan.

Obviously persons are capable of and occasionally do engage in conscious, deliberate, preinteraction planning, perhaps before interviews or public presentations; however, because planning is resource intensive in terms of time, energy, and cognitive operations, and because decisions concerning actions, including speech acts, to be deployed in conversations must be made on a split-second basis, such detailed, conscious planning cannot be accomplished during most social interactions. Given these limitations, it follows that:

Postulate 3: Persons frequently rely on plans they have used in the past to guide their present actions.

Rather than starting from scratch each time a new goal arises and applying rules to generate new plans, persons search their long-term memories for cases similar to the present circumstances as guides to present planning. Under this case-based approach to planning and reasoning (Hammond, 1989; Riesbeck & Schank, 1989), plans are indexed in memory by the goals they have been associated with in the past and the failures that occurred during previous applications of the plan. Indexing plans with respect to failures helps the planner avoid making the same mistake when the plan is applied in the present circumstances. Some evidence has been adduced to support certain aspects of this case-based view of planning (Berger & diBattista, 1992; Berger & Jordan, 1992).

Waldron (1990) demonstrated convincingly that thoughts concerning goals and plans occur relatively frequently during goal-directed social interaction episodes. Immediately after engaging in dyadic interactions, subjects in his study were asked individually to review videotapes of their conversations. When they came to points in the videotapes where they could remember what they had been thinking about during the conversation, they were asked to stop the tape and to indicate the content of their thoughts. Of the some 2,273 thoughts generated by subjects in this study, 44% were concerned with either the goals they were pursuing in the interaction or the plans they were using to attain their goals. This figure probably underestimates the extent to which knowledge of goals and plans influences the production of action during social interactions because, as was pointed out previously, knowledge of goals and plans can have impacts on action even when such knowledge is outside of conscious awareness. Thus, although conscious, preinteraction planning is relatively rare, knowledge concerning goals and plans apparently is brought to bear with considerable frequency on-line as social interactions progress.

A number of planning theorists have recognized that planners may anticipate counteractions to their projected actions and, as a result, integrate contingencies into their plans in order to counter potential goal blocks (Bruce & Newman, 1978; Carbonell, 1981; Wilensky, 1983). One study of spontaneous plan generation that employed social goals revealed little evidence of such contingent planning (Berger & Bell, 1988); however, another study of children's planning (Kreitler & Kreitler, 1987) found a positive relationship between one's belief in the efficacy of planning as an activity and the tendency to include contingent actions in plans. Presumably, then:

Postulate 4: The tendency to move to a sociocentric mode of planning, in which the projected actions of potential interaction partners are planned for, may be more pronounced when the planner is highly motivated to reach a particular goal or a set of goals.

Although the planning concepts discussed so far may appear to have a static quality, making them poor candidates for capturing the dynamics of relationships, such a conclusion is unwarranted. In general it is assumed that as persons interact with the physical and social world, their world knowledge is being updated constantly. Furthermore newly acquired information interacts with knowledge stored in memory to produce new memory structures. Consequently one does not necessarily incrementally add new knowledge to old, but in the process of dealing with new information, old knowledge is itself transformed. In short, memory is viewed as a dynamic process rather than as a mere repository in which knowledge accretes (Schank, 1982). In terms of the present discussion, an important implication of this dynamic view of memory is:

Postulate 5: Knowledge concerned with plans and planning, like other forms of knowledge, is constantly being updated and transformed. These transformations influence interpretations of past, present, and future action sequences.

Given this postulate, it would not be surprising to observe the same individual interpreting a similar sequence of events occurring on two different occasions in somewhat different ways, or the same individual interpreting a specific sequence of prior events differently on two separate occasions. Obviously, given both a dynamic view of memory and the passage of time, the descriptiveness of the phrase "same individual" is itself of dubious accuracy.

Goals, Plans, and Mutual Understanding

Having established the fundamental roles played by goals and plans in both the interpretation and the production of action and discourse, I now turn attention to the parts that goals and plans play in the development of social relationships. Underlying this discussion is the assumption that a considerable amount of the human action observed in everyday life is goal directed and plan guided. Granting the plausibility of this postulate, however, in no way warrants such claims as plan-guided behavior is always consciously monitored or persons are consciously aware of the goals they are pursuing at any given point in time. The hierarchical nature of plans allows for the possibility that actions may be identified at various levels of abstraction such that persons may not be aware that currently salient goals are in fact subgoals subserving more regnant goals (Vallacher & Wegner, 1985; Vallacher, Wegner, & Somoza, 1989).

Moreover, the assumption that persons' actions are goal directed and plan guided does not imply that communication is merely an instrumentality or a tool used by persons to assist them in reaching their goals. Although it is certainly the case that both verbal and nonverbal communication play central roles in the achievement of many social goals and that such communicative activity is plan guided (Levelt, 1989), it is also true that mental representations of goals and plans do far more than guide goal-directed action. These knowledge structures play a vital role in the comprehension and interpretation of directly observed action sequences and representations of such sequences in symbolic form. Both of these functions played by goals and plans are important contributors to various processes and outcomes observed in relationship life.

In light of individual plan-based understandings, the question is how such understandings become mutual. To answer this question, it is helpful to consider the following example. Assume that each member in a relationship likes the other but does not know whether these feelings are mutual. Further assume that each is interested in knowing whether the other individual shares these feelings of attraction, a situation that is prevalent in the early stages of many kinds of relationships and a condition that could arise in relationships that have persisted for a considerable period of time. Although this particular kind of problem has been addressed in productive ways under the rubrics of "secret tests" for assessing the state of relationships (Baxter & Wilmot, 1984) and affinity-testing strategies (Douglas, 1987), the difficulty with these "strategies" approaches to the present problem is that they do not answer the process question being posed; that is, isolating secret tests or affinity-testing strategies does not necessarily answer the question of how persons actually go about making such assessments of liking. Although individuals may use a number of strategies and the particular strategy or strategies employed may vary as a function of a number of personal and contextual factors, delineating conditions of strategy deployment does not explain how information is dealt with once it is obtained by using a particular strategy. Another way of viewing the problem is to focus on the term *use;* that is, what does it mean to *use* a strategy? The process is the issue here.

In light of the affinity-testing situation posed above, one possible plan of attack is for each person to become increasingly reciprocity sensitive. This kind of plan embodies the notion of the test-operate-test-exit, or TOTE, unit advanced by Miller et al. (1960) in which individuals assess where they stand relative to a desired goal; if there is a discrepancy, they execute some course of action to reduce that discrepancy. They then test to see whether the discrepancy has been reduced. If the desired goal has been achieved, they exit the loop. If the goal has not been achieved, they engage in further actions to reduce the remaining discrepancy. Within this conceptual frame, the operate phase of the TOTE unit could involve the deployment of a particular affinity-testing strategy designed to determine the degree of liking the other has for self, while the test phases could involve observations of the responses of the other person to the deployment of the strategy. In terms of the affinity-testing problem, one person might give the other person a particularly nice compliment not only to indicate liking but also to determine the degree to which the positive behavior is reciprocated. Reciprocated positive behavior then might be used as evidence for the hypothesis that liking is mutual, at least in the eyes of the individual tester.

In this case, reciprocal behavior serves an informational function instead of, or in addition to, the usual functions that have been postulated for the reciprocity phenomenon—that is, equity maintenance (Roloff, 1981) and social appropriateness (Brown & Levinson, 1978). In terms of the goal-plan framework advocated here, when positive behavior is reciprocated, it is interpreted within a knowledge structure that includes the proposition that under normal conditions, when persons like each other they tend to reciprocate positive behaviors; also, if persons have the goal of inducing other persons to like them, they will follow the plan of performing positive acts for the others. If positive behaviors are reciprocated, the inference is made that the others have some degree of liking for those performing the acts. Of course, there is the distinct possibility that the positive actions will not be reciprocated. In this case, the plan may provide the inference that lack of reciprocity may be indicative of lower levels of liking or that the targets may not have been aware that the compliments were sincere. In any case, lack of reciprocity might be as diagnostic of the others' feelings toward the self as reciprocity would be. The potential diagnostic value of reciprocity information may explain why initial conversations between strangers seem to follow the norm of reciprocity relatively closely and why, as relationships develop, such reciprocity may become less apparent. Once parties to a relationship build a fund of mutual understandings, it may become less necessary to acquire reciprocity information with which to make inferences about partners' feelings and beliefs.

Lest the reader still be unconvinced of the importance of goal-plan knowledge structures in the generation of the kinds of inferences examined in the example, consider a similar situation in which a given individual likes another person and wishes to induce the other to reciprocate the liking; that is, the planner's goal is to induce the affective state of liking in the other person. One plan to achieve this goal is for the planner to show positive behaviors toward the other, including complimenting the person. Here the plan to compliment the other is presumed to guide the planner's actions as they are produced. Notice, however, that the plan that serves this action production function could also be employed to interpret the actions of the other toward the self; that is, compliments directed toward the self may be expressions of affection by those who render them. Of course, plans like these may be framed in such a way that differential attributions concerning motives will influence interpretations of the other's goals. Positive actions may be sincere displays of liking, but they also may be deployed in the service of such ulterior motives as ingratiation (Jones, 1964; Jones & Davis, 1965; Jones & Wortman, 1971). Here again, however, it is assumed that not only are persons potentially able to detect such motivations in others' actions, but if they choose, they also can act in ways that actualize these states in their own behavior. Consequently it is reasonable to assume that the plans that guide inferencing during comprehension also direct actions during their production.

The example just discussed depicted an individual in search of an answer to the question of whether a particular other person shared feelings of liking. In the example, the person seeking the relevant information understood his or her feeling toward the other and endeavored to determine whether the other shared similar or dissimilar feelings; that is, the person sought information to make the determination. It would be misleading to believe that inferences about others' feelings for self necessarily are arrived at during or immediately after the planner concludes current information-seeking attempts. In fact, some evidence suggests that persons do not necessarily make large numbers of inferences on-line as they read texts (McKoon & Ratcliff, 1986). Indeed it seems quite possible that when out of the physical presence of target persons, individuals could recall a number of previous interactions with the targets to determine whether events that occurred during these interactions might have some bearing on the current goal of determining whether the other shares feelings of liking. This latter type of judgment process has been referred to by Hastie and Pennington (1989) as *memory-based inferencing,* and inferences that are made while the target individual is perceptually available to the social actor have been called *on-line inferences.* Although not employing explicitly the construct of memory-based inferencing, Duck, Pond, & Leatham (1991) suggest that individual reconstructions of relationship-relevant events in memory may exert powerful effects on the current attitudes and actions of relationship partners toward each other.

Several studies have revealed that the relationship between memory and judgments depends significantly on whether the judgments are made in on-line judgment contexts or are memory-based. For example, Hastie and Park (1986) reported that among persons who were told in advance that they would be judging the suitability of a job applicant after listening to a tape recording of an interview with him or her, no relationship was found between the amount of evaluative information presented in the interview that was recalled by subjects and their judgment of the applicant's suitability for the job across three replications of the experiment (median r = .09). By contrast, persons who viewed the same interview but were not informed in advance that they would be making suitability judgments later evidenced significant correlations (median r = .46) between the proportion of favorable statements recalled from the interview and ratings of the suitability of the applicant for the position.

Although these studies are based on the assumption that persons who were informed in advance about the judgment they would be making immediately after the interview made their inferences as they viewed the interview and that those who were not given these instructions relied on their memory of the interview to make their inferences, a crucial implication of this research is that many inferences that are important in the lives of relationship partners may be made when the other person is not physically present and providing information directly to the inference maker. This possibility may explain why some conflicts between relationship partners erupt at the beginning, rather than at the middle or the end, of particular interaction episodes that themselves were not immediately preceded by conflict-ridden episodes. In such instances, during the period of time between encounters, one partner may generate negative, memory-based inferences about the other person in the relationship that guide the inference makers' actions during the early stages of the next encounter. The partner, of course, may be mystified by the sudden change in the inference maker *for no apparent reason.* Of course, the difficulty here is that the partner does not realize that the inference maker has been thinking about the relationship during the period between encounters and that the partner is unaware that the inference maker may have searched his or her memory for numerous previous episodes before arriving at the present negative inference.

Although this particular example has emphasized the memory-based inferencing activity of only one person in the relationship, both persons might use the period between particular encounters to generate memory-based inferences that are highly similar, for example, judgments of mutual attraction for each other or judgments of mutual dislike for each other. In both cases, there would probably be very little mystery surrounding the mutual feelings of the persons involved in the relationship. Of course, it is also possible that during the period between encounters, persons may generate divergent memory-based inferences that, like those generated on-line, could become sources of potential disagreement and conflict between the partners. Whatever the final outcome of these inferencing processes, however, many of these inferences will be based on assessments of the goals and plans that partners believe each other to be following.

So far it has been suggested that plan-based inferences can be made either on-line as interactions unfold or between interaction episodes. It is worth considering briefly a special case of on-line inferencing that may be responsible for what can be called *spontaneous mutual understanding.* In the development of most relationships, it takes considerable time before individuals each develop a fund of unique, mutually plausible inferences for each other's and their own actions; however, it does happen that individuals meeting for the first time sometimes report that they understand each other exceptionally well after only a short period of interaction. Such phrases as "hitting it off," "understanding where each other is coming from," or "resonating with each other" are used to describe such experiences. One potential explanation of these instances is that they are the result of mutual overgeneralizations from a few superficial, mutually perceived similarities.

One implication of this overgeneralization explanation is that those involved in the relationship are bound to be disappointed to find that as they come to know each other better, they are not as similar as they first thought. Although this explanation is both plausible and the basis for a "go slow," conservative approach to making relationship commitments, it is also possible that spontaneous mutual understanding could be considerably deeper than that implied by this explanation. Some persons characteristically may reveal information about themselves that allows others to build extensive networks of inferences about them relatively quickly; others may not proffer information that allows the rapid generation of such elaborate networks. For example, persons who disclose information indicative of their basic values, values that presumably underlie a number of the more particularistic goals they pursue, may provide considerably more grist for their relationship partners' inference-generating mills than persons who dwell on more normative conversational topics during their initial encounters with others. Once value-relevant information is made available to partners, the partners may infer that they share not only similar value systems but also the sets of goals that these values implicate, as well as plans for reaching these goals. Again, of course, these inferences may not be accurate, and the individuals may be disappointed to find, later on, that they are not as similar as they first believed. Nevertheless, in contrast to the overgeneralization explanation, individuals' assessments of similarity can go far beyond a few, superficial attributes. One hypothesis that follows from this discussion is that the relationships of persons whose early judgments of similarity are predicated on more elaborate inferential networks will remain in those relationships longer, even after the inevitable dissimilarities are detected, than will persons whose early inferences are based on relatively few surface similarities. The plausibility of this hypothesis rests on the assumption that disconfirming more elaborate inferential systems will take more time than will disconfirming less complex systems. Moreover, complex systems may afford the inference maker greater opportunity to resolve apparent inconsistencies than will less complex systems, thus allowing the relationship to continue.

Given the preceding discussion, what can be said about the roles played by goals and plans in the development of mutual understanding? Understanding can be said to be mutual when persons in relationships believe that they know (a) what goals their relationship partner is pursuing relative to their own goals and (b) the plans they and their partner are using to pursue goals. Under this notion, mutual understanding is inference based. Persons may come to believe that they are pursuing similar, dissimilar, or incompatible goals. Furthermore, even though partners believe that they are pursuing the same or similar goals, they may believe that their plans for doing so are similar, dissimilar, or incompatible. No matter what combinations of beliefs about goals and plans obtain, mutual understanding arises out of these patterns of individual inferencing. Obviously the entire issue of the *accuracy* of these assessments has been avoided here; however, this is as it should be. Simply put, not only do individuals act on their beliefs, erroneous or accurate, but as was indicated earlier, the communication process itself is primarily an inferential game in which individuals do their best to make sense of sketchy patterns of sights, sounds, and markings on paper. This difficult and chancy inferential process is no less an important feature of relationship life.

Strategies, Stories, and Accounts

Persons involved in relationships have been depicted here as inference generators struggling mightily to apprehend the meaning of their own and their partners' actions by using their knowledge of goals and plans to make their experiences coherent. Recently some relationship researchers have suggested that the narratives or stories that persons tell about their relationships may provide considerable purchase in understanding how relationships work (Gergen & Gergen, 1983, 1984, 1987; Shotter, 1984, 1987). Although these researchers emphasize the oral telling of relationship stories, Harvey et al. (1990) have pointed out that such recounting can be done mentally with equally dramatic effects. They argue that the concept of *narrative* can be subsumed under the broader construct of *account,* although many accounts ultimately are rendered in the oral mode as stories.

From the perspective of mutual understanding in relationships, extremely important account-rendering venues are ones in which one or both parties to the relationship provide accounts to each other, or ones in which one or both partners create accounts and present them to a third party, while both relationship partners are present. Especially significant are accounts that involve the relationship itself, although accounts involving each individual in the relationship may prove to be enlightening to the other partner. A particularly significant relationship-relevant account might involve a married couple being

asked by a third party (perhaps their child) to explain how they
met and how they developed their relationship to the point of
marriage. These accounts might contain references to strategies
that were used to attain certain subgoals that were vital to the
development of the relationship. Thus, in the presentation of
such an account, one partner might reveal strategies that were
used to (a) meet the partner in the first place, (b) induce the
other person to go out on their first date, (c) attract the person,
and (d) interest the partner in a more serious relationship,
including the marital relationship. Requests for these kinds of
accounts could be made for persons involved in less close personal relationships—for example, dating relationships and relatively impersonal business relationships. In the latter case, business
partners might be asked to explain how they came together to form
their joint enterprise. Regardless of the degree of closeness of the
relationship, these occasions enable the partners to ask questions about the accounts rendered by each other and to offer
either confirmation of characterizations or conflicting interpretations of events. Not only may explanations for the "same
events" differ in such interactions, but there also may be disagreements over whether the events described in the account
happened the way the account giver presented them. In this kind
of communicative setting, the probability of mutual understanding is likely to increase because individual interpretations may
be made explicit. This is so even if similar interpretations of the
accounts do not result from the interaction; for mutual understanding certainly can involve the common knowledge that
interpretations differ significantly.

Although joint renderings of accounts may lead to higher
levels of mutual understanding, some evidence suggests that
even in these communication situations, marital partners may
interact in ways that may prevent such understandings from
developing. Sillars et al. (1984) found that when couples discussed issues involving instrumental activities, they showed
higher levels of mutual understanding than when they discussed
more abstract issues concerned with their relationship. Moreover, Sillars, Burggraf, Yost, & Zietlow (in press) reported that
couples who embrace a marital ideology emphasizing autonomy

evidenced more references to individual themes concerning personality and individual differences in their communication with each other and an interaction style they described as "differentiating." By contrast, couples whose dominant ideology featured interdependence evinced more communal themes in their interactions and employed an interaction style emphasizing "blending" of relationship themes. Apparently, then, both the level of abstraction of the issue under discussion, as well as the particular ideology that marital couples subscribe to, influence the degree to which mutual understanding can be achieved.

The notion of accounting itself may be viewed from a perspective somewhat different from the one described above. During the past 15 years, a considerable literature has developed focusing on various strategies that persons use to achieve a variety of social and personal goals. These goals include affinity seeking (Bell & Daly, 1984; Douglas, 1987), assessing relationship states (Baxter & Wilmot, 1984), comforting others (Burleson, 1984; Burleson & Samter, 1985), compliance gaining (Boster & Stiff, 1984; Cody, McLaughlin, & Jordan, 1980; Cody, McLaughlin, & Schneider, 1981; deTurck, 1985; Dillard & Burgoon, 1985; Falbo, 1977; Falbo & Peplau, 1980; McLaughlin, Cody, & Robey, 1980; Miller, 1987; Miller, Boster, Roloff, & Seibold, 1977, 1987; Rule & Bisanz, 1987; Rule, Bisanz, & Kohn, 1985; Schenck-Hamlin, Wiseman, & Georgacarakos, 1982; Tracy, Craig, Smith, & Spisak, 1984; Wheeless, Barraclough, & Stewart, 1983), information seeking (Berger & Kellermann, 1983, 1986, 1989; Kellermann & Berger, 1984), and relationship disengagement (Baxter, 1982). This general line of research has been conducted under the assumption that persons' goal-directed actions are guided by the strategies revealed in these studies. Most of the research done in this strategies tradition has been descriptive in that it has generated lists of strategies for achieving the variety of goals cited above. Some investigators have tried to determine the conditions under which various strategies are likely to be deployed in social interactions; however, a great deal of the research reported in this literature has been conducted in a theoretical vacuum (Berger, in press).

The purpose of mentioning this line of research here is not to remedy the lack of theoretical motivation behind it (see Berger, in press; Dillard, 1990; Greene, 1990, for such attempts), but to suggest two important points with regard to accounts. First, many relationship-relevant accounts seem to involve recollections about plans or strategies that were used to achieve goals in relationships. These accounts might include assessments of the degree of success or failure of the strategies; that is, persons might tell of their successful attempts to woo their partners, while others might indicate the strategies involved in their heroic but unsuccessful attempts to save their marriages. Consequently a significant point missed by strategies researchers, who generally have focused on issues related to strategy selection, is that the recollections of strategies used to achieve particular goals at one point in time may become integral to the construction of coherent accounts provided at a later point in time. Of course, general knowledge of plans or strategies for reaching social goals may intrude automatically in the account-making process and produce distortions in the recall of the specific episode being described, or, for self-presentational reasons, persons may alter their accounts intentionally (Gergen & Gergen, 1987). However, even in this latter case, intentional alterations require general knowledge of goals and plans for the production of coherent and plausible fabrications. A second point, and one that has been made previously, is that in order for persons to comprehend the accounts offered by their relationship partners, they must have the requisite knowledge of goals and plans. Without such knowledge, persons listening to the account are unlikely to get its point or to understand the moral underlying it. The ability to understand the point of accounts doubtlessly is related to the potential for accounts to produce significant outcomes for both individuals and relationships.

If the stories and accounts exchanged between relationship partners mainly consist of recollections of past efforts to use particular plans or strategies to reach goals that have a direct or an indirect bearing on the relationship, it is of potential theoretical interest to contrast those stories and accounts in which goals were successfully achieved with those in which the account renderer failed to reach the desired goal. It might be postulated that because of self-presentational concerns, persons are less likely to proffer accounts involving goal failure (Gergen & Gergen, 1987). However, an old and common story line in fictional narratives presented in both print and electronic media is one in which the protagonists initially follow plans to attain particular goals, but their plans are thwarted by other story characters or some event or events. In response to plan failure, protagonists devise new plans for reaching their goals, and they eventually succeed in doing so. Although protagonists usually ultimately succeed under this tried-and-true formula, thus enhancing their presentation of self, it is also true that the story itself is rendered potentially more interesting and engaging because it contains a plan failure episode that contrasts with successfully executed plans. Research conducted in the area of memory for narratives has demonstrated that successful and unsuccessful actions on the main causal chain of actions that make up stories are better remembered than actions incidental to goal attainment (Lichtenstein & Brewer, 1980; Mandler & Johnson, 1977; Omanson, 1982; Stein & Glenn, 1979; Trabasso & van den Broek, 1985), and successful goal-directed actions are better recalled than unsuccessful actions (Black & Bower, 1980).

When one or both parties to a relationship provide recollections or accounts of previous goal-directed action sequences, it is assumed that each person makes some judgment of the relative degree to which the goal under consideration was successfully achieved. For the sake of simplicity, assume that each person makes a determination of whether or not the goal was actually achieved. Given these individual determinations, partners may agree that goals were or were not attained; however, they also may diverge in their assessments of goal achievement. Moreover, relationship partners may or may not be in accord in their recollections of how the goal was achieved; that is, in addition to possible disagreements over goal attainment, partners may disagree concerning the plan used to try to achieve the goal. It is reasonable to suppose that conflict over both goals and plans is likely to be more severe than conflict over either one alone. More important, however, is the fact that although partners may agree that a particular goal was or was not achieved, they may disagree about the plan that was used to reach the goal. Disagreement at this level might be masked by agreement at the level of goals, thus creating the illusion of a common perception by both partners; or disagreement at the level of plans may interfere with the discovery of common evaluations of goal attainment. This latter possibility is not unlike the phenomenon commonly observed in arguments between persons who, after long and sometimes heated discussions, realize that they agree concerning a desired state of affairs—for example, reduction of crime—but disagree over the means for attaining the goal—for example, stricter law enforcement versus increased aid to the poor.

Given the limitations of human memory, especially for events long in the past, it is reasonable to expect that disagreements over accounts are more likely to occur when the time lapse between the occurrence of the events and the rendering of the accounts increases. However, a countervailing force that might reduce disagreements over accounts would be the frequency with which the account is rendered. The more frequently the account is given with both partners present, the more likely it is that the partners will develop a common interpretation of the events in question. By contrast, the infrequent rendering of accounts should potentiate disagreement as the interval between the events and the time the account is given increases.

In addition to passage of time, another factor that could affect the accuracy of recall, and thus the likelihood of disagreement, is whether the actions being recalled were successful or unsuccessful at reaching the goal or goals in question. It was suggested previously that actions that are successful at reaching subgoals nested under superordinate goals are better recalled than actions that fail to produce desired changes in goal states (Black & Bower, 1980). As a consequence, these findings suggest a potential bias that might create more disagreements in interpretation of failure sequences; however, testing this hypothesis might be made particularly difficult because of the tendency for some persons to be especially concerned with the positivity of their self-presentations. Such individuals might remember failure sequences but be reticent to report them, even to probing interviewers.

Implications for Relationships Research

An important implication of the preceding analysis is that a great deal of the work involved in achieving mutual understanding in relationships occurs at the individual level. This assertion calls into question the view advanced by some that individually oriented theories cannot provide adequate explanations for "relationship level" phenomena. One charge levied by such theorists is that individually oriented, atomistic theories are incapable of explaining such relationship-level phenomena as the contradictions that are inevitable features of any and all relationships (Altman, Vinsel, & Brown, 1981; Baxter, 1988, 1990, in press; Bochner, 1984; Rawlins, 1983, 1989). These theorists also allege that individually oriented theories do not adequately capture such notions as process and change and that dialectical theories are better able to explain the fluctuating behavioral patterns that are considerably more common in relationships than are smooth trajectories of growth and decay. This anti-individual theory view would seem to apply with equal relevance to such constructs as negotiation of meaning, mutual efforts after meaning, and mutual understanding, because these terms themselves seem to bespeak of relationship-level activity.

The case of mutual understanding, however, may not be as transparent as this relationship level of analysis suggests. What we commonly call *mutual understanding* may sometimes arise from the fortuitous confluence of individual systems of knowledge representation that are triggered by the exchange of arbitrary codes; that is, under such conditions mutual understanding in no way is "negotiated." When we, as researchers, speak of relationship partners "negotiating meanings" for their relationships, perhaps by dealing with the dialectical polarities inherent in them, we must be careful not to be mesmerized by the siren song of the conduit metaphor, only to founder on the Shoals of Misdirected Ideas. The process of interpretation is, in the final analysis, an individual affair. Persons can exchange patterned forms of physical energy that are potentially informative, but only potentially informative and informative within the context of existing knowledge. Moreover, the evidence suggests that even when persons involved in close relationships communicate with each other, their exchanges may act simply to trigger existing inferences rather than to create new ones, the latter process being implied by the term *negotiation* (Sillars et al., in press). Thus, what appear to be "negotiated meanings" for relationships may in fact simply be the result of the overlap of knowledge representation systems that persons bring with them to relationships. To clarify, the claim being made here is not that all instances of mutual understanding are the result of fortuitous confluences of systems of knowledge representation; however, mutual understandings between relationship partners may be considerably less "negotiated" than some may currently assume.

In this regard another problem concerns the relationship between terms used by researchers to describe processes and the ways the processes themselves actually work. As suggested previously, such terms as *mutual effort after meaning, shared meaning, negotiation of meaning, mutual understanding,* and the like seem to refer to "relationship-level" phenomena. In the extreme we could imagine a world in which individuals possess abilities that enable them to achieve these states to the ultimate degree. For example, in his interactions with others, Mr. Spock of the *Star Trek* series can engage in Vulcan mind fusion, Vulcan mind meld, and Vulcan mind touch so that he can read others' thoughts directly (Trimble, 1976). Alas, for humans, however, these states of unmediated, noninferential understanding are unattainable; not because there are no thoughts to be read directly, but because the code systems that link humans and the equipment that humans have to processes those codes have significant limitations. Nevertheless as humans we can imagine, label, and converse about such phenomena as mind fusion and mind meld, but we cannot experience them, unless we believe we are psychic. Similarly we can fabricate "relationship terms" that imply that their referents involve "mutuality," when in fact they may be considerably less "mutual" than the terms themselves suggest. This subtle Vulcanization of relationship terms leads to a distorted view of how both communication and relationship processes actually work.

In response to this general line of argument, one might point to the evidence that relationship partners develop "personal idioms" and "secret codes" that are only understandable to them (Bell, Buerkel-Rothfuss, & Gore, 1987; Bell & Healy, 1992; Hopper, Knapp, & Scott, 1981). The existence of these idioms is taken as warrant for the claim that relationship meanings are mutually negotiated. In light of the present perspective, this argument has at least three problems. First, persons involved in close relationships can generate relatively few such idioms when asked to do so. Bell et al.'s (1987) and Bell & Healy's (1992) respondents, who were involved in relationships at various intimacy levels, on average listed approximately six idioms, and some individuals generated none. Apparently, then, most relationship partners do not spend a great deal of time negotiating such terms, or, if they do spend large amounts of time so doing, the fruits of their labors are relatively meager. Second, couples participating in the Bell et al. (1987) study collaborated in generating lists of idioms. Consequently there is no guarantee that if relationship partners had been asked to generate such idioms independently, there would have been a great deal of overlap in partners' lists. The methodology used in this particular study virtually guaranteed some evidence of "mutual negotiation," as the authors themselves pointed out.

Third, previously cited evidence suggests that it is in the domain of relational or companionate attitudes, attitudes that are supposedly central to relationship life, that married couples demonstrate the *lowest* levels of mutual understanding (Sillars et al., 1984). Consequently it appears that even if couples spend considerable amounts of time trying to negotiate such mutual understandings, and as far as we know they may not, they are relatively unsuccessful. The analysis presented here suggests that one potential reason for failure to achieve mutual understandings is that general knowledge about the goals and plans that is integral to relational life and that is brought to bear in any particular relationship dominates potential idiosyncratic information that can be gleaned about a specific person in a specific relationship. Persons may employ easily retrieved general knowledge to interpret actions of specific relationship partners before they attempt to build knowledge structures focused on the particular individual in the relationship. This hypothesis makes considerable sense in terms of cognitive efficiency and cognitive effort because it is easier and less time consuming to employ extant general knowledge of relationships to interpret actions that occur in individual relationships than it is to build a fund of new knowledge for each relationship in which one is involved. This is not to say that specific knowledge is not and cannot be developed; however, the generation of such detailed knowledge is resource intensive and even when it is developed, it is used within the framework provided by the general knowledge of how relationships between people work.

Perhaps relationship researchers themselves tend to overestimate the extent to which individuals involved in relationships explicitly engage in "mutual efforts after meaning" and all of the effortful activity implied by such a phrase. Such a bias might arise because of the large amount of time these researchers themselves spend thinking and talking about relationships. This speculation is perfectly plausible in light of the evidence concerning the false consensus effect—that is, the tendency for persons to believe that others believe and behave the same way as they themselves do (Nisbett & Ross, 1980). Descriptive data collected from representative samples of persons involved in relationships, especially samples that represent noncollege student populations, are needed to determine the amount of time persons involved in relationships spend talking about their relationships. Given the time demands imposed on them by such activities as work, routine chores, and sleep, most adults probably have very little time to negotiate explicitly joint meanings for their relationships. As suggested previously, such "negotiations" may take place when individuals are alone, between interactions with their partners. It is during these periods that significant shifts in inferences concerning relationships may occur because memory-based inference processes are more likely to produce stimulus-based shifts in judgments than inferences made on-line, as interactions unfold (Hastie & Pennington, 1989).

Another implication that flows from the individually centered interpretative stance articulated in this chapter is that dialectical phenomena in relationships do not necessarily occur at the relational, as opposed to the individual, level of analysis, as has been claimed by some (Baxter, 1988, 1990, in press). Clearly individuals can and do wrestle with issues concerned with such dialectical poles as interdependence and autonomy in the absence of any interaction with relationship partners or confidants with whom such issues might be discussed. In fact, recent presentations explicating important dialectical poles in relationships in some ways resemble classical discussions of individually experienced conflict, especially conflicts of the approach-avoidance variety (Lewin, 1935). Decisions concerning whether or at what times one wishes to be independent of or connected with one's partner in a relationship might be analyzable under the rubric of double approach-avoidance conflict, for example. In any case, whatever terms are used to describe the phenomenon, in many instances such conflicts are dealt with within the heads of the individual social actors and not necessarily at the relational level. Individual cognitions about the conflict may be "social" in that they explicitly involve other persons, specifically relationship partners; but these social cognitions and the decisions they affect regarding such issues as autonomy and connection, which themselves may or may not be "polar opposites," are clearly individual-level phenomena.

When persons choose to talk about relationship issues with their relationship partners, they may be analyzable as relational-level phenomena; however, any particular issue, as discussed by the partners, is still subject to individual interpretations that may or may not coincide. Observations of interpretative divergences between relationship partners have led some to suggest that, at least to some degree, relationships exist within the heads of relationship partners (Duck, 1990; Duck, Pond, & Leatham, 1991). Moreover, as the literature on the effects of group communication on individual decision making teaches us, even when persons ostensibly discuss issues that may be relatively salient to them, the communication they engage in may be placebic in the sense that

it has little, if any, impact in shaping the final decision made by
the group; that is, one can predict the final group decision simply
by knowing the predispositions of each group member *before* any
group discussion is undertaken (see Hewes's, 1986, discussion of
his socio-egocentric model of group decision making).

Again Sillars et al.'s (in press) study of interactions between
married couples suggests that, at least under some conditions,
the conversations of couples about important issues in their
marriage resemble the episodes of parallel play sometimes observed in groups of young children; that is, the sequences of
communicative acts displayed by each individual may be meaningful, but when taken together, they are not integrated into a
coherent pattern. Furthermore it seems possible that, under
some conditions, couples involved in conversations might produce interleaved but automated sequences of actions that are
judged to be globally meaningful by observers but that have little
meaning to the interactants themselves. Thus interactions between relationship partners, including interactions involving
dialectical polarities, may not only fail to alter individual relationship meanings significantly but also may not necessarily take
place at the relational level of communication. Consequently it
is difficult to understand how dialectical approaches to the study
of relationships necessarily guarantee that communication in
relationships will be studied at the relational level of analysis
(Baxter, 1988, 1990, in press), because it is clear that dialectical
contradictions might be dealt with, at least in some cases, by
each individual in the relationship without explicitly engaging
the issue with the partner. Moreover, when the issue ostensibly
is discussed, individuals may not necessarily be "relating," in the
sense that they process each other's communicative activity in
a way that alters their individual interpretations.

In light of the dynamic view of memory structures advocated
in this chapter, discontinuous patterns of relationship growth
and decline, as opposed to the continuous trajectories of relationship growth suggested by social exchange theories (Altman
& Taylor, 1973; Thibaut & Kelley, 1959), would appear to be the

rule rather than the exception. Knowledge of relationship-relevant events may intrude in individuals' conceptualizations of relationships and may cause rapid and dramatic changes in such affective judgments as relationship satisfaction (Planalp & Honeycutt, 1985; Planalp et al., 1988). Moreover, the fact that the addition of new knowledge has ramifications throughout the memory system and affects interpretations of past events not only reaffirms the wisdom of Heraclitus's dictum that one cannot step into the same river twice but also suggests that relationship decline cannot simply be the reverse of relationship growth because it is not possible for individuals' conceptualizations of their relationships to return to some earlier point. Furthermore, because both goals and plans are a part of this dynamic system, ongoing changes in relationship goals and the means for attaining them are to be expected; and because the goals of relationship partners can and do change, it is probably misleading to think of relationships as reaching a particular state to be maintained. These dynamic properties of goal-plan knowledge structures also make the attainment of mutual understanding between relationship partners a difficult state to realize; and once such a state is achieved, it may not exist for a long period of time.

Finally, contrary to the intuitions of some, a positive relationship between mutual understanding and relationship satisfaction should not be expected. For instance, spouses may have very detailed mutual understandings of the reasons for the unfaithful acts of one of them. Such knowledge, even if it provides plausible explanations for the actions of the philandering spouse, is not likely to increase the relationship satisfaction level of the aggrieved spouse. Consequently mutual understanding does not necessarily direct persons down the royal road to relationship Nirvana, and, by implication, persons in relationships may experience more happiness when they do not know certain things about their partner. What needs to be better understood, then, are the conditions under which ignorance is bliss and the circumstances under which knowledge is power.

Memory Structures
for the Rise and Fall
of Personal Relationships

James M. Honeycutt

Individual cognition affects the ways in which the person acts in relationships just as much as it affects other behavior. Although much work has looked at social cognition in relationships, this chapter focuses specifically on the ways persons organize cognition about relational change, whether positive (growth) or negative (decline). It examines the ways in which beliefs are organized into memory organization packets (MOP) (Schank, 1982) that affect how the perceiver sees relationships and other people. Its major focus is on change, but it begins and ends by drawing parallels between the ways researchers view such change, compared to the "theories" held by ordinary folk. The chapter also offers a way of reconceptualizing the nature of "phases" in relationships that could re-enliven phase models; it does this by emphasizing the role of phases in the cognition of the subject.

Any view of the development of relationships assumes that individuals progress in some way, and most psychological models assume that this occurs via passage through various phases. Models of relationship development range from simple, three stage models, such as Levinger's (1974) old awareness model, to more complex multistage models that account for relationship decline (Duck, 1982; Honeycutt, Cantrill, & Allen, 1992; Knapp, 1984; Lee, 1984). The models present a linear view of growth that occurs in relationships with individuals sequentially progressing through early stages in order to develop close, interpersonal relations. The obverse is that although the relationship may end abruptly at any point, there is also the possibility of it going through a number of de-escalating phases (Baxter, 1985).

The simple linearity view has frequently been called into question (Baxter, 1985, 1988; Van Lear, 1992); as a result, developmental theorists have revised their models to reflect the dialectic view that relationships never really achieve simple phases or a steady state because there is continual negotiation and recalibration. Although movement tends nevertheless to be systematic, it may occur simultaneously at various speeds in various respects, or in various directions with a variety of results (Altman et al., 1981; Baxter, 1985; Duck & Craig, 1978; Knapp & Vangelisti, 1992; Taylor & Altman, 1987). The results may be positive or negative and can have a variety of effects on the level of certainty about the state of the relationship (Baxter & Wilmot, 1984; Planalp et al., 1988). Although the relationship is thus constantly evolving, it becomes a matter for developmental theorists to partition the concept of an intimate relationship into smaller, meaningful categories that provide an understanding of the properties and life cycle of relationships (Hinde, 1979). Thus the *phase* concept has been developed usefully to reflect relational properties in terms of the occurrence of systematic or repetitive behaviors.

As a development of such basic views, Duck (1990, 1991) argues that motion, rather than steady state, is the fundamental normative property of relationships, with partners attempting to negotiate or create an appearance of a steady-state in order to make relationships predictable, orderly, and manageable. Thus although relationships are dynamic rather than static entities, people tell narratives about relationships that help provide order to time-ordered events (Askham, 1981). Duck (1990) indicates how it is easier even for relational researchers to define relationships as states and to represent process or transitions as movements between so-called states because it is much easier to research definable states rather than continual movement.

When individuals provide relational narratives, we should find that individuals recall particular events rather than time-ordered process because relational "states" would be reflected through the expectancies that individuals have for the event-driven nature of the rise, maintenance, and demise of personal relationships. Martin, Hagestad, and Diedrick (1988) indicate how the recall of events is done usually through the telling of stories that capture occurrences of short duration. For example, when individuals are asked to tell the story of their marriage, their first response is often, "What do you want to know?" They ask this question to reduce processing and to concentrate on discrete events (Askham, 1981). Similarly, when asked to recall the development of any current relationship, individuals may tell stories of events of short duration such as an initial meeting, recognizing that the relationship was important through a disclosure episode, or overcoming a brief crisis.

A Memory Structure Approach
to Developmental Communication

From such evidence as mentioned above, we can create the position that these narratives are accessed through memory and that they set up expectancies for the categorization of relationship behaviors that may be observed or experienced in the future. In short, one way persons stabilize their relational worlds is through the organization of their cognitions about relationships. A fully developed approach focused on memory structure can be used to illustrate the existence and use of organized expectancies for the development or deterioration of close heterosexual relationships. (Although the memory structure approach also would apply to the description of same-sex relationships, the studies reviewed here have, for the most part, examined individual expectancies about the rise and demise of opposite-sex, intimate relationships.) Such an approach is based on the notion that individuals have cognitive representations for the actions that typify various kinds of relationships. Expectancies for the various kinds of relationships (e.g., acquaintance, platonic friend, best friend, romantic superior-subordinate, teacher-student) are accessed from memory based on direct and vicarious experiences. Expectations about the development of relationships are formed similarly. Relationship memory structures also are ordered hierarchically on the basis of recall of particular scenes (e.g., meeting an individual for the first time at a specific place) and scripts for behavior embedded within various scenes. By reliance on such an approach, researchers can begin to categorize behaviors in relationships and ascribe meaning to the actions.

Thus, even though relationships are in constant motion, relationship memory structures provide a perceptual anchor in which individuals can determine where they are in a relationship. To use a navigation metaphor, relational memory structures can act as a gyroscope to guide individuals through relationships because memory structures provide labels for ongoing experiences. Hence relational memory structures reflect and create stable expectancies for the dynamic behaviors that occur in relationships. They do not have to be activated by the observation of behavior, however, because, as Duck and Miell (1986) remind us, persons have knowledge about relationships even in the absence of an actual relationship partner. Indeed relationships can be viewed as changing mental (as well as behavioral) creations of persons who are bonded through communication. Duck (1990) indicates that the daily talk between relational partners is the observable relationship, yet persons still can have imagined trajectories for relationships in the form of expectancies for relationships independent of specific interactions in which they take part. These expectancies comprise schemata for relationships and allow individuals to categorize bits of seemingly related information into a structure for recognizing future behaviors as indicative of close or distant relationships (cf. Planalp, 1985).

A memory structure approach to relationship development thus provides a way of analyzing cognitive processes about relationships that can inform us about the thought processes of individuals as they think about relationships. Hence we can focus on relationships as intrapersonal creations that begin in the minds of individuals, as much as they can focus on expectancies derived in interaction from specific behavior.

Such an approach defeats the criticism, leveled at developmental stage theorists, that they propose arbitrary stage movement or that they cannot explain why some individuals move rapidly or slowly through different stages. A memory structure approach addresses this criticism by assuming that individual cognitive expectancies are a prime factor in determining the rate and direction of movement. This assumption has been tested indirectly through a series of experiments in which persons sort through a random set of escalating and de-escalating relationship behaviors (Honeycutt, Cantrill, & Greene, 1989). Sorting time is correlated with previous relationship history such that those who have been in more relationships take less time in sorting random actions.

The present approach to relational memory structure is based on Schank's (1982) theory of dynamic memory, which was designed originally to explain the categorization of information and which introduced the *script* concept (discussed by Schank & Abelson, 1977). *Scripts* were seen originally as schemata reflecting sequences of behavioral events, and persons were thought to have scripts for everyday activities such as opening lines on a date, greeting ritual, and introduction of others. Such scripts aided in the planning of activities and acted as a guide for behavior (Bower, Black, & Turner, 1979). The script notion is similar to Kelly's (1955) classical idea of *personal constructs,* in which individuals are represented as implicit scientists who have constructs or anticipations that reflect previous experiences. It is different to the extent that whole sequences of behavior are reflected in time-ordered series.

Schank (1982, 1986) describes a hierarchy of memory structures by distinguishing among scripts, scenes, memory organization packets (MOPs), and meta-MOPs. His interest was in computer science, as he and his associates designed artificial intelligence models for language and semantics. A computer analogy to the hierarchical ordering of knowledge structures is the idea of accessing microcomputer files through a DOS pathway. The root directory may be a directory entitled Escalating Relationship. Subdirectories in the root directory may symbolize the memory structures of dating, disclosure, and sharing activities. Within each of these directories may be files reflecting the scenes. The contents of the files reflect the specific scripts.

Scripts define the sequence of actions in recalled scenes and represent specific instantiations of more general scenes or help create plans for accomplishing goals. For example, an individual may have a *script* for things to talk about on a first date at a restaurant. The *scene* reflects imagery about a specific context and provides a physical setting that serves as the basis for reconstruction of memory. Schank (1982) defines a *scene* as a "general description of a setting and activities in pursuit of a goal relevant to that setting" (p. 90). Scenes point to specific scripts based on experiences within such a scene, and so a dating scene may involve the greeting ritual while picking up a date. An ordered array of scenes constitute a *MOP,* which is a memory structure composed of a variety of related scenes that are not contextually bound. For example, a memory structure for dating could contain scenes of first dates (and underlying scripts for greeting, small talk at a particular location), double-dating, informal dating, and so on.

According to Schank (1982), the primary function of a memory structure is to assist in rapid processing of new information that can be seen as reflecting a particular type of phenomenon. Such a memory structure provides expectations useful for rapid understanding of what is being perceived. Thus memory structures, as it were, are responsible for filling in information about events that must have happened but were left unstated. For example, a dating memory structure could include a number of dating scenes and would lead the individual to have expectancies of what would happen on "typical" dates or dates not yet experienced.

Collections of memory structures constitute what Schank (1982) refers to as *meta-MOPs.* A meta-memory structure for the development of personal relationships could contain underlying memory structures for dating, sharing activities, or disclosing intimate information. A meta-memory structure about escalation of relationships would contain relational actions that are not bounded by particular scenes, yet the actions could point to particular scenes (e.g., disclosing about a sibling's chemical dependency in the date's apartment).

Schank (1982) argues that long-term memory is arranged hierarchically through the above knowledge structures. For example, a dating memory structure for one person may be evoked by the recall of a first date at a movie with a particular individual. This structure may contain a movie-date script that includes the actions of queuing, buying tickets, buying refreshments, finding seats, watching the movie, and leaving the theater. The scene then could progress to an eating establishment. These two scenes compose the dating memory structure. Further, the dating memory structure is one of many memory structures that comprise the expectancies for the development of relationships. The dating memory structure also may be part of de-escalating expectancies as one envisions spending time with alternative partners.

Schank (1982) provides a brief example of a meta-memory structure for personal relations that contains memory structures for convincing another person and seduction. He also indicates that memory structures occur at physical, societal, and personal levels, where memory structures composing a relational meta-memory structure contain societal scenes. He defines a *societal scene* in terms of a social relationship between individuals who are "pursuing a goal that the other person is a necessary participant in, at a common time, with a communication link between them. The actions comprising the interaction between the participants define the scene" (Schank, 1982, p. 96). *Physical scenes* represent mental or visual images of our surroundings at a specified time. *Personal scenes* are idiosyncratic and may be thought of in terms of repetitive, private plans.

The physical scene is analogous to Burke's (1962) notion of scene in his dramatistic pentad model (scene, act, agent, agency, purpose) for explaining motives in discourse (cf. Chapter 7, this volume). These components have been referred to in terms of where, what, who, how, and why, respectively. Schank's (1982) reference to societal scenes is similar to Burke's notion of what transpired, or the "act," while the personal scene is reflected in the purpose, or why something occurred. Thus Burke's idea of ratios (in the scenic determination of act; see Chapter 7, this volume) is also implicit in Schank's conception.

The division of memory structures into these categories allows us to partition behavior into different scenes: Where did it happen? (physical scene) What societal conventions or norms were used, or what effect did the behaviors have on the individuals' social position? (societal scene) Were the individuals personally affected? What goals were achieved by the behaviors? (personal scene) Thus a dating memory structure may reflect an encounter at a movie theater (physical scene) and a disclosure at a restaurant so that the persons become more intimate (societal and personal scenes).

To test some of these ideas, Pryor and Merluzzi (1985) conducted a series of studies asking persons about the expected sequences of actions for "getting a date," as well as the actions for the "first date." Individuals were asked initially to generate a list of 20 actions that typically occur when a man asks a woman out for a date and the events that would occur on the date. Typical actions were the male noticing the woman, staring between the man and woman, smiling, and finding out about other persons from friends. Other actions included manipulating ways to accidentally run into the person, asking to be introduced by a friend, male beginning a conversation, finding similar interests in the conversation, male asking the female for her phone number, and male phoning female to ask her out for a date. Events for the first date included arriving at the female's domicile, meeting parents/roommates, having small talk, going to a movie, buying refreshments, getting something to eat after the movie, going back home, summarizing the night at the end of the date, kissing, and saying good night. (As an aside, it is important to note that a number of the above "getting date" behaviors could be perceived as sexual harassment. The generated list of actions assumes the willingness of the woman to be asked out, yet the actions could be perceived as unacceptable if the woman did not desire the actions. The possibility of such alternative interpretations of "the same" behavior reveals the conceptual importance of differentiating personal scenes from societal scenes.)

Pryor and Merluzzi (1985) found no differences between experienced and novice daters for the frequency of mentioning the various actions. The only observed difference in terms of expertise was in processing the expectancies in an intuitive "logical" sequential order. A second group of subjects had each action listed on an index card that was presented in a random deck; they were told to sort the deck into an intuitive logical order. Individuals with more dating experience, compared to persons with little dating experience, were able to arrange the randomly organized sequences of dating actions in a shorter time period.

The above study represents a detailed analysis of one of the actions (dating) associated with a larger meta-memory structure of escalating relationships. The dating memory structure contains scenes being at home, driving the car, being at the movie, going to a restaurant, and returning home. Within these scenes, scripts may be accessed (e.g., script for ordering a meal at the restaurant, script for saying good-bye).

Several exciting possibilities for investigation of relationships follow from these ideas. For example, the hierarchical organization of these types of knowledge structures (meta-memory structures, memory structures, scenes, scripts) provides a device that reveals how isolated events such as a single date or an argument can be viewed in broader relational terms within the idea of a meta-memory structure. To further elucidate these possibilities, I now briefly review studies using a relationship memory structure approach for the rise and fall of intimate relationships.

Redundancy and Ability
to Articulate Memory Structures

Early studies of script generation made an assumption in terms of information theory that if subjects were asked to list possible actions, these would be relevant and nonredundant. Persons were told to write down a list of actions for a given context, with each line representing one action. Consider the following hypothetical de-escalating meta-memory structure by Person A, who has been instructed to list typical actions that would occur in a relationship that has gone sour: (a) see less of the other person, (b) argue, (c) pursue other interests, (d) continue to argue, (e) spend less time with the other person, (f) spend more time in other interests, (g) continue arguing, and (h) end relationship. Person B writes the following actions: (a) see less of the other person, (b) argue about activities, (c) develop other interests, (d) see other people, and (e) talk about ending the relationship. A has generated eight actions, while B has generated five. Yet A is redundant because only four actions are unique. B has no occurrences of a repetition.

In fact, such research finds differences in the amount of generated actions, with some individuals writing more actions, and such differences were interpreted in terms of experience in the contextual area. However, counting the number of action lines may not be a good representation of the complexity of the meta-memory structure because individuals may repeat actions over a number of lines. Yet action repetition may reflect the *meaningful* recycling of actions throughout a relationship and the enduring pervasiveness of the actions; for example, arguing may occur throughout the history of a relationship. This interpretation is an entirely reasonable alternative to the usual one that repetition merely reflects an inability to generate a diversity of actions and that this reflects simplistic expectancies.

The meta-memory generation instructions assume Grice's (1975) maxim for relevance and nonredundancy in which individuals should write or speak to be informative without being too redundant. The calculation of a redundancy coefficient has revealed that this assumption is not totally supported (Honeycutt, Cantrill, & Greene, 1989). The coefficient is calculated in such a way that higher values reflect less redundancy. The redundancy coefficient is expressed as a ratio in which the number of unique actions is divided by the total number of action lines a person uses in the generation task. The mean redundancy for meta-memory structures about relational escalation is .70, which indicates a slight degree of repetitiveness (Honeycutt, Cantrill, & Greene, 1989). The calculation of redundancy has permitted researchers to be more precise in comparing the cognitive complexity of relationship meta-memory structures as a function of where the structures are formulated (sources of information), gender, and relationship history (novice vs. serial daters). It also has revealed that actions later in the meta-memory structures about escalation and de-escalation are interchanged more easily. Honeycutt, Cantrill, and Greene (1989) note that "once a certain action level is reached, there is a spreading activation in which behaviors may co-occur" (p. 77). Thus once again there may be meaningful reasons for repetition or redundancy that do not derive merely from simplicity of expectancies, but instead are important reflections of relational processes.

The lack of consensus in the ordering of actions later in (de)escalation reflects the diversity of scenes that may be used in generating the relational meta-memory structure and the increasing complexity of relationships. A person may recall quite particular scenes that allow an action to occur earlier in a relationship (e.g., display of physical affection), but in a later, developed, more complex relationship, this recall is less likely to be so predictable or driven by convention or commonality. Indeed Schank (1982) claims that individuals pursuing high-level goals are likely to use very personal memory structures. He notes:

> We may have our own way of pursuing goals on a date with a member of the opposite sex, that bear no relationship to the way anyone else behaves. . . . Some personal MOPs can be a variation on a more standard MOP, where some personal scenes are added to, or replace, one or more standard physical or societal scenes. (pp. 97-98)

In this regard it is important to note the extent to which various actions can be interchanged easily with other actions at different points of relational change. For example, subjects agree least on the ordering of the actions of verbal commitment and marriage, while there is wide agreement on the initial ordering of the actions of meeting, small talk, and calling the other person on the telephone. Also the de-escalating action of disagreeing about attitudes is more easily exchanged with the action "start seeing others," compared to the exchange of escalating actions such as small talk and making a verbal commitment.

Further, the action of stopping the expression of intimate feelings is more easily interchanged with final break-up than the action of meeting is with marriage. Stopping the expression of intimate feelings and meeting were ranked as the first two actions in their respective lists, while final break-up and marriage were rated as the last two occurring actions in the respective lists. These findings seem to reinforce Baxter's (1986) idea that there are many, rather than few, trajectories for declining relationships and that these are based on personal factors and the different sources from which people acquire information and expectancies about relationships.

Sources of Relationship Expectancies

Expectancies for relationship development are affected by direct relationship history, as well as by indirect experience gained through the media, reports of friends, and observations of others. The number of a person's previous intimate relationships is associated with a greater number of general expectations of what should occur in the development or deterioration of an intimate relationship, compared to those of persons never having been in any relationship. However, there is no direct association between relationship history and the number of actions generated.

One need not have extensive direct personal experience with intimate relationships in order to generate expectancies about what should happen in the course of these types of relationships. Our subjects have reported that the source of their expectancies for the rise of a relationship comes from talk with parents, followed by talk with peers (Honeycutt, Cantrill, & Greene, 1989). More women, compared with men, reported that they learn about relationships from siblings. Various other relationship sources include teachers, ministers, counselors, and the media. The source of expectancies for relational de-escalation in descending order was peers, parents, and siblings. Women reported learning more about breaking up from peers than men do. In no cases did men report learning about the rise or demise of relationships from a particular source alone. This finding is compatible with those of other studies indicating that women are more likely to monitor their relationships and to discuss them with other people.

Although one is quite likely to learn about relationships directly from others before one experiences them directly oneself, obviously direct experience is another source of expectancies. Previous findings indicate that individuals having been in no relationships, compared to individuals having been in one or two relationships, had fewer expectancies of what should occur in an escalating relationship and tended to stress, somewhat naively, that small talk and marriage signified a bonded relationship (Honeycutt & Cantrill, 1991). Further, compared with individuals having been in three to five relationships, zero-history respondents were less likely to mention talking about future plans as a couple, showing physical affection, or making a statement of love to the partner. The escalating meta-memory structure for the zero-history individuals seems to be idealistic. Only marriage and small talk were stressed as relational indicators more often by this group, and for them, marriage may be a prototypical symbol of an intimate relationship. On the other hand, individuals who have been in one or two relationships were less likely to mention marriage as part of their meta-memory structure for an escalating relationship. Perhaps those with a relationship history can distinguish more easily a potential intimate relationship from other "typical," but inherently nondevelopmental, dating relationships.

Another source of expectancies is what my colleagues and I previously have referred to in more than a dozen studies as *imagined interactions* (e.g., Honeycutt, Zagacki, & Edwards, 1989). These are covert dialogues that individuals imagine having with significant, living others that serve a variety of functions such as message rehearsal, catharsis, and self-understanding. Individuals report having imagined interactions with dating partners, followed by family members and friends. A few persons have reported imagined interactions with prospective and former partners. The most common topics of the imagined interactions were dating and conflict/problems.

One function of imagined interactions is to psychologically create or maintain a relationship (Honeycutt, 1989). Individuals report negative, positive, and mixed emotions while having the imagined interactions with relational partners. Expectancies also may be created, instantiated, and developed through imagined interactions. Knapp and Vangelisti (1992) argue that in decaying relationships there may be an increase in covert dialogue because open communication is at a standstill due to the partners believing they can predict how an actual interaction will go. Yet covert dialogue occurs in planning initial encounters, reliving positive experiences, dealing with conflict, and in the aftermath of relationships. The topics and interaction partners in the imagined relationships help relive prior encounters and prepare for anticipated ones. The content of the imagined interactions can act as a repository for relationship expectancies and form a basis for judgments of "typicality."

Perceived Typicality and Necessity of Relational Actions

Abelson (1981) discusses the notion of *gap-filling*, in which individuals may report that a given action is typical on seeing it even though it is not frequently mentioned in a spontaneous generation task. Individuals tend to rate more relationship actions as being typical than necessary for a relationship to grow or deteriorate. The gap-filling phenomenon represents the availability heuristic as base rates of previous responses by others are incongruent with subsequent ratings of typicality. Instances of the action may be easier to recall, available in memory due to recognition of the action. The gap-filling phenomenon is important in explaining how individuals can relate to others' personal experiences. Consensual meta-memory structures can exist in terms of recognizing actions, while there may be more idiosyncrasy in generating sequences of relational actions because some actions are harder to access in a free generation task.

Studies conducted by Honeycutt and his associates have revealed that the most frequently mentioned escalating action is initial meeting, with 97% of respondents mentioning this action. The next highest mentioned action was dating (92%). The least mentioned escalating actions were overcoming crisis (13%) and talking about future plans as a couple (16%), even though both actions were mentioned by a separate group of subjects as highly typical and necessary.

The most frequently mentioned de-escalating action was final break-up (58%), followed by avoiding the other (40%). The least mentioned de-escalating actions were talking with friends about relationship problems (10%) and giving excuses for not being able to go out (11%). These actions also were rated as very typical, though giving excuses was seen as less necessary (Honeycutt et al., 1992).

Gender Differences
in Meta-Memory Structure Processing

Females have reported more unique meta-memory actions than men when controlling for redundancy of actions in escalating and de-escalating relationships. In addition, Honeycutt and his associates (Honeycutt, Cantrill, & Greene, 1989) found that women reported having more general expectancies of what should happen in the development of an escalating romance, while there were no differences between the sexes for having generalized expectancies of what should occur in the breakdown of a relationship.

Honeycutt and his associates (1992) found that women were more likely, in the generation of a de-escalating meta-memory structure, to make what they referred to as *commissions*. These were distinguished from *omissions* by use of a semantic language perspective. Ross (1977) discusses the informational value of occurrences and nonoccurrences, and Honeycutt and associates find that people tend to notice actions in forming impressions, while neglecting to consider the information value of noticing when actions do not occur. By contrast, in a de-escalating meta-memory structure, the person is more likely to focus on omissions and to write "He/she was not spending enough time with me" as opposed to "He/she was spending too much time with his/her job or activities."

It is clear that de-escalation is largely typified by similar omissions, and they seem to be equivalent to the awkward silences between people forming relationships. Honeycutt and associates have found that the de-escalating meta-memory structure contained the following omissions: stop expressing intimate feelings, decrease physical intimacy, spend less time together, avoid other, and call less. Conversely the following actions could be classified as commissions: argue about little things, disagree about things to do, antagonize the other, criticize partner, make sarcastic remarks, give excuses for being busy, talk about cause of disagreements, enacting a trial rejuvenation, talk with friends about relational problems, talk about breaking up, assess comparison alternatives, develop outside interests, see others of opposite sex, spend more time with same-sex friends, and end the relationship. Even though men and women both mentioned more commissions than omissions, women mentioned more de-escalating commissions than men. This finding may be explained in terms of female monitoring of relationship decline as more attention seems to be concentrated on what is occurring as opposed to violation of an expectancy that is expressed in terms of what is not happening. Additional support for the idea of female monitoring is seen in the processing times of randomized de-escalating meta-memory structure actions in which females are able to sort a randomly arranged set of de-escalating actions in a shorter time than males.

If women are more attuned to cognitions of relational trajectories, they may rate a variety of actions as being more typical or necessary than do men. The data indicate that women rate more of the escalating actions as being typical than do men (Honeycutt, Cantrill, & Greene, 1989). For example, women rate sharing joint activities, overcoming a crisis in the relationship, meeting parents, talking about future plans, making verbal expression of love, stating a commitment, and making other-oriented statements as more typical. Regarding necessity, women rate meeting parents and talking about future plans as more necessary, than do men. The only action mentioned by men as more necessary for the intimacy to develop in a relationship compared with women is sexual intercourse.

Inferential Biases in Generating
a De-Escalating Meta-Memory Structure

An intriguing phenomenon occurs when individuals are asked to generate relationship expectancies about de-escalation. Individuals mix emotional inferences with reports of behavioral actions. Table 3.1 shows a possible hierarchical relationship that relates observable behaviors to a factor of emotional intensity in a relationship. Inferences of love and anger reflect instances of emotional arousal such that a love/hate relationship has intensity of feelings. It is interesting how individuals mix emotional inferences with reports of behavioral actions when generating de-escalating meta-memory structures. For example, in Table 3.1, individuals may report that they expect anger to occur in the breakdown of a relationship, as well as expectancies of yelling, shouting, and profane language, which may be operational indicators of anger. This appears to be more of an information processing problem when thinking about the breakup of relationships.

The mixing of inferences and behaviors continues even when individuals are given examples of emotions that may be felt during the breakdown process. For example, Honeycutt and colleagues have told respondents that they are interested in people's expectations about behaviors that occur in decaying relationships (e.g., arguing about what to do) and that behaviors should not be confused with reports of feelings, emotions, or how oneself may view the other. The example given is that a person saying, "feeling bored, doubts the relationship" is reporting not on expectancies of behavior but on feelings and emotions associated with what may be expected to occur in the relationship. Subjects still mention inferences even when these instructions are provided.

Carlston's (1980) dual-memory model of impression formation is relevant in explaining this inferential bias. He posits that individuals select specific behaviors, as well as draw on inferences, in making impressions of others. Inferences may be made about unarticulated behaviors. Smith (1987) reports that viewers of a videotaped couple's interaction reported both inferences and behaviors in rating the intimacy of the couples.

Table 3.1. Hierarchical Relationship Between Categorizations of Behaviors, Prototypes, and Inferences

Observed behaviors:	Kissing, hugging, smiling	Slapping, kicking, frowning
Prototype:	Physical affection	Physical aggression
Inference:	Love	Anger

It would be interesting to investigate the underlying scenes and scripts associated with various inferences. For example, is boredom associated with repetitive actions that are well-learned or novel situations that the individual does not understand, such as talking technical jargon? Other inferences are feelings of annoyance, bitterness, jealousy, moodiness, feeling hurt, and sadness. The inferences may be associated with scenes of arguing. Cody (1982) provides examples of inferences in the strategies that people use to end relationships. He reports inferences such as telling the other that the self felt too dependent on the partner, feeling unable to trust the other, feeling the other's personality was incompatible, and telling that the self cared very much for the other but that the relationship had to end anyway.

The citing of inferences may reflect a basic inability to articulate the underlying actions. The inference reflects a convenient category that subsumes unarticulated behaviors. The top-down processing does not permeate to root behaviors. For example, it may be easier to label actions of yelling with a high pitch and voice volume by concentrating on the perceived emotional outcome: anger. On the other hand, therapists speak about how difficult it may be for spouses in counseling to articulate relationship problems (Hatfield, 1982). Cupach and Metts (1986) provide an example of the difficulty of verbalizing feelings of not being loved. Instead the clients may verbalize a list of proposed changes for the other ("I want my partner to share in household errands."). More research is needed that examines categorization of events and their relationship to emotional inferences at different points in the trajectory of relationships.

Impact of Expectancies on Relationship Messages

Relationship memory structures reveal the mental creations of our relationships. The mental creations may be reflected in the messages communicated by individuals. On the one hand, memory structures prescribe what should be said in a given scene. On the other hand, reactions to messages become assimilated into the memory structure, thus affecting future expectancies for relationships. A given individual may expect another to be relatively sociable, sincere, and outgoing on an initial date. Initial dates may confirm or reinforce the expectancy. Disconfirming experiences may result in the modification of initial dating expectancies. Different messages may be discussed in subsequent dating experiences.

Kellermann, Broetzmann, Lim, and Kitao (1989) analyzed initial interaction MOPs. These researchers found a progression of topics for initial encounters that was relatively stable though adaptable to situational needs. The initial interaction MOP contains speech acts of getting facts, discussing facts, evaluating facts, providing explanations, discussing goals/intentions, and discussing the enabling conditions for goals.

The structure of interaction for persons who have more knowledge about another allows greater variability in topic sequencing. Conversational norms encourage turn taking, topic continuation, and topic transition relevance (Goodwin, 1981). The violations of these norms are more tolerated when individuals have specialized knowledge of each other and have created special relationship rules for interaction so that pursuance/avoidance of particular subjects is exhibited. It would be useful to investigate the messages that individuals expect to occur at transitional points in relationships. For example, Baxter and Wilmot (1984) found that direct questioning was not used as often as other indirect strategies for individuals wanting to find out where their relationship stood in terms of intimate involvement. Indirect strategies such as hinting, "jealousy tests," joke telling, and introducing the self and partner to outsiders as a couple were used more often.

Honeycutt and colleagues are using the content of escalating and de-escalating meta-memory structures to construct scenarios that take subjects up to a certain point in a personal and "typical" relationship. Personal and typical relationships are manipulated to contrast expectancies for own and stereotypes of prototypical relationships. Subjects are prompted to reveal what they think will be said next to promote a "stage" transition, as well as what would be said instead of something else. The prompting procedure allows us to determine the influence of meta-memory structures on message production. This approach also reflects what we have called a *proactive imagined interaction* (Honeycutt, Zagacki, & Edwards, 1989). Individuals imagined conversations with others in which they may rehearse for anticipated encounters and re-create earlier encounters, as well as attempt to increase self-understanding. Imagined interactions can help create relational meta-memory structures as a person engages in self-talk with an imagined other.

In a related vein, Duck (1990) has wondered about the role of "future talk" in the trajectory of relationships. The relationship can be seen as an evolving mental creation based on expectancies and re-creation of previous encounters. Duck, Pond, and Leatham (1991) found that reports of the quality of communication at different time periods were related to current relationship satisfaction rather than to predicting subsequent relationship satisfaction (cf. Gottman & Krokoff, 1989). Hence memory about communication is re-created in the present to be compatible with current relationship quality.

The re-creation of communicative encounters can occur through having imagined interactions (Honeycutt, Zagacki, & Edwards, 1989). This imaging of communication can help create expectancies for subsequent encounters and relationships. The memory structure approach to developmental communication assumes that relationships are indeed mental creations. Duck and his associates (Duck, Pond, & Leatham, 1991) have written: "Insofar as subjects clearly invest interactions with their own private and symbolic meanings, researchers will grasp the relational significance of relational events only when they attempt to study and interpret those symbolic meanings that are the arches of the mental creation of relationships" (p. 34). I concur and believe that the study of meta-memory structures for the trajectory of relationships provides an intriguing way to examine the mental creations of personal relationships.

Phases of Relationship Revisited

The above considerations emphasize the importance of the organizing role of cognition in the conduct of relationships and also offer me the chance to return to the issue of phases in relationships and to offer a new perspective on them. In brief, the argument is that it is the structure of cognition that produces phases rather than the nature of the phenomena themselves. The *relational meta-memory structure approach* especially offers a cognitive perspective on the linearity problem associated with phase models in which it is assumed that individuals sequentially progress through objective stages in a systematic fashion. The *memory structure approach* argues, by contrast, that phases exist in memory in the representation of expectancies for prototypical behaviors that occur within intimate relationships. The expectancies represent internal guides for behavior that help individuals recognize behaviors and promote labeling of their experiences. Therefore the developmental models, whether of subjects or of researchers, serve a heuristic function in conceptualizing the idea of phases of interaction.

Developmental models of relationships have proven to be useful devices to researchers in bringing order to what otherwise may be seen as a series of unrelated or chaotic events. The *phase* concept allows researchers to place behaviors into meaningful categories on the basis of co-occurrence. Kelley and his associates (1983) indicate that "when a relationship changes markedly in a property, it is reasonable to say that it has moved to a new stage or level" (p. 38). Thus they view dating, self-disclosure, and learning about another's personal habits as reflecting the intensification of a relationship. Such developmental models serve a critical function in depicting "motion" in relationships.

Another advantage of developmental models is their ability to represent the direction of movement in relationships through the identification of researchable phases. Change may be bidirectional and may fluctuate in intensity, or there may be alternating periods of growth and decline as movement is primarily based on need, exchange, and social background (Surra, 1990). Nonetheless individuals may progress differently through various stages even though common patterns are identified, but Duck (1988) notes that "it is nevertheless safe to conclude that some sequencing of influences has been shown by several authors but that no precision or specificity as to their exact operation has been advanced" (p. 73).

Knapp and Vangelisti (1992) indicate that stages can be identified by researchers in terms of the preponderance of recurring communication behaviors. Although behaviors may occur at any point in a relationship, it is the clustering of similar behaviors that provides the foundation for the labeling of a phase. For example, intimate disclosure may occur during initial encounters, but it is more likely to be observed over a number of topical areas and in greater depth for affable persons who have known each other over a history of repeated encounters. Thus "intimate disclosure" is a better defining characteristic for researchers investigating personal relationships than for social relationships (e.g., strangers). Such a view is reflected in research showing that an individual's meta-memory structure for relationships tends to place disclosure at later time periods in the developmental trajectory (Honeycutt, Cantrill, & Greene, 1989); that is, individuals typically report that disclosure takes place at later points in the development of a relationship.

All the same, when people's own descriptions of relational change are examined, we find that some persons do not mention disclosure as part of the escalating meta-memory structure and that some actions may be skipped, while others are never experienced. For example, issues of relational dissatisfaction may not be disclosed in some declining relationships, while in other relationships, dissatisfaction may be discussed superficially (Baxter, 1985). Lee (1984) found in a retrospective study of 112 breakups that 26.8% omitted so-called stages. He surmised five stages of breakdown reflecting (a) discovery of dissatisfaction, (b) initial discussion of dissatisfaction, (c) serious discussion of dissatisfaction, (d) one or both individuals reaching a decision concerning the relationship, and (e) a transformation stage in which a change occurs in the relationship. Lee also reported that 31.2% of the breakups involved the omission of some stages early in the decline process (e.g., discussion of dissatisfaction), while later recycling back to previously omitted stages. There was nonlinearity in breakups rather than a systematic universal trajectory leading to termination of the relationships.

The failure to find nonlinearity in subjective reports should not, however, be confused with the idea that reports of breakups do not reveal regular patterns. Rather, some patterns of relationship escalation and de-escalation are not necessarily linear. On the other hand, if developmental theorists allow for too much random movement, the theory becomes chaotic, and we are left with the old imprecision of "it all depends on the particular relationship." All relationships would be idiosyncratic without similarity in the progressions of behaviors across relationships, and individual quid pro quos would be negotiated in each relationship. By contrast I argue that memory structures for relationships provide the initial information by which relationship rules are negotiated and that these provide for the stability of relationships and identify boundaries for the categorization of different types of relationships (Argyle & Henderson, 1985). For example, a rule "Thou shalt be faithful" can be viewed as an expectancy that characterizes an exclusive marital relationship. As an individual thinks about the rule, various personal scenes and scripts may be accessed. Some individuals even report thinking about scenes from the movie *Fatal Attraction,* in which the consequences of infidelity were portrayed as murderous.

Although individuals are idiosyncratic, this assumption is not compatible with information-processing studies in which individuals display relative consistency in categorizing information. A pioneer study by Dornbusch, Hastorf, Richardson, Muzzy, and

Vreeland (1965) revealed that children who were asked to describe two other children at a summer camp used the same categories of description 45% of the time. However, the same child describing two other children used categories that overlapped 57% of the time. Other cognitive researchers have noted that consistency is greater within individuals generating categories than it is between individuals (Wegner & Vallacher, 1977).

The meta-memory structure approach assumes that individuals likewise have relatively consistent personal expectancies of what should happen in the progression of a relationship that can be used as an anchor prototype for categorizing the type of relationship observed between others as well as one's own relationships. If the categorization consistency extends to relationship expectancies, this would help explain why some people appear to get involved repeatedly in similar types of relationships even when they seem to be nonrewarding or dissatisfying affiliations. Relationship expectancies may be reinforced as observed behavior is assimilated into existing categories, but accommodation occasionally takes place in which the expectancies are modified to account for new observed behavior (Honeycutt, 1991b). For example, a general type of relationship expectancy involves the idea that relationships are "profitable," such that individuals seek positive outcomes while minimizing negative outcomes (Sabatelli, 1988). Thus individuals may endure costs in hopes of receiving deferred rewards (Nye, 1982), as well as changing perceptions on the magnitude of costs endured. When current costs are redefined, expectancies are accommodated to the existing situation so that it may be seen as less costly.

Thus, although phase models have considerable intuitive appeal, they have a number of problems, and one perhaps can reconstrue them as researchers' expectancy models. An initial problem with phase models is that they imply an end state, and the original social-penetration model included a stage of "stable exchange," which reflected communication patterns of spontaneity, efficiency, openness, and flexibility. Knapp (1984) refers to a bonding stage representing the highest level of intimacy. The end state for decaying relationships has been referred to as "termination," "grave-dressing," and "dissolution" (e.g., Baxter,

1985; Duck, 1982). Even after relationships have "ended," the former partners may see each other through custodial arrangements, chance encounters, or integrated social networks. Some individuals may maintain an intrapersonal communicative link by having imagined interactions with a former partner (Honeycutt, 1991a).

Second, if relationships are phasic, then how are one-night stands, holiday romances, and lifelong platonic friendships to be classified in terms of sequential movement? Further, the differential rate of movement through stages makes the *stage* concept difficult to falsify in terms of behavioral observation if the stages are objectively real. Other critics raise the question of regression to earlier stages to stabilize a relationship at perhaps a lower level of intimacy if one has been trying to advance it too far while the other disagrees with the transitional movement. Yet due to the repository of memory and experiences, one can never go back to the "way we were" (Knapp, 1984).

Third, what is the demarcation between unilateral, bilateral, or mutual awareness of each other? These concerns also reflect the falsifiability problem of relationship phases if they are presumed to be "real." Murstein (1986, 1987) and Lewis (1973) discuss the development of roles in which relationships evolve from impersonal roles to more personal roles. Levinger (1974) discusses increasing levels of awareness toward another such that the individuals share relative levels of knowledge and intimacy about each other. Alternatively Delia (1980) notes that many relationships are characterized by increasing information but stable and restricted intimacy. Over time the division between impersonal and personal roles is thus less clear.

Fourth, considerable work shows that dialectical tensions exist in relationships such that smooth, linear progression is not really what occurs in either the development or decline of relationships. Phase models assume systematic movement through stages of interaction, and Knapp (1984) provides examples of stabilizing movement within stages. Movement may occur forward, backward, and laterally. According to the social penetration model, individuals tend to progress through adjacent stages rather than to skip stages. Knapp (1984) indicates that "each stage contains important presuppositions for the following stage; 2) sequencing makes forecasting adjacent stages easier; and 3) skipping stages is a gamble on the uncertainties presented by the lack of information that could have been learned in the skipped step. Some social norms even help to inhibit skipping steps" (p. 51). Yet social norms may be recalled only in terms of societal scenes that then become part of relationship meta-memory structures.

The problems of behavioral falsification, stage parsimony, direction of movement, and rate of movement through relationship phases seem on the face of it to signal the demise of developmental models that assume the objective reality of phases. A saturation point also seems to have been reached with the diversity of models (e.g., Altman & Taylor, 1973; Baxter, 1985; Coleman, 1977; Duck, 1982; Knapp, 1984; Lee, 1984; Levinger, 1974; Murstein, 1986).

Even the reliance on exchange principles to explain movement through phases is open to challenge. Lannaman (1991) has criticized this perspective for its neglect of unintended consequences and the emphasis on hedonistic drives. Relational partners typically are depicted as conscious decision makers who could list material, symbolic, and affectional rewards and costs. The basis of these criticisms is the notion that the researchers' explanation for movement through stages has been exhausted insofar as it centers universally on satisfaction of interpersonal needs or assessment of the cost-benefits of relationships. As an alternative to social-exchange principles that seek to explain relationship stability on the basis of maximizing profit given available comparison alternatives (Hinde, 1979), some authors have proposed that relationships proceed through the reduction of uncertainty (Berger & Roloff, 1982). Stability generally can be enhanced through the reduction of uncertainty to sustain predictable and coordinated interactions even though some events increase uncertainty, which may result in the relationship ending (Planalp & Honeycutt, 1985). However, other relationships were redefined, while others were kept at the same level of intimacy. A few events caused the relationship to become closer such that there was a change in the definition or stage of the relationship. Yet the uncertainty-increasing events resulted in beliefs about confidence of predicting the partner's future behaviors a few weeks after the event. Hence uncertainty was increased momentarily. On the other hand, Berger and Kellermann (in press) discuss how the assumed rationality of individuals in a variety of communication models has gone unquestioned and without analysis of the habitual nature of much of our communication behaviors.

However, this issue can be reconceptualized by use of the above approach to memory structure. The argument could be made that progression through relationships is the result of cognitive structures that lead to behaviors being routinely enacted such that the person is on "automatic pilot." Once the pilot light is disrupted, the individual may be more mindful. Some scholars have taken the position that mindful processing precedes mindlessness so that through repeated experiences, new behaviors are assimilated within existing categories (Nisbett & Ross, 1980). A person with more dating experience might see increased disclosure as indicative of a particular state of intimacy, compared to a person with little dating experience (Honeycutt & Cantrill, 1991).

A development of this idea is found in the meta-memory structure approach adapted here. *Memory structure theory* assumes that the habitual nature of behaviors is the result of an individual following the script for a particular goal. More specifically, processing information about events in relationships is a function of the content of the individual's relationship expectancies. The expectancies may be well developed or relatively unarticulated, but are certainly personal. The idea that individuals have expectancies derived from previous experiences thus directs attention toward intrapersonal thought processes. Hence it may make more sense for research to assume that developmental phases exist in the minds of individuals rather than in "the reality" of relationships, independently of them. This statement says nothing about behavioral support for parsimonious categorizations of phases. The developmental models may serve as a heuristic anchor for processing relationship behaviors, and the *stage* concept simply may offer prescriptions for so-called appropriate behaviors.

How Do I Love Thee?
Let Me Consult My Prototype

Beverley Fehr

What relationship knowledge should ordinary people possess in order to navigate successfully through their interpersonal worlds? Even though this may sound like a simple question, there is no single, simple answer. One could reply that relational competence requires knowing how to initiate interactions, how to classify or categorize the nature of one's interactions, how to maintain relationships once they have been initiated, and how to bow out of relationships. Close personal relationships researchers have, in fact, directed attention toward these kinds of relationship knowledge. A focus of such research has been the issue of how people think about or make sense of their relationships. Consider, for example, Elizabeth Barrett Browning's famous question (from *Sonnets from the Portuguese*, no. 43) in the title of this chapter. It seems reasonable to suggest that "How do I love thee?" can be

AUTHOR'S NOTE: I would like to express appreciation to Art Aron, Mark Baldwin, Steve Duck, and Dan Perlman for their very helpful comments.

answered only by referring to the knowledge that one has accumulated concerning the meaning of love. One then can evaluate the extent to which one's current experience matches or resembles one's conception. One also might consult this knowledge base to determine the *kind* of love that is felt for the other person. It can be assumed, more generally, that people approach relationships with some knowledge about relationships, classes of relationships, emotions and types of emotion, and love and types of love.

The issue of how laypersons organize and use knowledge is not a new one. In cognitive psychology, for example, research has been conducted on the structure and content of natural language categories such as furniture, vehicle, and bird. For example, we recognize robins, ducks, turkeys, sparrows, and eagles as different sorts of birds. Although we are all familiar with both the species and the general class of such objects, a fund of interesting psychological issues is actually created by the human ability to categorize objects or events into classes. The concern in this chapter is, of course, not with such natural phenomena as birds. Rather the focus is on knowledge of social categories—in particular, those pertaining to relationships and emotions.

To address the general issue of the kinds of knowledge structures that facilitate competent behavior in relationships, a necessary first step is to assess what laypersons know about concepts such as *love* (and the extent to which these are shared representations). Fortunately many of the approaches and methods developed in cognitive psychology can be applied fruitfully in the social domain (Fiske & Taylor, 1991). This chapter examines such research on laypersons' knowledge of relationship-relevant concepts, particularly the concept of *love*. Key questions to be addressed include: What does the everyday person have in mind when asked about love? How do people differentiate love from related concepts such as liking, being in love, and commitment? Do conceptions of love differ from one person to the next? Stated differently, are people's categorizations purely personal, cultural, or some combination of both? Finally, how do cognitive representations of love influence people's behavior in relationships? These are important questions because everyday conceptions of love affect, if not determine, when love is attributed to one's partner and to oneself, how feelings of love are communicated in a relationship, and ultimately the course and expression of love in relationships (e.g., Kelley, 1983).

In this chapter, research on laypersons' knowledge of love and related concepts, conducted from a prototype perspective, are presented. These studies tell us what it is that laypersons know, not explicitly what laypersons *should* know, to function well in their relationships. However, certain implications for competence can be drawn from this literature. These implications will be spelled out later. First a brief description of the prototype approach is presented, followed by the findings of prototype studies on close relationships.

The Prototype Approach

Research on natural language concepts conducted in cognitive psychology by Eleanor Rosch has fueled an interest in everyday thought (see Mervis & Rosch, 1981, for a review). Rosch argues that many natural language concepts do not lend themselves to a classical definition, whereby concepts are defined by a set of individually necessary and jointly sufficient criterial attributes. Instead, in her view, many natural language categories are organized in terms of *prototypes,* which are defined as the clearest cases or best examples of a category. Other members can be ordered in terms of their degree of resemblance to these prototypical cases. For example, apples and oranges are very clear instances of the category fruit, whereas figs and pomegranates are less so. Some members, such as tomatoes, blend into neighboring categories such as vegetable. The prototypical instances share the greatest number of attributes with other category members, whereas nonprototypical instances share fewer attributes with the typical cases and more features with members of neighboring categories. Consider, for example, some of the attributes used to classify birds: coat: feathers; oral opening: beak; primary mode of locomotion: flying. Mervis and Rosch point out that robins and sparrows, prototypical birds, possess all of these qualities. Less typical birds such as turkeys do not share the primary mode of locomotion feature with robins and sparrows; penguins, which are even less typical, have scaly flippers for swimming rather than feathered wings for flying. Rosch demonstrated that the prototype structure of natural object categories such as fruit and bird affects virtually every information processing variable that has been examined in cognitive psychology. For example, in reaction time studies (e.g., Rosch, 1973), subjects take longer to verify the category membership of nonprototypical, than prototypical, instances.

This approach to natural language concepts seemed promising for application to other areas in psychology where key concepts consistently have defied classical definition. For example, Fehr and Russell (1984) documented the many unsuccessful attempts of emotion theorists and researchers to generate an agreed-on definition of the term *emotion.* They suggested that the conflict and confusion were understandable if one entertained the possibility that the concept of *emotion* was not classically definable, but rather organized in terms of prototypical cases. A series of studies supported a prototype conceptualization: Subjects reliably rated love, anger, and happiness as prototypical emotions; awe, boredom, and calmness were considered to be nonprototypical. These goodness-of-example ratings were found to affect information processing in a number of ways: how readily an instance came to mind, how likely it was to be labeled as an emotion, how easily it could be substituted for the word *emotion* in a sentence, and the degree to which it shared features with other emotions. Fehr and Russell concluded that the concept of *emotion* could best be understood from a prototype, rather than a classical, perspective.

The Prototype of Love

The success of the prototype approach when applied to emotion suggested that it also might be applied fruitfully to the specific emotion that laypersons consider to be most prototypical of the concept—one with profound relational "residues" and impact—namely love. As with emotion, there is no widely accepted definition of love. Fehr and Russell (1991) comment that failure to achieve consensus on definitions and typologies of love indicates that social scientists are unclear on what should be included under the heading of love. From a prototype perspective, this lack of agreement is understandable: "There may be no small set of criterial features common to all and only instances of love. There may be no fixed number of subtypes into which love can be divided" (Fehr & Russell, 1991, p. 427).

As this quotation implies, when applying prototype theory to a particular domain, a two-pronged approach is possible. One approach is to demonstrate that the concept has an internal structure such that some types are considered to be prototypical, while others are regarded as nonprototypical of the concept. An alternative approach, outlined by Fehr (1986, 1988b) is to focus on features, rather than types, of concepts. Fehr posited that not only might prototype concepts lack a set of defining features but also the listed features themselves might vary in terms of typicality. For example, the feature "feathers" might be very prototypical of, or central to, the category of bird. On the other hand, the feature "is eaten by humans" would apply mostly to nontypical members, such as turkeys and chickens, and would be shared with members of adjacent categories (e.g., cows and pigs). Most prototype research on love has taken a features approach, although Fehr and Russell (1991) studied *types* of love from a prototype perspective. As will be seen, these two ways of uncovering what the layperson knows about the concept of *love* are complementary. Studies on types of love are described first, followed by prototype research on love's features. [This chapter is restricted to a discussion of prototype research on layperson's views of the generic concept of *love*. Research on romantic love is included only in cases where the purpose was to delineate the similarities and differences between it and the general concept of *love*. Readers who are interested in lay conceptions of romantic love are referred to Marston, Hecht, & Robers (1987) for an analysis of the subjective experience of romantic love (and ways in which love is communicated). Davis and Todd's (1982) paradigm case analysis of romantic love and friendship is also highly recommended.

Types of Love

Fehr and Russell (1991) conducted six studies designed to test the hypothesis that kinds of love vary in their degree of membership in the category love (prototypicality), with no sharp boundary separating members from nonmembers. In Study 1, 93 instances of love were listed by more than one person. The most frequently listed type was friendship, followed by sexual, parental, brotherly, sibling, maternal, passionate, romantic, and familial love. In Study 2, when 20 target types were rated for prototypicality, the highest ratings were assigned to maternal, parental, friendship, sisterly, romantic, brotherly, and familial love. These kinds of love match Hatfield and Walster's (1978) conceptualization of companionate love as a low-key emotion characterized by friendship, trust, respect, caring, and so on. The kinds of love captured by Hatfield and Walster's description of passionate love as an intense, emotional, sexualized experience received the lowest typicality ratings: sexual love, passionate love, infatuation, and puppy love.

In the remaining studies, Fehr and Russell (1991) demonstrated that the category membership of typical kinds of love was verified more quickly than that of nonprototypical instances. The consensus was also greater that typical members were, in fact, genuine cases of love. In addition, prototypical members were more easily substituted for the word *love* in sentences. Finally typical kinds of love shared more features with one another and with love itself than did nonprototypical members. (The latter finding is discussed later.) These studies revealed that companionate kinds of love are at the core of what the term *love* means to the layperson; passionate varieties are less likely to come to mind and are regarded as peripheral.

Feature-Listing Approaches

Does a different picture emerge when laypersons are asked to list features, rather than types, of love? An answer to this question was provided by Fehr (1988b). In the first of six studies, university students generated 68 nonidiosyncratic features of the concept of *love* (see Table 4.1). The most frequently listed features were caring, happiness, want to be with the other, friendship, and feel free to talk about anything. One of the largest groupings referred to positive feelings (e.g., happiness, contentment, affection, excitement, euphoria). However, the concept was not described in uniformly positive terms; the features of uncertainty and scary were included, albeit with low frequency. The prototype of love also consisted of behaviors that reflected the positivity of affect (smiling, laughing, gazing at other) along with altruistic acts (e.g., helping, doing things for the other, sacrifice, put the other first). Cognitive kinds of features depicted a rational component in which the other is admired and respected, as well as more irrational cognitive activities, such as rumination (think about the other all the time) and positive distortion (see only the other's good qualities). Physiological concomitants also were mentioned (e.g., heart rate increases, butterflies in stomach, sexual passion). The absence of inhibition when with the loved one was another theme (e.g., feel free to talk about anything, feel relaxed with the other, openness). There was also a social support grouping: supportiveness, sharing, empathy, and comfort the other. Finally some of the features, such as commitment, security, and long lasting, implied an expectation that the relationship would endure.

In Study 2 the 68 features were rated for prototypicality. Those receiving the highest ratings were trust, caring, honesty, respect, and friendship. The lowest ratings were assigned to euphoria, gazing at the other, see only the other's good qualities, butterflies in stomach, uncertainty, dependency, and scary. Fehr (1988b) noted that the features receiving the highest typicality ratings map on to descriptions of companionate love, whereas the features receiving the lowest ratings portray passionate love. Thus, consistent with Fehr and Russell's (1991) studies on types of love, Fehr's (1988b) studies revealed that companionate or friendshiplike *features* are central to the layperson's conception of love. Passionate, romantic features are seen as part of the concept but as much more peripheral.

Since the publication of Fehr's (1988b) findings, several replication studies have been conducted. For example, Button and

Table 4.1. Features of Love

Attribute	F^a	B & C	L & A	
			1	2
Trust	x	x	x	x
Caring	x	x	x	x
Honesty	x	x	x	x
Friendship	x	x	x	x
Respect	x	x	x	x
Concern for the other's well-being	x			
Loyalty	x		x	
Commitment	x	x		x
Accept the other the way he or she is	x	x	x	x
Supportiveness	x			
Want to be with the other	x		x	
Interest in the other	x			
Affection	x	x	x	x
Closeness	x			x
Understanding	x	x		x
Sharing	x	x	x	x
Want the best for the other	x			
Forgiveness	x			
Intimacy	x	x	x	x
Other is important	x			
Openness	x			x
Feel relaxed with the other	x			
Liking	x			x
Compassion	x	x	x	x
Devotion	x			x
Giving	x		x	x
Happiness	x		x	x
Feel free to talk about anything	x			
Do things for the other	x	x		
Feel good about self	x			
Responsibility	x			
Warm feelings	x		x	x
Patience	x	x		
Long-lasting	x			x
Miss the other when apart	x			
Comfort the other	x			
Attachment	x	x		
Sex appeal	x			
Touching	x		x	x
Sexual passion	x	x	x	x
Need each other	x			
Mutual Contentment			x	
Put the other first	x	x		

Table 4.1. Continued

Attribute	F^a	B & C	L & A 1	L & A 2
Unconditional	x			
Wonderful feelings	x		x	
Physical attraction	x	x		
Laughing	x		x	
Sacrifice	x	x	x	x
Helping	x			
Empathy	x			x
Admiration	x			
Positive outlook	x		x	
Kind	x		x	x
Protectiveness	x			
Have a lot in common	x			
Excitement	x		x	x
Security	x		x	x
Think about the other all the time	x		x	
Energy	x			x
Heart rate increases	x		x	
Euphoria	x		x	
Gazing at the other	x			
See only the other's good qualities	x			
Butterflies in stomach	x			
Uncertainty	x		x	x
Dependency	x		x	
Scary	x			x

NOTE: 1. F = Fehr (1988b); B & C = Button & Collier (1991); L & A 1 = Luby & Aron (1990) Script Instructions; L & A 2 = Luby & Aron (1990) Attribute Instructions.
2. Only identical or nearly identical responses were combined for this table. For example, Button and Collier's feature "accepting each other no matter what" was coded as Fehr's feature "accept the other the way he or she is"; "putting the other before self" was coded as "put the other first."
a. Fehr's features are rank-ordered from high to low typicality.

Collier (1991) asked university students and patrons of a shopping mall in Newfoundland to list features of love. More than half of their 39 features overlapped with Fehr's list (see Table 4.1), and the majority of these were prototypical, which suggests consensus on the core meaning of the concept. Button and Collier commented, "the features for love agree remarkably well with those reported by Fehr's (1988[b]) subjects, lending external validity to her findings" (p. 6). In the authors' second study, university students and government employees provided typicality ratings for the features of love derived in Study 1. As in Fehr's Study 2, companionate features of love such as trust, communication, honesty, respect, friendship, and understanding received the highest ratings; passionate features such as physical attraction, passion, and sex received lower ratings.

Luby and Aron (1990) also replicated Fehr's (1988b) Studies 1 and 2 with students at the University of California, Santa Cruz. They noted that their 69 and 93 features of love (depending on the instructions used) overlapped substantially with Fehr's feature list. In Study 2 their sample also assigned high typicality ratings to the features that were considered to be most prototypical in Fehr's study 2 (e.g., honesty, trust, caring, and respect).

As Table 4.1 illustrates, there is considerable agreement between the four data sets. This accord is remarkable, considering that all of these studies required coding of subjects' open-ended responses. This0 is a complex task because coders are required to make a series of judgments about which features should be combined without the benefit of hard-and-fast rules (see Fehr, 1988b, for a description of this process). The consensus on which features of love are central to the concept and which are not is underscored when one correlates the sets of typicality ratings of Fehr's 68 love features; Fehr's, Luby and Aron's, and Button and Collier's four sets of typicality ratings (men's, women's, students', and government employees') are highly intercorrelated, ranging from .80 to .93. (Similarly the correlation between Fehr's typicality ratings and those gathered by Aron and Westbay, 1991, is .86 [Aron, 1991, personal communication]).

The overlap is greatest for the features that Fehr (1988b) found to be prototypical. In fact, agreement was unanimous for the five features that received the highest typicality ratings in her study, a particularly impressive result, given the diversity of the samples; subjects residing on the Canadian West Coast, the Canadian East Coast, and the American West Coast all listed trust, caring, honesty, friendship, and respect as features of love. Moreover, the various groups all considered these features central to or prototypical of the concept; in fact, in all of the data sets, these five were ranked at least among the top eight features in terms of typicality. Other prototypical features that appeared in all four data sets were accept the other the way he or she is, affection, sharing, intimacy, and compassion. The results of these studies, taken together, suggest that Fehr's (1988b) finding that friendship-based, or companionate, love is central to the layperson's conception of love is a robust one.

Passionate features were listed in all of the studies, but not with the same consistency across samples as was found for the companionate features of love. Passionate kinds of features were considered to be nonprototypical of love in Fehr's research and received ratings below the median in each of the replication studies. It can be concluded that the layperson's prototype of love is rich and complex, consisting of many features that depict both companionate and passionate components, but with the former weighted more heavily in cognitive representation than the latter.

Other Approaches to Uncovering the Prototype of Love

Other approaches to uncovering the prototype of love have been taken by Shaver, Schwartz, Kirson, and O'Connor (1987), Fitness and Fletcher (1991), and Buss (1988). Buss (1988) focused specifically on *behaviors* in his prototype analysis, while Shaver et al. and Fitness and Fletcher explored prototypes of emotion *episodes.*

Shaver et al. (1987) asked subjects to describe love, sadness, joy, and fear episodes. Coders then distilled a prototype for each emotion. The prototype of love included several features that were classified as antecedents: finding the other attractive, realizing that the other has something that one wants or needs, and feeling wanted/needed by the other. Other elicitors of love included the other inspires feelings of openness, trust, and security; special times shared with the other; and enjoying good communication. Features classified as responses included wanting to be physically close to the other, and engaging in physical closeness (e.g., touching, hugging, kissing, sex). Behaviors such as expressing one's feelings, gazing, and smiling also were listed. The response of a physiological nature was feeling excited, high in energy, fast heartbeat, etc. The feelings listed were uniformly positive: happiness, joyful, exuberant, warm, and so on. Finally cognitive biases such as being obsessed with the person and positive distortion (e.g., seeing only the positive side; everything seems wonderful) were also part of their love prototype.

Fitness and Fletcher (1991, Study 2) hypothesized that emotion prototypes may be influenced by the social context in which they occur (e.g., a marital relationship). They asked students in New Zealand and their spouses to describe the most typical incident that would produce feelings of anger, love, hate, or jealousy in one partner toward the other. Typical love experiences were elicited by events such as the partner giving time and support, sharing happy times, and thinking about the partner. Positive cognitions, particularly about the partner, were common. Almost all subjects mentioned an urge to be physically close to the partner and listed related behaviors such as hugging and kissing. Other behaviors included verbally expressing one's love, giving presents, or doing nothing. Physiological symptoms tended to be rather low-key: relaxed muscles and warmth or heat were the most common responses. Fitness and Fletcher concluded that their prototype of love, unveiled in a marital context, bore many similarities to the prototypes of love presented by Fehr (1988b) and Shaver et al. (1987), who did not specify a particular context.

Buss (1988) asked subjects to list behaviors that typify love. A second sample then rated each act for typicality. Acts suggesting commitment (e.g., She agreed to marry him.) received high ratings, as did acts involving resource display (e.g., He bought her a special present.). Other prototypical acts signaled exclusivity and fidelity (e.g., She remained faithful to him when they were separated for more than 1 month; She gave up going out with other men for him.). Sexual intimacy was depicted in acts such as He made love to her. Finally, consistent with Buss' evolutionary interpretation, certain behaviors revolved around sexual reproduction (e.g., He told her he wanted to have children with her.). Some acts were not predicted on the basis of evolutionary theory. For example, behaviors indicative of social support were listed by subjects in the first study and received high typicality ratings in the second study (e.g., He gave her verbal support for her tough decision.). Other behaviors portrayed self-disclosure and confiding, as well as making sacrifices for the other. Finally subjects also listed acts such as gazing at the other, holding hands, and losing sleep because of thoughts of the other. These behaviors also emerged in the prototypes of love uncovered by the feature-listing approaches.

Buss (1988), Fitness and Fletcher (1991), and Shaver et al. (1987) used coding procedures and instructions different from Fehr's, thereby precluding direct comparisons with her study or with Button and Collier's (1991) and Luby and Aron's (1990) replications. However, some similar themes are revealed by these different approaches. For example, all of these prototypes included positive cognitions, physiological reactions, behaviors indicating physical closeness, social support, and positive affect. (Negative affect appeared mainly in the feature-listing studies.)

It seems surprising that the prototypes of love acts and episodes do not include the "big five" features of trust, friendship, respect, honesty, and caring, which were ubiquitous in the feature-listing studies (and received the highest typicality ratings). Perhaps the instructions in the episode and act studies elicited fewer abstract and more concrete responses. This possibility would seem especially true for Buss' study, in which subjects were told specifically to list love acts. Some of these acts can be interpreted as behavioral instantiations of more global, abstract features such as caring (e.g., He called her when she was feeling down.) or trust (e.g., She told him a very private secret about her past.). It is also possible that in the Shaver et al. and Fitness and Fletcher studies, the broad coding categories (relative to Fehr's) resulted in these features being combined with others. For example, in Shaver et al.'s study, "O inspires openness, trust, security, etc. in P" was one of the features with the highest frequency. The *etc.* might well refer to other features such as honesty. The "big five" features also could have been excluded due to lack of fit with the classification schemes. Fitness and Fletcher, for example, categorized responses into events, cognitions, behavior, verbal expressions, physiological responses, and so on. It is not clear how abstract features such as trust, caring, and respect would be coded.

At any rate, the results of these studies indicate that multiple levels of analysis are possible when exploring laypersons's knowledge structures. Buss (1988) conducted a very fine-grained, micro-level analysis of the behaviors of love. Fehr's (1988b) features approach strikes a middle ground, while Shaver et al. (1987) and Fitness and Fletcher (1991) focused on broader, macrolevel categories. Thus a specific act from Buss' study, such as She lost sleep thinking about him, could be classified as Fehr's think about the other all the time feature and as Fitness and Fletcher's cognitions: positive, partner category. The various levels of abstraction reveal different, but complementary, information about the layperson's conception of love (Vallacher & Wegner, 1987).

In sum, the results from the prototype studies just described suggest that laypersons refer to a very complex knowledge base when asked about love. The findings support Fehr and Russell's (1984) claim that to know the meaning of a single word such as *love* is to know a script, complete with antecedents, behavioral responses, beliefs, physiological reactions, and so on. We can refer to this script when deciding whether we love someone (and vice versa) or how to express our love once we have made that decision. For example, according to Shaver et al. (1987) and Fitness and Fletcher (1991), laypersons have knowledge of love's antecedents: The other possesses something one wants or needs, thinking about the person, sharing happy times, or finding the other attractive. People's knowledge of love also includes physiological reactions, many of which indicate a high level of arousal: butterflies in one's stomach, heart rate increases, sweating, and so on. However, the layperson acknowledges that low arousal also can be a part of love; subjects in these studies reported feeling relaxed, calm, and comfortable with the loved one. Similarly the affective component includes both intense emotions such as euphoria and excitement, along with lower key emotions such as contentment. Emotions are overwhelmingly positive in hedonic tone, although feelings like scary, jealousy, and insecurity are listed occasionally. The positive affect experienced has a number of visible expressions (e.g., smiling, laughing).

The provision of social support seems to be an important component of love, along with altruism (giving, making sacrifices for the other). In addition, a physical or sexual component is mentioned in all of the studies. According to laypersons, the prototype of love also includes cognitive activities such as ruminating about the other and seeing only the other's good qualities. Intimacy-related features are prevalent, as are features describing self-disclosure and open communication. Finally many prototypes contain a cluster of commitment features or acts that are indicative of relationship longevity (e.g., a bond, long-lasting, marriage).

It may seem counterintuitive that both intense and nonintense emotions, high and low physiological arousal, are included in the prototype of love. This apparent contradiction is resolved, however, when one examines the typicality ratings assigned to these features. These ratings suggest that people make a basic distinction between companionate and passionate love. The "rational," low arousal, low intensity features depict the former and receive the highest typicality ratings. The mirror image features (high arousal, intense emotions) characterize passionate love and receive the lowest ratings. The companionate features lie at the core of what the layperson means by love, as is compellingly demonstrated by the fact that trust, caring, honesty, respect, and friendship were universal across the four sets of feature lists described, and they received the highest typicality ratings in each study.

Prototypes of Love Versus Related Concepts

Although it seems reasonable to suggest that being cognizant of the culturally shared love script will facilitate competent relating, the issue is actually much more complex. Knowledge of the prototype of love alone is not sufficient to ensure relational success because there are a myriad of ways we can feel and behave toward others. We can feel committed to a relationship with someone; we can feel passionately in love. At times, rather than invoking our generic prototype of love, we might make finer discriminations and refer to feelings of romantic love or affection or infatuation. Thus one can assume that part of relational competence is knowing not only what love is but also what love is not. In other words, competence may entail being able to disambiguate love from related emotions, feelings, or states and being able to differentiate between various kinds of love. In this section, research that situates the prototype of love in a nomological net of relationship concepts is described. One would expect that features of concepts such as *liking* and *commitment* would overlap with the companionate features of love. In contrast, concepts such as *romantic love* and *being in love* should intersect with the passionate features of the prototype of love.

Love and Liking

The concepts of *love* and *liking* were compared by Luby and Aron (1990). (Luby and Aron [1990] reported findings from two data sets, which varied in terms of the instructions given to subjects [a scriptlike example vs. an attribute-list example]. In the interests of brevity, only the features obtained from the script-listing instructions will be reported because only these features were later rated for typicality.) Nearly the same number of features were found for both—60 for liking and 69 for love, 20 of which were shared. Both companionate (e.g., caring, friendship, sharing, want to be with the other) and passionate features (e.g., attraction, excitement, nervousness, touching) were common to love and liking. Features unique to liking included comfortable, want to please the other, sharing their sense of humor, and interest in their life. Many shared features received high typicality ratings, as did several of the unique features of each concept. For both love and liking, the features that received the highest ratings were companionate ones, including trust, caring, friendship/companionship, communication, happiness, and respect. Although the authors concluded that *love* and *liking* are qualitatively different concepts, the overlap between them is fairly substantial. Moreover, the shared features tended to receive high typicality ratings for both concepts.

Love and Commitment

Some theorists have argued that love and commitment are synonymous. Others maintain that love and commitment overlap, although they differ in how they conceptualize the nature of the intersection. Still others believe that love and commitment are completely independent concepts. In an attempt to discover which theorists' model the everyday view resembled most, Fehr (1988b, Study 1) had subjects list the features of love and/or commitment. A sizeable proportion of the respondents listed love as a feature of commitment and vice versa. Further, 21 of the 68 features listed for love were also among the 40 features listed for commitment. These shared features received higher prototypicality ratings in a subsequent study than did the features that were unique to each concept, suggesting a substantial degree of relation. From these and other findings, Fehr concluded that the layperson's view of the relation between love and commitment mapped most closely onto Kelley's (1983) description of these concepts as largely overlapping but partially independent.

The features that were listed for both concepts (e.g., caring, trust, sharing, honesty, respect, devotion, giving, and loyalty) indicate that the companionate component of love is related most closely to commitment. Features that were unique to commitment depicted themes of obligation, as well as making a decision and following through on it. The affective features (e.g., affection, contentment) suggested more placidity and lower intensity than many of the features of love. Love attributes that depicted a passionate component (e.g., excitement, euphoria, wonderful feelings, sexual passion, heart rate increases) generally were not shared with commitment. This finding is consistent with Kelley's (1983) observation that companionate love and commitment are closely associated, whereas "love based on unstable causes, for example, on transient passion, will not promote commitment" (p. 313).

Love and Romantic Love

As mentioned earlier, Fehr (1988b) found that the companion-ate features of love were seen as more central (prototypical) to the concept than were passionate features. She conceded that if subjects had been asked specifically about romantic love, the passionate features might have assumed greater importance. Button and Collier (1991) designed a study to test that possibil-ity. Subjects listed the features of either love or romantic love. The final lists of 39 love and 41 romantic love features over-lapped considerably—29 features were common to both con-cepts. Features that were unique to romantic love included romantic walks, obsession with the other, longing, candle-light, going out for dinner, picnics/sunsets, playfulness, and fantasy. Features listed for love but not romantic love were patience, independence, putting other before self, possible marriage, and making other feel wanted. The results of their second study were surprising—the features that received the highest typicality ratings were similar for both concepts: trust, caring, communication, honesty, friendship, respect, understanding, and having fun together. Significant differ-ences were found for only 3 of the 29 shared features: Attrac-tion, physical attraction, and passion received higher ratings for romantic love than for love. The authors concluded that Fehr's finding that companionatelike features constitute the core of love also extends to romantic love. They elaborate on this point:

> The current research . . . suggests that passionate attributes did not emerge as central in Fehr's (1988[b]) study of love because they are not central in people's conceptions of love. The use of a "romantic love" probe probably would not have changed the [her] results because passionate attributes are secondary in both love and romantic love concepts. (p. 11)

The relation between love and romantic love also was exam-ined by Fehr and Russell (1991, Study 5). They asked subjects to list features of 20 different kinds of love. The types of love ranged from having 18 to only 3 features in common with Fehr's

(1988b) prototype of love. Romantic love shared 12 of its 29 features with love. Although the feature lists themselves were not presented in that article, an examination of the romantic love prototype reveals that many of its unique features depict romantic behaviors (e.g., candlelight dinners, taking walks, soft music, sitting in front of a fireplace), which is exactly what Button and Collier (1991) found. Romantic fantasies (e.g., dream about the person, like a fairy tale) are also represented to a greater extent than in the general love prototype, as are exclusiveness and absorption (e.g., your world revolves around the person) and idealism (e.g., idealistic, problems seem to vanish). As one might expect, more features depict a physical/sexual component (kissing, glowing, sweaty palms). Interestingly the features shared by love and romantic love are both companionate (friendship, caring, sharing, honesty) and passionate (think about the person all the time, sexual, physical attraction).

More recently, I have asked subjects to rate the romantic love features in terms of how typical each is of romantic love. The highest typicality ratings are assigned to the companionatelike features that are shared with the love prototype (e.g., happiness, caring, honesty, friendship, feel free to talk about anything). Features unique to romantic love receive the lowest typicality ratings: don't know the person very well, sweaty palms, giving gifts, like a fairy tale, and your world revolves around the person. Thus, consistent with Button and Collier's (1991) findings, there are a number of similarities between the prototypes of love and romantic love. Moreover, it is the features that are shared with love itself that are regarded as most central to romantic love, whereas the unique romantic love features are seen as peripheral to that concept.

The finding that a companionate component is shared by romantic love and love prototypes and, in fact, even may be central to that intersection seems counterintuitive, given that romantic love and passionate love are often treated as synonymous. Perhaps passionate features spring to the fore only when subjects are asked to focus explicitly on the experience of being in love. Fortunately Luby and Aron (1990) asked their subjects to do just that.

Love and Being in Love

Luby and Aron (1990) extracted 69 love features and 58 being in love features from their data, 28 of which were shared. As with love and romantic love, love and being in love had both companionate (e.g., caring, friendship, communication, respect, trust) and passionate (e.g., sweating, dreaminess, excitement, sex, jealousy) aspects in common. Features such as intense emotions, unrequited, sudden, loss of sleep, ecstasy, and including the loved one in one's future were unique to being in love. The shared features, especially companionate ones, received the highest typicality ratings for each concept, leading Luby and Aron to conclude that the concepts of *love* and *being in love* share a common core. They speculate that love simply may be characterized by less intensity than being in love.

Thus companionate features continued to play a central role even for the concept of being in love, with all of its passionate connotations. What does one make of this fascinating, albeit perplexing, finding? Fehr and Russell's (1991) studies on the prototypes of different kinds of love, taken with the findings from the feature-listing studies, may shed some light on this issue.

Love and Prototypes of Kinds of Love

Fehr and Russell (1991, Study 5) assessed the degree of overlap between the superordinate prototype of love and the prototypes of several kinds of love, in addition to romantic love (described earlier). Love had the fewest number of features in common with infatuation and puppy love. The greatest overlap existed between the generic love prototype and kinds of love between family members, along with friendship and committed love. These kinds of love also received the highest typicality ratings when asked how good an example they were of the concept (Fehr & Russell, 1991, Study 2), which further indicates that they lie at the heart of what love means to the layperson. It is interesting to note that central to all of these kinds of love is a companionate component. For example, caring, trust, friendship, and respect received among the highest typicality ratings recently gathered for committed love, friendship love, and the familial kinds of love. Thus, in the same way that Fehr (1988b) found that the companionate features of love were seen as most central to the concept, so too are the types of love for which a companionate component is at the core. Further, consistent with Fehr's (1988b) finding that the passionate features of love were seen as peripheral to the concept, Fehr and Russell (1991, Study 5) found that passionate varieties of love (e.g., passionate love, sexual love, puppy love, infatuation) had the fewest number of features in common with the superordinate category love and also received the lowest typicality ratings.

In sum, there is substantial overlap between the features of love and those of related concepts such as *commitment, being in love,* and *liking,* as well as between love and the features of certain types of love (e.g., romantic love, friendship, and love between family members). It seems safe to say that if the concept being compared possesses companionate features, it is these attributes that will be shared with love. This is true for liking and commitment and even for romantic/passionate concepts such as *romantic love* and *being in love.* As one would expect, the latter also share passionate features with love. Nevertheless the companionate features of love receive high typicality ratings even for those concepts, suggesting that companionate features represent the most substantive link with love itself.

The overlapping nature of these various concepts provides fascinating fodder for research on the dynamics of close relationships. For example, expressions of love can be interpreted as expressions of commitment, romantic love, or being in love. Conversely expressions of liking risk being taken as expressions of love. Abbey (1982), for example, found that men tend to mistake women's friendliness for sexual attraction. These kinds of mistakes may not be very common; people seem to find ways of navigating through the fuzziness and making these kinds of discriminations. The context (e.g., whether one is interacting with a same- or other-gender person) often will clarify what is intended by an expression of love. For example, a heterosexual person probably does not invest much time trying to decipher whether a same-sex person's friendliness signifies an interest in friendship or romance. How has contextual factors disambiguated the meaning of communications have been a major focus of research in the discipline of communication studies (see, for example, McLaughlin, 1984).

People also may deal with the inherent blurriness of these concepts by paying particular attention to unique features when deciphering the meaning of another person's expression of love. On the one hand, if the person says, "I care about you," any number of relationship possibilities are suggested. On the other hand, if the person displays unique romantic love features such as kissing you, serving you dinner by candlelight, and telling you that he or she dreams about you, you probably will infer that this person has romantic love in mind. It would be fascinating to explore whether people do, in fact, use distinctive features as diagnostic information.

Individual Differences in Prototypes of Love

Despite variations in instructions, coding schemes, and subject samples, the prototypes of love uncovered in the various studies discussed so far displayed an impressive degree of similarity. However, agreement in terms of a general concept of *love* at the nomothetic level does not preclude differences at an idiographic level. In other words, despite consensus on the general prototype of love, there also may be considerable variation in conceptions of love from one person to the next. Presumably such differences would be systematically tied to individual difference variables such as gender, sexual orientation, age, intimacy status, personality, and attachment style, for which effects have been found in related domains (e.g., the experience of romantic love). The study of individual differences in conceptions of love is important because these differences are associated with differences in the subjective experience or phenomenology of love (Dion & Dion, 1985).

Gender

"Simone de Beauvoir once wrote that men and women have different concepts of love, and that's why they fail to understand one another. I don't doubt this is true" (Solomon, 1988, p. 69). Do men and women, in fact, have different concepts, or prototypes, of love? The answer seems to be yes and no, depending on how one asks the question. Generally gender differences are not found. For example, Fehr (1988b) found that male and female university students did not differ in terms of the features they considered central and peripheral to love. In fact, their typicality ratings were highly correlated. Rousar and Aron (1990) obtained similar results with a much more heterogeneous sample. They asked heterosexual and homosexual men and women (students and nonstudents) residing in the San Francisco area to rate 20 of Fehr's love attributes for typicality. No gender differences were found in ratings of the prototypical and nontypical features. Aron and Westbay (1991, Study 1) also did not obtain gender differences in ratings of the Passion, Commitment, and Intimacy factors that were found to underlie Fehr's love features (see section on Intimacy Status). However, in a validation study, women assigned higher typicality ratings than did men to the Intimacy factor features.

When Luby and Aron (1990) compared men's and women's ratings of their prototypical and nontypical love attributes, no differences were found. In a subsequent exploratory feature-by-feature analysis, men provided higher ratings for 11 of the 69 attributes. These results must be interpreted with caution, however, given the lack of overall gender effect and because of the small sample sizes (e.g., fewer than 10 men).

In Button and Collier's (1991) first study, male and female subjects tended to list the same features for love (and romantic love). Moreover, the frequency with which the features were listed was comparable. Contrary to other research, however, a number of gender differences emerged in the typicality ratings study—gender differences were found for 20 of the 41 love and romantic love features. Women rated the cluster of attributes that formed the core of love and romantic love as more important than did men (e.g., friendship, trust, respect, commitment, honesty, sharing, caring, compatibility). They also assigned higher ratings to several unique love attributes (patience, independence, encouragement, and possible marriage), as well as to two unique romantic love features (love and special feelings). Only fantasy, a unique romantic love feature, received higher ratings from men.

Buss (1988) predicted, from an evolutionary perspective, that men and women would differ in the kinds of acts generated as exemplifying love. In general terms, men were expected to nominate acts involving resource display (e.g., money, possessions), whereas women were predicted to nominate acts that would signal their reproductive capability (e.g., youth, beauty). As expected, men were more likely than women to nominate sexual behaviors and acts pertaining to the possession of tangible resources. Women were more likely to list acts depicting fidelity and having children. No gender differences were found in frequency of listing for acts involving marriage or commitment. Unfortunately men's and women's typicality ratings of the 100 love acts were not compared.

Finally Fehr and Russell (1991) asked female and male students to provide typicality ratings for 20 types of love. No gender differences were found. In subsequent research (e.g., Fehr & Broughton, 1991), subjects were presented with feature lists depicting 15 of the kinds of love targeted by Fehr and Russell. Instead of typicality, they were asked to rate how similar the view of love depicted in each feature list was to their own view. Thus the focus was shifted to the subject's personal conception of love. Gender differences consistently have been obtained in studies using this methodology. Men regard romantic love, sexual love, infatuation, puppy love, sibling love, and passionate love as closer to their own conceptualization of love than do women. Women rate the prototypes of sisterly love and friendship love as more similar to their view of love. Finally men and women do not differ in their ratings of most of the kinds of love between family members—familial love, parental love, maternal love, and brotherly love—nor have gender differences been found for committed love, platonic love, and affection.

To summarize, when asked to rate which features (or kinds) of love are prototypical and nonprototypical of the concept, men and women tend to agree with one another. Gender differences emerge, however, when a more personal response is requested, as in Fehr and Broughton's (1991) studies. (Similarly Button and Collier (1991) asked subjects to rate the features according to *importance*, which may have prompted subjects to respond in terms of their own view of love or relationships, rather than in features-of-concepts terms.) The gender differences that are found by using these kinds of instructions are consistent with the frequently reported finding that companionate love figures prominently in women's beliefs and experience of love, whereas men's orientation is more romantic (see Fehr & Broughton, 1991, for a review).

Intimacy Status

Aron and Westbay (1991) factor analyzed their's and Fehr's typicality ratings of her 68 features of love. The three factors that were extracted resembled the components of Sternberg's (1986) triangular theory of love and therefore were labeled Intimacy, Passion, and Commitment. Features with high loadings were treated as items on scales that were developed to measure each factor. The authors reasoned that endorsement of the scale items would differ, depending on the psychosocial stage of the respondent. Specifically they predicted that subjects who had successfully completed Erikson's intimacy versus isolation stage, in which the individual is developmentally ready to enter a close, intimate, relationship, would rate the items of the Intimacy scale as more prototypical of love than subjects at preintimate stages. Ratings on the Passion and Commitment scales were not expected to vary. The hypothesis was confirmed: Subjects classified as intimacy-ready rated the Intimacy scale items as more prototypical of love than did preintimacy subjects, while the groups did not differ in their ratings on the Passion and Commitment scales. These findings were replicated in a validation study.

Sexual Orientation, Attachment Style, and Age

Rousar and Aron (1990) compared the typicality ratings assigned by male and female heterosexual and homosexual respondents to a subset of Fehr's prototypical and nontypical love features. Ratings did not differ as a function of sexual orientation. With regard to attachment style, a significant interaction was obtained but was not regarded as substantive; secure subjects assigned slightly lower ratings to the nonprototypical love features than did anxious/ambivalent subjects. The ratings of subjects in three age groups—17-24 years, 25-34 years, 35 and above—also were compared. No differences were found.

Personality

So far, no studies have been published on personality differences in endorsement of the features of love. However, Fehr and Broughton (1991) conducted a series of studies on personality correlates of the 15 prototypes of love referred to earlier (e.g., romantic love, friendship, maternal love). The model used, the interpersonal circle, provides a theory-based definition of interpersonal behavior organized around the primary personality dimensions of dominance and nurturance. Subjects completed the Interpersonal Adjective Scales (Wiggins, 1979), which assess eight different personality categories based on combinations of these two orthogonal dimensions. Thus *extraversion,* for example, is conceptualized as a blend of high dominance and high nurturance, while *introversion* is comprised of low dominance and nurturance. It was predicted that prototypes of family kinds of love and friendship, which are characterized by closeness, interdependence, intimacy, commitment (kinds of love in which companionate features are central) would be related to traits that fall on the "warm," or high nurturance, side of the interpersonal circle. Prototypes that depict love in more passionate, transient, and less intimate terms (e.g., infatuation, puppy love, sexual love) were expected to be aligned most closely with traits on the "cold," low nurturance, side of the circle. Results supported predictions. For example, ratings of the prototype of friendship love were correlated most strongly with endorsement of the high-nurturance trait, *warm-agreeableness,* whereas the sexual love prototype (which contains such features as using the other person for your own gratification) showed the strongest relation with the low-nurturance trait, *cold-hearted.*

Self Versus Typical Prototypes of Love

Some researchers have examined whether different proto-types of love are elicited depending on whether subjects are asked to describe their own personal experience, as opposed to a typical experience, of love. For example, in Shaver et al.'s (1987) study, some subjects were asked to "Think of a real incident in which you felt particularly IN LOVE or LOVING," whereas others were asked to describe their impressions of typical emotion episodes—"What generally happens when a person becomes loving?" (p. 1072). For most emotion prototypes, subjects in the typical condition were more likely to mention behaviors that are easily observed in others (e.g., smiling, for the joy prototype), whereas the self accounts focused more on internal subjective experience. Thus, for love, subjects in the self condition were more likely to list feeling relaxed, calm. However, they also mentioned smiling more frequently than did subjects in the typical condition. Subjects in the typical condition were more likely to mention being forgetful, distracted, etc., and seeing only the positive side, which suggests that "people are not very aware of their own narrow focus and cognitive biases when describing personal experiences of emotion" (Shaver et al., 1987, p. 1080). However, differences were found only for these 4 of their 23 features of love, indicating a high degree of similarity between self and typical accounts.

Fitness and Fletcher's (1991, Study 2) research on typical experiences of love toward a marital partner was described earlier. They compared the results of that study with their first study, in which subjects recounted the most recent time they had experienced love for their spouse. As expected, recalled events were more likely to include idiosyncratic features than typical accounts of love. Also, in the recalled accounts, although subjects reported wanting to hug and kiss their partners, they sometimes felt unable to do so (e.g., being in public). (Typical accounts tended not to include such obstacles to expressions of love.) Overall the two sets of accounts were very similar.

In sum, when one surveys the studies that have examined individual differences in prototypes of love, the results suggest more similarity than diversity. For example, gender, age, sexual orientation, and attachment style differences in typicality ratings usually are not found, nor have gender differences in feature-listing frequencies been reported. On the other hand, Aron and Westbay's (1991) studies on intimacy stage demonstrate convincingly that individual difference factors may influence ratings of conceptually relevant subsets of features.

Presumably individual difference factors will have the most powerful effect when the focus is explicitly on the individual, as when Fehr and Broughton (1991) asked subjects to respond in terms of their own view of love (rather than provide typicality ratings, as is usually done). Under these conditions, gender and personality differences have emerged. These findings, taken with those of Aron and Westbay (1991), suggest that against a backdrop of consensus on the meaning of love, there is potential for disagreement between individuals. Such disagreements might well have implications for perceptions of and harmony in ongoing relationships. This issue is considered in the next section.

Prototypes of Love: Behavioral Implications

It is assumed that the way people think about love will shape the kinds of decisions they make and the actions they take in their close relationships. For example, Kelley (1983) points out, "People's beliefs about love are part of the causal conditions governing the behavior and feelings that occur in love" (p. 271). This statement also applies to conceptions of the dynamics of love "and, of course, people's conception of their own love constitutes an important criterion for what they do toward their partner and for how they respond to their partner's actions" (p. 271). The effects of people's conceptions of love on various relationship processes and outcomes have not been studied extensively. This is an important issue, however, because the nature of these conceptions is bound to affect the competence with which interpersonal relationships are conducted.

A preliminary step was taken by Fehr (1988b), who wondered what people pay attention to when evaluating their relationships. Fehr (1988b, Study 5) predicted that when deciding whether a relationship is developing in the direction of greater love, people would monitor changes in typical, rather than nonprototypical, features. The rationale was: If prototypical features capture the core meaning of a concept, then changes in the level of love in a relationship should be reflected in the applicability of those features. For example, greater caring, a prototypical feature of love, should be taken as more indicative of increased love in a relationship than greater security or passion (nontypical features of love). To test this idea, subjects were provided with relationship descriptions ranging from low to high in love. They were asked to rate the applicability of prototypical and nontypical love features to each description. Results showed that although both kinds of features were seen as more applicable as the relationships became more loving, the applicability of the typical features increased systematically, whereas the applicability of nontypical features was not as closely tied to the level of love in the relationship description. Instead nonprototypical features tended to be rated as moderately applicable regardless of the level of love. Thus, according to Fehr, changes in prototypical features of love (e.g., greater caring, respect, trust, happiness) are taken as barometers of increased love in a relationship.

In a subsequent study, Fehr (1988b, Study 6) examined the opposite side of the coin—namely, how people decide whether a relationship has become less loving (or committed). Subjects were provided with a description of a loving, committed relationship. They then were asked to assess the impact of violations of typical and nontypical features of love on the relationship. It was hypothesized that violations of prototypical features of love would threaten the relationship more seriously than violations of nonprototypical features. As predicted, a loss of sense of caring, trust, honesty, or respect, or a feeling that friendship was no longer a part of the relationship were all seen as seriously threatening or undermining the extent to which a relationship was regarded as loving. On the other hand, ceasing to feel euphoric, to gaze at one's partner, to be dependent, or no longer seeing only the partner's good qualities were not regarded as diagnostic of diminishing love in the relationship.

Fehr (1988b) concluded that these two studies demonstrate that lay people's conceptions of love influence their views of the dynamics of close relationships. She suggests that people may pay particular attention to prototypical attributes and changes in these attributes when assessing the state of their relationships.

Implications of conceptions of love in terms of actual behaviors were investigated by Fehr (1988a). Specifically this study focused on the relationship repercussions resulting from matches or mismatches in romantic partners' prototypes of love. It was hypothesized that partners who shared very similar conceptions of love would experience greater love, liking, commitment, and satisfaction in their relationship than those who held dissimilar conceptions. Further, it was predicted that the former group would experience greater relationship longevity than the latter. These predictions were tested in a longitudinal study of dating couples. Results indicated that the degree of correspondence between the partners' conceptions of love did not predict levels of love, liking, satisfaction, and so on. Instead *perceived* similarity in conceptions of love proved to be the important variable. Couples who believed they held similar conceptions of love at both testing times exhibited high levels of love, liking, satisfaction, and commitment. All of these relationships remained intact over a 3-4-month interval. Those who believed their views of love were dissimilar at Time 1 but perceived greater similarity by Time 2 showed a dramatic rise in the quality of their relationship from Time 1 to Time 2. These relationships, too, remained intact. The dating couples who perceived similarity at Time 1 but not at Time 2 showed a decrease in their scores on all of the measures. This group was an especially volatile group; they experienced the highest rate of breakups. Finally couples who believed their views of love were dissimilar at each testing period scored low on the love, liking, satisfaction, and commitment measures at both testing sessions. These couples were not as likely to break up as couples who believed they had become more dissimilar. However, the probability of dissolution was much higher for them than for couples in the first two groups.

Thus the way one perceives the correspondence between one's own and one's partner's prototypes of love has profound implications for the quality and even existence of a relationship. The finding that perceived similarity emerged as the critical variable raises a number of questions: What might cause couples who hold similar prototypes of love to mistakenly believe they do not? One also wonders at what point perceptions meet reality—Can couples who have very different views of love but believe their views are similar continue to sustain that belief over a long period of time? Planalp (1987) suggests that when people approach an interaction with different conceptions, metacognition may play a role: "Each person has knowledge of the other person's relational knowledge that makes it possible to anticipate and explain the other's actions even if their relational knowledge is not in synchrony" (p. 186). The effects of and ways of resolving discrepancies in partners' prototypes is an interesting topic for future research.

Conclusions and New Directions

Investigations of conceptions of love from a prototype perspective is a fairly recent scientific venture. This line of work should be continued with an explicit focus on the implications of such conceptions for competent relating. Fehr (1988b) remarked that people presumably rely on their existing notions of love and commitment when attempting to answer questions such as: Do I love this person? She went on to suggest that people might engage in a prototype-matching task in which the features of their actual relationships are compared with their cognitive representations of the concept of *love*. This process probably also occurs in the other direction. For example, there is considerable evidence that people rely on their prototypes to fill in gaps when they encounter missing information (e.g., Fiske & Taylor, 1991). In fact, Fehr (1988b, Study 3) found that presenting subjects with only a subset of the features of love led them to believe they had seen other, prototypical features that had not been presented. This gap-filling function of prototypes is useful because, for the most part, someone who can be trusted, for example, probably is also worthy of respect. However, prototype-based inferences will not always be correct. Relational competence may entail knowing when data-driven processing of information is appropriate and when prototype-based processing should be used.

Ways in which people's knowledge structures may contribute to dysfunctional relating is another intriguing topic for future investigation. This issue could be explored empirically in a variety of ways. For example, conceptions of love held by people in unhappy relationships should be compared with those held by nondistressed couples. Perhaps one or both partners in a distressed relationship subscribe to views of love that are impossible to attain. Or perhaps people who are dissatisfied with their relationships place undue emphasis on aspects of love (e.g., excitement, sexual passion, dependency) that are regarded as peripheral by those who enjoy satisfying relationships. Alternatively people in unhappy relationships may be acutely aware of the "normal" view of love and feel distressed because they realize that their relationship is not characterized by prototypical features of love, such as respect, caring, or honesty. The kind of intervention that would foster competent relating would differ depending on which of these possibilities was supported by research.

The origins of people's conceptions of love, both in clinical and nonclinical contexts, and their relation to competence also merit investigation. A related, important topic is the extent to which one's own experiences in relationships shape personal conceptions of love toward or away from competent relating. Duck (1988) commented that experiencing relationship dissolution, for example, affects the ways future relationships are initiated and maintained: "Break-up today sets the scene for tomorrow's relationships; the degree of eagerness with which they are sought, the amount of wariness with which they are approached, and the extent to which the person specifically watches out for or guards against particular features of the new relationship" (p. 114). Presumably, significant relationship experiences can cause people to revise their prototypes of concepts such as *love,* resulting in either enhanced or diminished interpersonal functioning.

In conclusion, let us return to the question with which this chapter began: How do I love thee? If, in fact, laypersons consult their prototype, they are tapping into an impressive body of knowledge. Fehr's (1988b) study, for example, yielded 68 different features; Luby and Aron (1990) reported 93! Despite the large number of attributes, the layperson's concept of love is remarkably tidy: Companionate features lie at the core; passionate features are regarded as part of the concept but are relegated to a peripheral status. This finding is very robust; subject groups from New Zealand and various parts of North America: Male and female, homosexual and heterosexual, psychology students and nonpsychology students, patrons of a shopping mall, government employees, and married subjects focusing on love in a marital context, agree on the features and internal structure of the prototype of love. This prototype structure seems to serve as diagnostic information when people check on the health of their relationships: If the companionate features are thriving, the relationship is declared to be in good health; if those features are deteriorating, the relationship is regarded as declining. The importance of the companionate component was underscored in the research on prototypes of kinds of love; again the types that possessed a substantial companionate component were regarded as closest to the core meaning of the concept of *love.*

In addition to a commonly agreed-on generic representation of love, it seems that people also construct their own personal conceptions. These representations appear to be related systematically to individual difference variables such as gender and personality. Perhaps laypersons possess several levels of knowledge of concepts: a culturally shared, general prototype of love, along with equally complex representations of their own view of love (and of different types of love). If so, when one asks, "What do you mean by love?" the layperson may be able to give several answers; one answer reflecting what they and everyone else means by love, and another answer reflecting their own, more idiosyncratic view. Researchers have only begun to mine the knowledge (and perhaps levels of knowledge) about the concept of *love* that the everyday person carries around in his or her head. Yet uncovering this knowledge is critical as a first step toward the goal of determining the cognitive structures that underlie relational competence.

5

Knowledge Structures and Explanations in Intimate Relationships

Garth J. O. Fletcher

Julie Fitness

The study of people in social contexts possesses a fascinating and distinctive feature; that is, the phenomena of interest (human beings) are often engaged in the same pursuits as social scientists—namely, the development of theories to explain, predict, and control human social behavior and experience. Nowhere is this feature more apparent than in the study of personal or close relationships.

Personal relationships are primal in human society. We learn how to be human, social beings largely in the context of close relationships with our parents, relatives, and friends. And in adult life, for most people, our identities and lives are dominated by those nearest and dearest to us. The importance and nature of such relationships in society are both reflected in and created by the mountain of relationship-relevant information foisted on us daily in pop songs, agony columns, self-help books, romantic novels, TV plays and sitcoms, advertisements, stage plays, movies, and more.

Small wonder, then, that people think about personal relationships and develop theories about specific relationships as well as relationships in general. Given the need to control and predict behavior in this area of life, with its attendant uncertainties, it should also come as no surprise that people will at times attempt to explain their own and others' close relationship behavior. Indeed the study of cognition in relationships has been dominated by an interest in such explanatory processes (Fletcher & Fincham, 1991b). The associated body of attributional research has, in turn, been theoretically dominated by the standard attributional account drawn from *attribution theory,* a generic term applying to the clutch of classic attribution statements produced by Heider (1958), Jones and Davis (1965), Kelley (1967), and Weiner (Weiner et al., 1972).

Attribution theory was in its heyday in social psychology in the 1970s, although it remains popular today partly through its widespread exportation to other areas, including the study of personal relationships. To understand the weaknesses and gaps in attribution theory, however, it is important to note that it was developed prior to the cognitive revolution in psychology and its offshoot of social cognition in the 1970s. Indeed the proponents of social cognition were so carried away with their new bag of toys—concepts and methodologies borrowed from cognitive psychology—that many of them simply ignored attribution theory (see, for example, the first handbook of social cognition by Wyer & Srull, 1984).

Present-day social cognition theories also have weaknesses, one of which, in our view, involves paying insufficient attention to attributional processes. On the other hand, it would be surprising if the old attributional war-horse did not require refurbishment, and that is the task we have set for ourselves here operating within a relationship context. We have attempted to develop a model that locates attributional processes and the standard attributional model within a social cognitive perspective that emphasizes the role of the layperson's theories of personal relationships (termed here *knowledge constructs*).

This is not the first time such a task has been attempted, similar models being developed by Bradbury and Fincham (1989) and Fletcher and Fincham (1991a). However, the theory proffered here differs in a few crucial respects from these earlier versions. First, these earlier models were directed specifically at attributions within dyadic interaction. The present model is much more general, taking into account the obvious point that attributional activity concerning relationships may take place outside the context of dyadic interaction. Second, as the title of the chapter implies, the model explicated here is more concerned with the nature, content, and interaction among distinct knowledge structures than is the case with these previous accounts. In broad terms, then, this chapter is concerned with the nature of and links between the two constructs alluded to in the title—relationship knowledge structures and explanation.

Personal Relationship Knowledge Structures and Attributional Processing: A Proposed Theoretical Framework

The general model we explicate is shown in Figure 5.1. It is not intended as a detailed information-processing account, but rather is offered as an organizing theoretical framework—as a starting point. Before detailing the components of the model, the following example should help provide a general idea of its workings: Joan's husband unexpectedly pays her a compliment, which leads her to feel particularly happy (eliciting event and affect) because she recently had begun to think that her husband was taking her for granted (relationship account). She recalls with pleasure other occasions on which her husband had similarly demonstrated his qualities of generosity and sensitivity (controlled, conscious thought). Thus she produces a relationship-positive attribution, "My husband is a sensitive person"

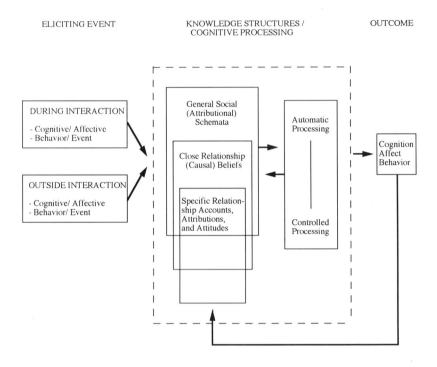

Figure 5.1. Knowledge Structures and Processing Within Relationships: An Attributional Model.

(cognitive outcome), based on general attributional schemata and her specific relationship account. She decides to cook him a special meal (behavioral outcome), and her general belief that close relationships need work to stay vibrant (close relationship causal beliefs) is buttressed (feedback arrow from outcome to knowledge constructs).

We now outline and discuss the different elements shown in Figure 5.1: the three categories of knowledge structure, the factors that elicit knowledge constructs, the cognitive processing component, and, more generally, the role of affect in the model. The remaining outcome category is not considered separately, but rather is dealt with as it arises within each section. Relevant research findings are cited, and a variety of important issues are raised as we proceed.

What Are Knowledge Structures
and Why Are They Important?

The category of *knowledge structures* refers to any relatively permanent set of cognitions or cognitive structures that reside in our long-term memory store. These are a vast array of items, including beliefs, attributions, expectations, and memories of behavior. As previously noted, personal relationships are central elements in people's lives. Accordingly we would expect people to develop relatively elaborate theories, beliefs, expectations, and so forth about such relationships.

The notion that we store every single event and behavior experienced as memory traces in long-term memory has generally been discarded as implausible. Instead, according to stock cognitive theory, people encode, organize, store, and recall events and behaviors in terms of stored structures (cf. Chapter 3, this volume). Of course, a small amount of information can be retained in working memory, but this memory store is severely limited in terms of the amount of information it can retain and the length of time the information remains available. Hence, stored knowledge structures are inextricably intertwined with cognitive processing, and this intimate relation is represented in Figure 5.1 and is illustrated in our previous example.

The knowledge structures in Figure 5.1 are organized in terms of a global-specific dimension, which is a typical kind of division in theories of memory (Anderson, 1983; Schank, 1982) and also a critical assumption in recent theories of social cognition in personal relationships (e.g., Fletcher & Fincham, 1991a; Surra & Bohman, 1991). We now consider the most abstract category of knowledge schemata and discuss the links between this knowledge structure and attributional judgments in relationships.

General Social (Attributional) Schemata. A problem for any theory of attribution is that laypersons produce an almost infinite variety of causes to explain social behavior. The classic attribution theories of Heider (1958), Kelley (1967), and others deal with this issue by assuming that it is not the content of the causes that matter, but where the putative causes are located along a handful of causal dimensions such as stability, locus of attribution, and controllability. Hence, it can be seen that the classic attribution theories posit abstract knowledge constructs that slot into the topmost box shown in Figure 5.1.

Almost all of the attribution research in relationship contexts uses the same standard attributional theory that postulates links between the attribution dimensions, derived from the classic attribution approaches, and relationship satisfaction. The basic idea is simply that people in happy relationships make attributions that maximize the favorable implications of positive behavior but that minimize the implications of negative behavior. Conversely those in unhappy relationships adopt the opposite pattern of attributions in relation to positive and negative behaviors, respectively. For example, a man in a happy sexual relationship is likely to explain his partner's gift of flowers with a stable, internal, and global cause (e.g., she is a sensitive, caring person) but to attribute his partner's insensitive remark to an unstable, externally located, and specific cause (e.g., she did not have much sleep last night). In contrast, a man in an unhappy relationship is more likely to attribute the gift of flowers to an unstable, externally located, and specific cause (e.g., she has had a rare win on the horses) and to attribute the cutting remark to a stable, internal, and global cause (e.g., she is an insensitive, bad-tempered person). The two sets of attributions can be described as relationship-positive and relationship-negative, respectively.

A good deal of research generally has supported the validity of the standard attributional model, using a range of investigative techniques and including both cross-sectional and longitudinal designs. This literature has been reviewed extensively elsewhere, so we spare the reader a repeat of the exercise here (for reviews, see Bradbury & Fincham, 1990, and Fletcher & Fincham, 1991a). But we make two general points.

First, this body of research supports the supposition that these attribution dimensions possess psychological reality; that is, they are not merely convenient explanatory fictions. This is perhaps not surprising, given that without the possession of such content-free knowledge structures, it is difficult to see how people could ever generalize knowledge or rules gained from particular areas to other domains of interest (see Schank, 1982).

The second point is related to the way attributions operate, in the standard account, to maintain existing levels of relationship satisfaction regardless of whether positive or negative interactive behavior is produced. This feature is linked to a central tenet in classic attribution theory—namely, that naive dispositional theories, judgments, or knowledge structures are inherently resistant to change. This tenet is hardly surprising if one considers the nightmarish alternative in which our partner and relationship judgments would shift according to every nuance and change in behavior. Attributions can, thus, be viewed as one powerful means by which the relative permanence of our relationship theories are protected against the apparently contrary and shifting behavioral evidence that is part of the typical personal or close relationship.

This claim is that knowledge structures are *resistant* to change, not *incapable* of change. Obviously relationship judgments and satisfaction often change over time, not uncommonly leading to relationship collapse. We shall return to the issue of relationship stability and change, vis-à-vis attribution processes, in a later section. For now we turn to a category of knowledge construct that simply is absent from the standard attributional framework— beliefs about the causes of successful relationships.

Relationship (Causal) Beliefs. This second level of knowledge structure concerns beliefs that pertain to relationships in general. Specifically the class of beliefs we deal with here concern the perceived factors that lead to relationship success or failure. A recent attempt by Fletcher and Kininmonth (in press) to develop and test a scale measuring such relationship beliefs in the domain of intimate, sexual relationships (the Close Relationship Beliefs Scale) is informative about both the nature of such beliefs and how they might function in terms of our model. Hence we describe this research in some detail.

To develop the Close Relationship Beliefs Scale, Fletcher and Kininmonth (in press) first designed a study to unearth the set of prototypical beliefs about the causes of relationship success. A university-based student sample and a nonuniversity sample wrote down all of the factors that they believed would produce a successful and loving sexual/romantic relationship (either married or unmarried). Eighteen beliefs subsequently were derived from these statements, and three Likert scales were used to measure each belief: Subjects were required to indicate with each item, on 6-point scales, the extent to which they held each belief (anchored by *do not hold this belief at all* and *hold this belief very strongly*). An exploratory factor analysis of the subtotals for each belief (*n* = 981) revealed four interpretable factors labeled intimacy (e.g., in happy relationships partners totally accept one another), external factors (e.g., money is as important as love in close relationships), passion (e.g., without good sex, relationships do not survive), and individuality (e.g., each partner has a right to absolute personal privacy).

This four-factor structure was remarkably stable across several samples: comparing men with women, and comparing subjects who were currently involved in romantic, sexual relationships with those not in such relationships. Two further studies also provided convergent and discriminant validity for the four belief factors, using a variety of other scales. Importantly, there was good evidence that these relationship beliefs differed from judgments concerning actual relationships, specifically relationship satisfaction and memories of belief-related behavior. Relationship satisfaction, for example, was unrelated to how strongly the beliefs were held (except for a small correlation of .28 between intimacy beliefs and relationship satisfaction).

Consistent with our previous reasoning, however, it was found that general relationship beliefs moderated the relations between self-reports of behaviors in close relationships and relationship satisfaction. For example, a sample of subjects who had strong beliefs in the importance of intimacy had significantly stronger links between their levels of relationship satisfaction and their self-reported levels of intimacy behavior (e.g., good communication) in their relationships (*r* = .69) than another group of subjects who had relatively weak beliefs in the importance of intimacy ($r = .32$). This pattern of correlations was repeated across the other three belief scales.

Taken together, then, these findings support three key conclusions. First, general close relationship beliefs and relationship-specific judgments and constructs are represented separately in human cognitive architecture. Second, relationship beliefs influence judgments in specific relationships by channeling attention to particular categories of behaviors. Third, stable individual differences exist in the extent to which people hold content-specific beliefs concerning the causes for relationship success.

Of course, the Close Relationship Beliefs Scale is not the first scale to be developed to measure beliefs or other knowledge constructs that operate at this mid-range, content-loaded level. Other popular scales already exist specifically designed for romantic, sexual relationship contexts, including the Love Attitudes Scale (Hendrick & Hendrick, 1986) and the Relationship Belief Inventory (Eidelson & Epstein, 1982). However, on the basis of some of the thinking behind our model, we believe that such scales suffer from some important theoretical cum methodological problems. Let us elucidate.

First, scales that purport to measure relationship beliefs, attitudes, or other knowledge structures typically include a mishmash of items comprising attitudes, expectations, intentions, beliefs, attributions, memories of behavior frequency, and so forth (see Baucom, Epstein, Sayers, & Sher, 1989). Second, and more seriously, scales often also haphazardly mix items measuring different categories of knowledge construct shown in Figure 5.1; namely, they often include items that apply to a respondent's specific relationship with items that apply to relationships in general.

To give an example and to illustrate the unfortunate consequences that can follow from these moves, we take the Relationship Belief Inventory (Eidelson & Epstein, 1982)—a scale often used in relationship research. This scale measures five categories of beliefs (eight items per subscale) that are thought to be dysfunctional in intimate, sexual relationships: (a) disagreement is destructive, (b) mind reading is expected, (c) partners cannot change, (d) sexual perfectionism, and (e) the sexes are different. The items from the scale, however, include a large range of categories, including general beliefs, attitudes, expectations, and behavioral or affective reports from the respondent's own current romantic, intimate relationship. By our count, 21 of the 40 items apply to a specific relationship—for example, I take it as a personal insult when my partner disagrees with an important idea of mine; I get very upset if my partner does not recognize how I am feeling and I have to tell him/her; I cannot tolerate it when my partner argues with me.

To compound the problem, the above sorts of item clearly are set up along a positive-negative dimension. The result is that such scale items are similar to those included in widely used measures of relationship satisfaction such as the Dyadic Adjustment Scale (Spanier, 1976) and the Marital Adjustment Test (Locke & Wallace, 1959). This sort of item overlap is unfortunate because most published research using the Relationship Belief Inventory has focused on the relations between the Relationship Belief Inventory and relationship satisfaction or other constructs that are strongly related to marital satisfaction, such as positivity of communication (e.g., Bradbury & Fincham, 1988; Epstein, Pretzer, & Fleming, 1987; Fincham & Bradbury, 1987; Gaelick, Bodenhausen, & Wyer, 1985).

The *disagreement is destructive* subscale suffers the most from this problem, with all eight items referring to positive or negative aspects directed at the current relationship. Consistent with our reasoning, two studies that have examined the relations between marital satisfaction and each construct separately (Eidelson & Epstein, 1982; Epstein et al, 1987) both found that of the five belief constructs, the disagreement is destructive belief attained the highest correlations with relationship satisfaction (−.57 and −.54, respectively). In short, the correlations between the Relationship Belief Inventory and relationship satisfaction are not necessarily evidence for the construct validity of the scale (as claimed by Eidelson & Epstein, 1982), but are more likely to be the result of item overlap between the measures.

We stress that these problems are not confined to the Relationship Belief Inventory but are a common problem with scales in the relationship arena. One moral of this story is that social scientists need to pay more attention to the *content* of scales and not just rely on internal reliability coefficients, Eigen values, correlation coefficients, and all of the other statistical paraphernalia of modern-day psychometrics.

Specific Relationship Accounts, Attributions, and Attitudes. Finally, in this section we consider the most specific level of knowledge structure (see Figure 5.1), which embraces the relatively elaborate accounts people develop concerning their own important relationships. Such accounts may be storylike in outline but will contain many causal elements (Harvey et al., 1989; Planalp & Surra, in press). This class of structures overlaps with the previous categories but, as we already have argued, represents a distinct category.

As already outlined, it is likely that the more abstract knowledge structures will affect these relationship-specific naive models. It is important to note, however, that causal influence also may flow from such relationship-specific structures upward, to influence the more general and abstract relationship beliefs. For example, Harvey et al. (1989) reported that students who identified particular difficulties in their relationships as causes of previous breakups, such as a difficulty with communication, also believed they would need to work especially hard on those factors to make their future relationships successful.

We shall return later to some of the intricate connections among the three postulated knowledge structures when the cognitive processing component of our model is discussed. Before doing so, the issue of when knowledge structures become activated is dealt with.

When Do Knowledge Structures Become Activated?

One central class of factors here concerns the nature of the construct itself. A potentially huge number of knowledge structures are *available* for retrieval, but such structures will vary in terms of their *accessibility*. Some knowledge structures may be retrieved only on certain occasions within relationships; for example, specific beliefs and memories concerning a partner's relationship with his father may be retrieved only when a rare visit is made to the in-laws. However, other constructs will be what is termed *chronically accessible.* Such constructs can prime relatively permanently the generation of thoughts or feelings quite unconsciously and unintentionally. For example, levels of relationship satisfaction may routinely help generate attribution processes in relationship contexts—simply being with one's partner may be a sufficient condition to elicit this knowledge construct with its powerful overlay of affect.

The remaining class of factors, shown in Figure 5.1 under the heading of *eliciting event,* concerns events or conditions that prime particular knowledge constructs or elicit cognitive processing that, in turn, invokes such constructs. Such events may occur either within or outside relationship interaction. For example, one's partner may induce a relationship-positive attribution by paying an unexpected compliment. However, watching a play, reading a book, or merely noticing a stranger who resembles one's partner also may evoke some thinking and associated affect concerning one's relationship, with an attendant attribution or two. Alternatively thoughts and feelings of anger or love or daydreaming about one's loved one (or hated one) also may trigger attributional processing.

Finally, it may be noted that the eliciting events have been split into those that occur either externally (behavior, event) or internally (cognition, affect). Research that implicates both classes of factors is cited later. For the moment, we simply note that both classes of variable are plausible candidates for eliciting cognitive processing and for activating knowledge structures.

The Cognitive Processing Component

It is difficult to see how ordinary dyadic interaction, with its multiplicity of cognitive processing demands, would be possible unless a large number of processes were carried out simultaneously (in parallel). Hence a tremendous amount of cognitive processing must occur rapidly and unconsciously. Indeed the distinction shown in Figure 5.1 between automatic processing and controlled processing, or similar kinds of distinctions, are commonplace in cognitive psychology (see Fletcher & Fincham, 1991b). This distinction has been characterized in a variety of ways, with *automatic processing* variously described as fast, unconscious, effortless, not readily verbalizable, and carried out in parallel. In contrast, *controlled processing* typically is considered to be relatively slow, conscious, effortful, controllable, and serially produced.

A continuing debate concerns whether and to what extent such features are necessary or most important in relation to definitions of the two processing modes (see Uleman & Bargh, 1989). Indeed we agree with Bargh's (1989) argument that it remains an open question concerning the extent to which these different "defining" characteristics of the automatic/controlled processing distinction might operate independently of one another. However, certain points appear to be commonly agreed upon. First, the distinction is better represented as a continuous dimension, rather than two discrete categories. Second, a key difference between clear-cut examples of the two processing modes is that controlled processing has marked attentional capacity constraints, whereas automatic processing has relatively little capacity constraints. This characteristic is related to the idea that automatic processing is carried out in parallel, whereas controlled processing is serially produced.

Before dealing with the topic of automatic processing in more detail, we focus on controlled attributional processing and deal with the point that people do not always ask why or indulge in tortuous conscious analysis of their relationships. Thus the questions are raised: (a) Just how common is conscious, controlled attributional processing in everyday relationships? and (b) Under what conditions do people indulge in such controlled attributional analysis in their relationships?

Controlled Processing. Attributional research in relationship settings typically requires participants to consciously consider and provide answers to attributional questions provided by the experimenter. Hence the results are almost certainly the products of controlled, attributional processing. A thorny problem with this standard methodology is the distinct possibility that experimenter-supplied attributional questions may instigate attributional processing different from that occurring spontaneously in everyday life. An even nastier possibility is that in the absence of experimenter-supplied questions, explicit, conscious attributional processing typically will not occur at all. To investigate these possibilities, several researchers have assessed unsolicited attributions by asking subjects what they would think and feel in response to hypothetical positive and negative interactive behaviors in their relationships. Causal attributions occurring in the resultant protocols then are coded into relationship-positive or relationship-negative attributions. The results from these studies show that spontaneous attributions are plentiful and demonstrate the same attributional differences between happy and unhappy couples in their unsolicited attributions as those found in studies that use structured experimenter-supplied ratings (Fletcher, Fitness, & Blampied, 1990; Grigg, Fletcher, & Fitness, 1989; Holtzworth-Munroe & Jacobson, 1985).

This genre of attributional research also can be interpreted as providing evidence related to the second question posed above, namely, When does conscious, controlled attributionalizing occur? The results have shown two key variables to be important elicitors of controlled attributional processing: negative events and unexpected outcomes. We would expect such conditions to occur most frequently in relationships that are unstable or having problems. Indeed there is evidence that conscious, attributional activity is heightened in such relationships (Fletcher, Fincham, Cramer, & Heron, 1987). More generally, this line of research suggests that attributional activity is tied to the development of the relationship and to the changes that occur in relationship-specific models (the feedback loop in Figure 5.1). When the needs for control and prediction are heightened in relationships, then so, apparently, is the need for satisfactory explanations. (For more extensive research reviews and discussions of the role of attributions in relationship development, see Planalp & Surra, in press, and Surra & Bohman, 1991).

To return to the issue of ecological validity, the skeptic could press harder and question just how "spontaneous" these attributions are in the previous research cited. If, as seems likely, attributional processing is a natural component of conscious, explicit analysis, then it could be argued that these attributions are not truly spontaneous, as subjects are explicitly requested to think about and analyze the behavioral events. Thus the question remains whether people spontaneously produce on-line attributions during interaction with their partners.

Fortuitously, we possessed a set of previously published data (Fletcher & Fitness, 1990) that could be used, in reanalyzed form, to address the issue just described. In addition, this set of reanalyzed data concerned the relations between the kind of on-line attributions produced (relationship-positive vs. relationship-negative) and depression, relationship satisfaction, and both verbal and nonverbal behavior. As these analyses are unpublished and address some critical gaps in attribution research (such as the links between attributions and actual interactive relationship behavior), we present them fully here. In this research, 38 couples in long-term, unmarried relationships each had 10-minute discussions of important problems in their relationships. Using a technique initially developed by Ickes, Robertson, Took, & Teng (1986), subjects then independently and immediately reviewed videotapes of the discussions. Subjects were instructed to stop the videotapes whenever they remembered experiencing a thought or a feeling and to verbally describe it (these descriptions were recorded on audiotapes). A range of evidence suggests that the resultant protocols represent reasonably veridical accounts, provided that these videotape reviews are carried out immediately following the discussions and it is stressed to subjects that they must not manufacture their thoughts afresh (see Fletcher & Fitness, 1990; Fletcher & Kininmonth, 1991; Ickes et al., 1986).

In this study we also required subjects to complete measures of depression and relationship satisfaction and obtained observer ratings of both the positivity of the content of verbal behavior and nonverbal behavior (voice tone, facial expression, and posture) (see Fletcher & Fitness, 1990, for further details). For the current analysis, we went back to the transcriptions of the thought and feeling protocols and had two raters pluck out the causal attributions, categorizing them according to whether they were relationship-positive, relationship-negative, or neutral. Inter-rater ratings were reliable, ranging from 90% to 97% agreement.

The first finding of note is that the thought/feeling protocols were loaded with causal attributions. Subjects stopped the tape a mean number of 10.2 occasions and produced a mean number of 8.6 attributions (M = 2.0 relationship-positive attributions, M = 4.1 relationship-negative attributions, and M = 2.5 relationship-neutral attributions). Table 5.1 shows the results of a hierarchical multiple regression (and zero-order correlations) using the percentage of relationship-positive attributions as the dependent variable. This analysis treats each partner as an individual subject (cf. Fletcher & Fitness, 1990).

As can be seen, all of the zero-order correlations were significant in the predicted directions. In light of the amount of measurement error, these correlations underestimate the real effect sizes: When corrected for attenuation, the correlations range from .30 to .45. Subjects with more relationship-positive attributions were happier, less depressed, and produced more positive nonverbal and verbal behavior. However, these relations are difficult to interpret because of shared variance. For example, in accord with much previous research, people who were more depressed were also less satisfied with their relationships (r = −.43). This relation between depression and relationship satisfaction casts doubt on the documented relation between relationship satisfaction and attributions because it is entirely possible that people in unhappy relationships think more negatively about their relationships because they are depressed, not because they are dissatisfied with their relationships. However, the regression coefficients do not support this hypothesis. As can be seen (Table 5.1), the regression coefficient for depression was close to zero, while the regression coefficient for relationship satisfaction remained significant. This particular set of findings is remarkably similar to those reported by Fletcher et al. (1990), although this earlier study used a quite different technique whereby subjects described their thoughts and feelings in response to imagining hypothetical scenarios in their relationships.

Finally the regression coefficients in Table 5.1 show that the positivity of verbal behavior maintains a reliable relation with

Table 5.1. Zero-Order Correlations and Standardized Regression Coefficients From a Hierarchical Multiple Regression With the Percentage of Relationship-Positive Attributions as the Dependent Variable

Independent Variables	r	Beta
SET 1		
Problem seriousness	−.11	−.04
Relationship happiness	.32**	.28*
Depression	−.21*	−.08
R^2 Increase over problem seriousness	.10*	
SET 2		
Positive nonverbal	.28**	.05
Positive verbal	.32**	.32**
R^2 Increase over Set 1	.11*	
Total R^2	.22**	

NOTE: The sample size was 76.
*$p < .05$; **$p < .01$.

the percentage of relationship-positive attributions but that the relation between nonverbal behavior and the positivity of attributions sinks close to zero. This result is in line with those reported in the original study (Fletcher & Fitness, 1990) and is consistent with the idea that verbal behavior is monitored more closely and under tighter intentional control than nonverbal behavior. Accordingly, what people say in these dyadic discussions receives more conscious, in-depth analysis than does the gamut of nonverbal behavior accompanying the content. Hence it follows that the occurrence of conscious attributions will be more influenced by verbal than nonverbal behavior and also that such conscious attributional thinking will have a stronger influence on verbal than nonverbal behavior.

These results are important. They show that conscious attributions that occur in the midst of interactive discussions are related to behavior and knowledge structures in ways consistent with, but beyond, previous research. In addition, the results support the proposition that controlled attributions are alive and well in relationships and are not simply a product of the fevered imaginations and investigative procedures previously used by psychologists. Finally the findings intriguingly suggest that automatic processing is a central component of relationship interaction—a thesis we take up in detail in the next section.

Automatic Processing. It is important, first, to make a distinction between two basic categories of automatic processing (Bargh, 1989). The first category consists of automatic, data driven, perceptual processing that occurs prior to conscious awareness. This kind of automatic processing implies that a person will process information about his or her partner even when the TV is on, the baby is crying, and he or she is trying to read the newspaper. The second category of automatic processing is theory driven and is concerned with the automatic retrieval of knowledge structures that may be activated by a conscious and controlled activity. This section deals only with this latter category of automatic processing. In particular, we outline a theory specifying how the interactions between the middle-level category of attributional knowledge construct and the most relationship-specific level (see Figure 5.1) are instrumental in driving the automatic processing of relationship information.

To begin, a plausible hypothesis already alluded to is that relationship beliefs, even if they change under the harsh light of reality, guide and focus the processing of relationship interaction and so influence the theories or models that people construct of their own relationships and the attendant relationship evaluations and judgments. For example, a person who believes that romance and passion are essential ingredients of a successful intimate relationship is likely to pay particular attention to the occurrence of related behaviors (candle-lit dinners, admiring glances, surprise gifts, etc.). Romance and passion will, thus, play a central role in the development of the mental model of such a relationship and also strongly influence relationship satisfaction. In contrast, someone who believes that romance and sex are generally unimportant factors in determining relationship success should pay less attention to this category of behaviors and not base his or her relationship evaluations of the relationship on the quality and quantity of romantic behavior and sex. Indeed we earlier cited evidence consistent with this claim (Fletcher & Kininmonth, in press).

To put this point more technically, strong relationship beliefs should operate as chronically accessible constructs that automatically will generate processing of behavior or events in relationships that are strongly related to these beliefs. To test this hypothesis, Fletcher, Rosanowski, and Fitness (1992) exploited a critical feature of automatic processing previously described—namely, that automatic processing, in contrast to controlled processing, does not excessively draw on the limited attentional resources available in working memory. In the present context, this statement means that strongly held relationship beliefs, in contrast to weakly held beliefs, should allow the automatic processing of belief-relevant behavior without excessively drawing on the limited resources available in working memory.

Fletcher et al. (1992) tested these predictions by using the Close Relationship Beliefs Scale described earlier. Initially two categories of close relationship belief were assessed: beliefs in the importance of intimacy, and passion in producing successful relationships. Subjects with strong or weak beliefs in these two belief categories decided whether a succession of adjectives (e.g., *warm, boring*) accurately described their own relationships. Through use of computers, subjects' speed of response was measured in two conditions. In one condition subjects answered the questions with no distractions, but in another condition other subjects answered the questions while concurrently memorizing digits, a procedure that has been shown typically to place more demands on working memory and to lengthen the decision latencies (Bargh & Tota, 1988).

The results can be summarized readily. As predicted, when deciding whether belief-relevant adjectives described their relationships, subjects with strong beliefs made judgments equally as fast under cognitive-load conditions as when no extra cognitive load was present; in contrast, weak-belief subjects were considerably slower in the cognitive-load condition, compared to the no-load condition. In addition, both strong- and weak-belief subjects were slower in the cognitive-load condition than the no-load condition when judging belief-irrelevant adjectives. This latter finding precludes an explanation for the central findings in terms of the possibility that people with strong beliefs in particular domains may differ in other (unknown) ways that enable them to process automatically any information about their close relationships.

In sum, the results of this experiment support our supposition that strongly held beliefs concerning the importance of intimacy or passion in causing relationship success facilitated the automatic processing of belief-relevant information about subjects' own relationships. Causal relationship beliefs appear to influence how everyday material is processed in a quite unconscious and unintended fashion. A general related point is that research and theorizing carried out by relationship researchers almost invariably equate thinking or cognition with the kind of verbally reported judgments that are most likely to be part of conscious, controlled cognitive processing (see Fletcher & Kininmonth, 1991). If, as we believe, rapid and automatic cognition is endemic in relationships settings, then this often tacit assumption is clearly problematic.

The Role of Affect and Emotional Attributions

One of the problems with adopting a cognitive approach to personal relationships is that it neglects what surely is a vital and central component of such relationships: the role of affect and emotions. It is difficult to do justice to this massive, if little studied, topic here, but we think it is important to sketch how a knowledge structure approach might contribute to our understanding of how emotions are linked to attributions in relationships.

As shown in Figure 5.1, affect appears as both a possible eliciting event and an outcome. It is a popular idea in emotion theories that autonomic arousal is part of a system especially evolved for alerting and directing the organism to some potentially dangerous or threatening state of affairs (see Berscheid, 1983). Accordingly it is not surprising that the important triggers of emotional arousal are identical to those that have been found to instigate explicit attributional processing—for example, negativity and unexpectedness (Fitness & Strongman, 1991). In addition, emotional attributions (outcomes) are likely to be theory driven, in part, by attribution processes. Weiner's (1986) theory posits that an initial crude appraisal of an emotion occurs along a positive-negative dimension. Next a more elaborate attributional analysis, along the attribution dimensions of locus, stability, and controllability, determines the appropriate emotional attribution.

A study by Fitness and Fletcher (in press, b) adds some weight to Weiner's general thesis concerning emotional attributions in relationship settings. In Study 1 of this research, 160 married subjects recalled an incident of love, hate, anger, or jealousy in their marital relationships and wrote accounts of their physiological symptoms, urges, behaviors, and general appraisals. In addition, subjects rated each emotion on a range of cognitive appraisal dimensions, including the attributional dimensions of stability, controllability, locus, and globality. To illustrate some of the findings generally related to Weiner's thesis, the causes of love were perceived as global and internally located in both partner and self. In contrast, the causes of hate were seen as a function of the partner, but not the self, and were perceived as specific rather than global in nature.

However, the overall findings also suggest that subjects possessed prototypical knowledge structures for each emotion that went well beyond attributions, including characteristic urges, actual behaviors, control mechanisms, types of triggering events, and perceived physiological symptoms. Some interesting similarities and differences emerged among the four emotional concepts. For example, the negative emotions (hate, jealousy, and anger) invariably were elicited by the negative behavior of the partner, whereas, perhaps surprisingly, the most popular eliciting event for love was not partner behavior per se but the act of daydreaming or thinking about the partner. Interesting differences also were found among the negative emotions. For example, anger typically was accompanied by active interactive behavior (e.g., yelling), but hate was more often associated with passive behavior such as emotional withdrawal.

To test whether the detailed emotion accounts assembled from Study 1 actually represented knowledge structures (possessed psychological reality), two further studies were undertaken. In the second study, 80 married subjects wrote hypothetical accounts describing typical love, hate, anger, and jealousy incidents in marriage. The results were generally in accord with Study 1, suggesting that both kinds of account (recalled and hypothetical) are generated from the same emotion knowledge constructs. The third study was the flip side of the first study. Subjects (university students, most unmarried) were given varying amounts of information derived from Study 1 concerning each emotion in the form of short interactional vignettes (love, hate, anger, and jealousy) and were required to select the correct emotion from a list of four positive and four negative emotions. Results indicated that the accuracy of emotion identification was a linear function of the amount of information provided. A mean accuracy rate of 26% was attained when the event only was described, and 69% accuracy was achieved when the event descriptions were combined with information concerning prototypical cognitive appraisal features (such as causal locus and stability), behavioral urges, actual behaviors, and physiological symptoms.

In general, then, the results from this research confirm the existence of relatively elaborate knowledge structures concerning specific emotions in relationship contexts. It is worth noting here that in spite of the growth in the study of both emotion and personal relationships during the last two decades, this research is one of the first to investigate the nature and function of emotion knowledge structures in romantic, sexual relationships. The results generally suggest that social cognitive theories concerning such relationships have construed the role of emotions rather too narrowly (see, for example, Fletcher & Fincham, 1991b); that is, specific emotional attributions are driven, in part, by relatively elaborate knowledge structures that include but go beyond attributional schemata.

Conclusions

Psychological theories rise and fall according to whim and fashion. Yet attribution theory has maintained its status as a major area in (social) psychology with surprising vigor for more than two decades. Doubtless, its longevity is owed, in part, to the way basic attribution theory has been exported successfully to many other areas, including relationship research. But we think there is another more basic reason for its continued popularity that some of the research described above confirms—namely, attribution structures and processes are a central and vital component of human cognition. Simply put, humans seek to understand and explain the world, especially the social world. However, as has been made clear in this chapter, we believe the way ahead is best charted with theories that integrate attribution processes and structures into more general social cognitive models. The research described here deals with a few components of the model offered but, we hope, illustrates the way such an overarching theory can be exploited, developed, and tested.

Studying social cognition within relationship contexts is a difficult proposition, to put it mildly, both theoretically and practically. However, we think the fruits to be gained from the endeavor make it worthwhile. As noted earlier, cognition and behavior are predominantly learned and developed within social settings, especially dyadic close relationships. Thus much of our cognition and emotion, including both knowledge structures and ongoing processing, is social in nature. A psychology that grapples with the links between social cognition and dyadic relationships has the potential to inform our understanding of both basic cognitive processes and the way relationships function in the real world.

You, Me, and Us: Perspectives on Relationship Awareness

Linda K. Acitelli

*[T]he threads between minds
are very thin and hard to hold.*
Elaine in "A Sepulchre of Songs"
Orson Scott Card (1991)

Sarah and David just met. He asks her to dance. They begin. He steps on her toes. She smiles. He winces. She thinks, "What a clod." He thinks, "What a martyr." He says, "I'm sorry. I'm not a very good dancer." She says, "You're doing fine." He thinks, "How can I get out of this mess?" She thinks,

AUTHOR'S NOTE: The preparation of this chapter was supported, in part, by a grant from NIMH (1 R29 MH46567-O1A1). I would like to thank Joseph Veroff and Steve Duck for their valuable feedback, which was crucial to the development of this chapter. Thanks also go to Rosalie Burnett, who has shared her ideas and provided the inspiration for the title of this chapter.

"Please let this dance be over." Obviously Sarah and David are not impressed with each other. But how do we know that? By their actions? By their speech? Or by their thoughts about one another? Perhaps all three. But change the scene slightly. The words and actions will be exactly the same, but the thoughts will be different. Sarah and David begin to dance. He steps on her toes. She smiles. He winces. She thinks, "I hope I didn't make him do that." He thinks, "She must think I'm a clod." He says, "I'm sorry. I'm not a very good dancer." She says, "You're doing fine." He thinks, "Thank goodness she is so nice." She thinks, "How kind of him to apologize." Here it looks as though Sarah and David are getting along just fine. The actions and speech in these scenes are identical, yet the meaning of the exchanges between them are entirely different. This admittedly simple dramatization illustrates what researchers of social cognition and researchers of personal relationships have been discovering that they have in common. This research from different fields has been coming to the same conclusion—namely, that very important relationship processes take place in the partners' minds (e.g., Duck & Sants, 1983). Although David's stepping on Sarah's toes was the catalyst for their thoughts about each other, the reader can readily see that the interpretations that each of them made for the action are more important for determining how they feel about one another than the action itself. (Of course, if they had been acquainted previously, their earlier feelings about each other may have colored their interpretations of their behaviors. So for the sake of simply demonstrating the point that perceptions and thoughts of a person can be more important in determining how people feel about their behaviors than the behaviors themselves, Sarah and David have just met.)

This chapter focuses on individuals' perceptions of themselves, their partners, and their relationships. As Berger and Kellner (1964) posit that marriage is the construction of a social reality, others (particularly Laing et al., 1966) have shown that interpersonal perceptions may be the threads from which the fabric of the shared reality is constructed. Partners' threads may be of different textures and colors, yet through the weaving together of their lives, they may create a unique relational cloth.

The resulting fabrics may be loosely or tightly knit, rough or smooth, solid or patterned. They can tear and be repaired, stiffen or soften, expand or shrink, stretch and grow. Or one fabric can have all of these characteristics at different times or all at once in the same cloth. Although the fabric becomes more than the sum of its threads, a primary objective of this chapter is to examine these threads or perceptions within relationships and to see how these perceptions influence relationship and individual well-being.

The chapter centers around the model depicted in Figure 6.1. It provides a framework within which to integrate the existing research and literature rather than a causal model in the strict sense of the term. Rather than providing us with a smooth continuum from which to construct the next logical steps, the earlier research emerges from a patchwork of different areas within the social and behavioral sciences. Although the model is admittedly broad, the chapter identifies and explains ambiguous causal directions, specifies the domains in which the model proves to be useful, and points the reader to directions for future research.

Note that the boxes can be viewed in rows (A, B, or X) or in columns (1, 2, or 3). The boxes in Rows A and B represent individual phenomena relating to Persons A and B; the boxes in Row X are interpersonal. The columns represent order in time, such that Column 1 represents phenomena that exist *before* Persons A and B meet; Column 2 depicts thoughts and behaviors that occur *after* Persons A and B meet; and Column 3 represents the *outcomes* of both thoughts and behaviors that occur in Column 2. Phenomena in Columns 2 and 3 occur within the *context* of the relationship, represented by the area surrounded by broken lines. The length of time represented in this model can vary widely. It is assumed that the causal directions implied by the solid arrows hold for relationships in their initial stages. Over time, it is possible that the phenomena occurring in Columns 2 and 3 can affect the phenomena in Columns 1 and 2, respectively, hence the broken arrows going from Columns 2 and 3 to Columns 1 and 2.

An example will help clarify the components of the model. Say that Persons A and B have just met and are about to form

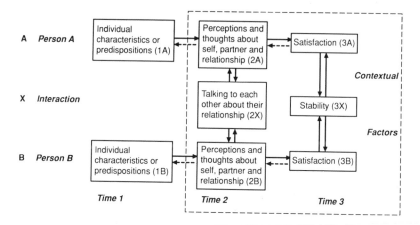

Figure 6.1. General Framework for Studies on Relational Thinking and Talking

some kind of relationship with one another. They each have their own individual characteristics (1A, 1B) that can influence how they think about one another (2A, 2B). Over time (the length of time will differ between partners and relationships), partners become aware (2A, 2B) that they have a relationship and begin to talk to each other about it (2X). What they say may be concrete ("I'm glad we like the same kinds of movies") or abstract ("Isn't it interesting how two people with such different backgrounds seem to like the same things?"). Such statements can, in turn, influence their thoughts about one another and the relationship (back to 2A and 2B). These cognitions can affect each partner's evaluation of and satisfaction with the relationship (3A, 3B). Partner satisfaction also influences how long they are likely to stay in the relationship (stability–3X). The length of the relationship and a sense of stability also can influence satisfaction with the relationship.

The above example depicts a relationship in its beginning stages and in an apparently positive context. Length of relationship and emotional tone of the situation are just two of the contextual factors expected to influence the frequency, content, and consequences of relational thinking and talking. This chapter demonstrates how previous work fits into the general model depicted in Figure 6.1. Concepts are followed by the label of the box (1A, 2A, etc.) into which they can be integrated.

A major assumption that usually is made for such models is that the arrows imply influence. An additional assumption made for this model is that the arrows imply meaning. For any one of these phenomena to influence any other, it (more often than not) has meaning to the individual. (The individual need not be aware of the influence for it to have meaning.) That is, if Person A starts thinking about Person B, the way that Person A will perceive Person B has much to do with Person A's characteristics such that Person A's characteristics (e.g., personality, expectations, mood) will provide an interpretive filter through which Person B is perceived or through which Person A constructs the meaning of Person B (cf. Kelly, 1955). Person A may try to convey the meaning of these thoughts through speech. Of course, speech is constrained by a host of factors (e.g., impression management, politeness) that do not govern thoughts, such that talk is rarely, if ever, a direct translation of thoughts. Nevertheless the point is not how the speech is constructed, but rather whether or not the person conveys his or her thoughts about the other person or the relationship through talk. Such talk may or may not occur. But if it does, it influences (has meaning for) subsequent thoughts about the relationship. These thoughts have meaning for the value that the person may place on the relationship (or his or her relationship satisfaction). Note that no arrows link talk to satisfaction. This model requires that some sort of interpretation or thought process mediates that link.

If relationship talk does not occur, thoughts about the partner and the relationship still will influence the partner's relationship satisfaction. However, this may be a case where illusions take over and, if they are not shared, may lead to trouble (dissatisfaction and/or instability) in the relationship. A sense of stability, coupled with relationship length, also can have meaning for the relationship partners (and influence their satisfaction). Thus a bidirectional influence of satisfaction and stability is postulated.

Although the model in Figure 6.1 is presented as a useful framework for organizing existing literature and for generating hypotheses, it cannot account for every possible nuance or characteristic of the interactions it is meant to represent. Interactions are rarely as simplistic and mechanistic as portrayed in two-dimensional models that look more like plumbing than living. Meaning can infuse or permeate experiences such that assigning it to a link in a causal chain seems illogical. With help from Watzlawick, Beavin, and Jackson (1967), one can state that perceptions, thoughts, behaviors, interactions, in short, experiences, cannot *not* have meaning. Thus perhaps it is more appropriate to talk about how meaning changes, becomes transformed and transforming, rather than how meaning is created or how it causes certain behaviors and thoughts. But most of us still live in Flatland (Abbott, 1884) when modeling human behavior. (While pop psychology books exist, I have yet to see the pop-up versions.) Because it is very difficult to model, let alone measure, the complexities involved in the transformation of meaning, this simplified approach in Figure 6.1 will remain as an example of a model that satisfies the scientific criteria of parsimony, utility, testability, and heuristic value. As such, the model also can be compared with other models that take this approach.

The model in Figure 6.1 can be contrasted with the more detailed model presented by Fletcher and Fitness (Chapter 5, this volume). Their model is more specific in that it elaborates in more detail the "cognitive architecture" of an individual partner's mind. Whereas Figure 6.1 refers simply to perceptions and thoughts about self, partner, and relationship (Boxes 2A or 2B), the Fletcher and Fitness model depicts separate components of such perceptions and thoughts as general social schemata, relationship beliefs, and specific relationship accounts, attributions, and attitudes. Thus, in the Fletcher and Fitness model, the entire area surrounded by broken lines can be fit into Box 2A or 2B of the model in this chapter.

Although the hierarchical categorization of and the relationships between the components of cognition are valuable to the understanding of cognitive processing, the focus of the present chapter is not whether thoughts about the relationship are general or specific, but whether they occur at all and the consequences of such occurrences; that is, when people think during

an interaction, are their thoughts focused on the self, the partner, or the relationship? For example, whether an attribution
focuses solely on one partner or the relationship itself can have
different consequences for affective outcomes.

Furthermore Fletcher and Fitness explain cognitive processing in more detail. Although it is expected that automatic processing may underlie the conscious, more controlled processing
that occurs when people think about their relationships, this
distinction does not fit easily into the model in this chapter. For
example, to talk about the relationship, one might assume that
some conscious, controlled thought about the relationship occurred before or during such talk. However, whether the individual is aware of (or controlling) the fact that his or her speech
is phrased in relational terms may not be so clear cut.

Thus the model in this chapter simply focuses on a hypothetical sequence of events that occur when two people in a relationship think and talk about their relationship. The outcomes
of such thinking and talking are modified by contextual factors
that may be compared to the "eliciting event" column in the
Fletcher and Fitness model. Both models show that relationship
satisfaction (or outcomes) can influence and be influenced by
cognitions occurring within the context of a relationship.

As a starting point, the research discussed is on intimate
heterosexual relationships. As numerous researchers have demonstrated, there are strong links between the quality or presence
of a special intimate relationship and an individual's physical and
psychological health. Thus such relationships are the focal point
of the studies discussed in this chapter. Nevertheless an additional goal of the chapter is to stimulate hypotheses for researchers to apply the concepts discussed here to other types of
relationships.

Studying Relationship Awareness

The concept of *relationship awareness* (2A, 2B) has been
introduced to provide a framework for studying the effects of
thinking and talking about relationships on individual and rela-

tionship well-being. Acitelli (1986, 1988, 1992) defines *relationship awareness* as a person's thinking about interaction patterns, comparisons, or contrasts between himself or herself and the other partner in the relationship. Included are thoughts about the couple or relationship as an entity. The assessment of relationship awareness denotes the act of thinking in relational terms or focusing one's attention on the relationship and is not meant to judge the quality of an individual's portrayal of a relationship. Talking in relational terms (2X) is considered to be a behavioral manifestation of relationship awareness because, as Burnett (1984) points out, "the focus of awareness, the giving of attention, which accompanies both [thinking and talking about relationships], is what is at issue" (p. 3).

Although relationship awareness is a process and is not defined here as a personality disposition, there is evidence that thinking about relationships (like thinking about the self or private self-consciousness) may be a personality trait (Snell, 1988). Yet relationship awareness as defined here is not to be confused with Snell's concept of the same name. Snell defines *relationship awareness* as consisting of three personality dispositions: (a) *relationship consciousness,* the tendency to think about internal, dynamic features of a relationship; (b) *relationship monitoring,* the tendency to think about the public impression created by one's intimate relationship; and (c) *relationship anxiety,* the tendency to experience anxiety and shyness in an intimate relationship (Snell, 1988). Because further discussion of this concept would not sharpen the focus on the process of thinking about relationships, I will not go into more detail here. (See Acitelli, 1992, for more detailed distinctions between relationship awareness and other relevant concepts such as relational schemata [Planalp, 1987], interpersonal and relationship attributions [Fincham, 1985; Newman, 1981], and intentional metacommunication [Perlmutter & Hatfield, 1980].)

Figure 6.2 is a visual representation of the cognitions of interest in Boxes 2A and 2B of Figure 6.1. An individual can think about a partner and about the self and not necessarily think about the relationship. Such thoughts could be represented as two separated circles, a representation that McCall (1988) refers to as the more conventional "interpersonal" depiction of a relationship. Relationship awareness (or thinking about the relationship), on the other hand, involves a person's thinking about the middle circle in Figure 6.2, not just where the self and the partner circles might intersect. The relationship itself becomes a distinctive entity. This representation is similar to what McCall (1988) refers to as the "organizational" depiction of a relationship: "In the interpersonal depiction, the two individuals see only one another; in the organizational depiction, the two individuals see not only one another, but also their relationship" (p. 409). McCall's organizational depiction is different from Figure 6.2 in that, in his figure, the box that represents the relationship does not overlap with that of the relationship partners. Instead it is drawn above the partners and is connected by "organizational" lines (much as kinship ties are depicted in anthropological kinship networks). In Figure 6.2, however, the relationship circle purposely overlaps with those of the self and the partner. Granted, for some people these boundaries may overlap more or less than they do here, but self and relationship, in general, are overlapping entities.

In fact, various conceptions of relationships could be drawn with just these three circles. For example, the egocentric partner's mental model of self, partner, and relationship may be represented by one huge circle (the self) and two small circles (partner and relationship) that are completely surrounded by the border of the larger circle, indicating that there is nothing about the partner and relationship apart from the self. Or partners who see themselves as completely enmeshed may represent themselves and their relationship as just one circle. While many representations are possible, Figure 6.2 is the generic one.

An important distinction guiding the focus of the work on relationship awareness is the difference between thinking or talking *within the context* of a relationship and thinking or talking *about* a relationship. Cognitions and communications may occur within the context of a relationship yet not focus on the relationship per se.

Other theorists of relationship thinking (Burnett, 1987; Cate, 1991) include thinking about partners as well as thinking about

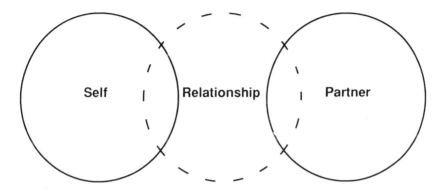

Figure 6.2. One Possible Representation of Self, Partner, and Relationship

the relationship in their conceptions of relationship thinking. (See Acitelli & Holmberg, 1993, for a more complete description of and distinctions between the work of Acitelli, Burnett, and Cate.) Relationship awareness, on the other hand, focuses solely on the relationship, represented by the center circle in Figure 6.2.

Distinguishing between thinking about persons and thinking about relationships is important for two main reasons. One reason is that the consequences of such thinking and talking can be different, depending on the focus of the thought. Bernal and Baker (1979) point out that couples in conflict are less likely to remain in conflict if their conversations can shift from an individual partner (or blaming) focused discussion to one that is more relationship oriented. Consider a spouse reacting to a particular problem by saying, "You've got a problem" instead of "We've got a problem." Phrasing the conflict as a relationship problem is perceived as being more helpful in resolving the conflict than if it is deemed some other kind of problem (Acitelli, 1988). Perhaps the perception of being helpful arises because of the degree of closeness implied by the message. The use of the pronoun *we* can indicate closeness, intimacy, or acceptance and can increase the amount of inclusion of the other in the partners' statement (see Duck, 1992, or Mehrabian, 1971). This degree of closeness (or distance) in a message is referred to by Mehrabian

(1971) as *immediacy* and can help create and define a relation-ship. In a similar vein, spouses who see themselves as a couple are happier than those who see themselves as two separate people (Acitelli & Antonucci, 1991; Scott, Fuhrman, & Wyer, 1991). Perhaps people who see themselves as a couple face everyday marital tasks in terms of "we" rather than "I" alone. The "we're in this together" attitude may help them through con-flicts by placing them on the same side, rather than as two adversaries pitted against one another.

A second reason to make the distinction between thinking about partners and thinking about relationships is for precision of definition. If researchers say they are studying relational thinking, then it is logical to require that such thinking involve two people and their relationship to each other (just as it is logical for relationship researchers to study both partners in a relationship, as opposed to just one). Thinking about one's self or one's partner is not the same thing as thinking about the relationship, or how these two people relate to each other. However, thoughts and perceptions of self and partner are nec-essary components of relationship awareness and are important research foci in their own right. Thus an important prelude to the study of relationship awareness is the study of its components—spouses' perceptions of self and partner, and the relationship between these perceptions—often referred to as *interpersonal perception.*

Awareness of Self and Partner (2A, 2B)

Several studies point to the central role that interpersonal perceptions play in close relationships. *Person perception* in-volves studying one person's perception of another (e.g., think-ing a partner is fun); *interpersonal perception* involves studying the relationship between partners' perceptions of one another (e.g., similarity of partner perceptions or each partner thinking the other is fun; Sillars & Scott, 1983). Such perceptions are posited to be the threads through which a social reality is woven (Berger & Kellner, 1964; Laing et al., 1966). Such perceptions are also the basis for perceptions of the relationship (which is discussed in the section that follows).

Interpersonal perceptions can be formed through several combinations of perceptions of self and other, but like Kenny and Acitelli (1989), this section focuses on three: (a) When both partners' self perceptions are congruent, partners' perceptions are said to be *similar;* (b) when one partner's perception of the self is congruent with that partner's perception of the other, there is *perceived similarity* for that partner; and (c) when a partner's view of the other corresponds with the other partner's view of him- or herself, there is *understanding.* Acitelli, Douvan, and Veroff (1993) have referred to similarity, perceived similarity, and understanding as *perceptual congruence* variables. Whether the partners recognize the congruence (*know* that they are similar or understanding) is another matter that has not been sufficiently addressed (see Duck, 1991, for further elaboration of this point).

Early studies (e.g., Byrne & Blaylock, 1963; Levinger & Breedlove, 1966) indicated that perceived similarity is greater than actual similarity between spouses and that perceived similarity is a stronger predictor of marital satisfaction than is actual similarity. As Sillars (1985) and White (1985) warn that the consequences of perceptions of similarity and understanding may depend on the nature of the referent of perception, it is important to note that most of these early studies were assessing the congruence of partners' attitudes and preferences. Thus there may be an untapped myriad of perceptual referents, the congruence of which could have different consequences for marital well-being; that is, congruence of perceptions may be more important for some targets of perception (e.g., attitudes, role expectations) than others (e.g., food preferences, leisure activities).

A more recent study (Acitelli et al., 1993) focuses on spouses' perceptions of each other's behaviors during conflict and demonstrates the importance of further specifying the perceptual referent by differentiating between the constructive and destructive nature of the behavior. Thus, when looking at spouses' perceptions of each other during conflict, the authors emphasize that the consequences of perceptual congruence may depend on whether the behaviors perceived are constructive or destructive to conflict resolution. For example, it may be more important to a marriage for partners to agree that they do not insult each other—because insult is *destructive* to conflict resolution—than to agree that they try to look at the conflict in a new light, which is *constructive* to conflict resolution. The context of conflict is important as a major arena for marital communication and relationship negotiation. How partners perceive one another during conflict can play a major role in shaping their shared reality, exposing differences they may not have "seen" before, and can have consequences for their marital well-being, especially in the early years of marriage.

Interviews with newlywed couples provided data for this study (Acitelli et al., 1993) and are part of a larger project on the first years of marriage (Veroff et al., 1985). Spouses were asked (separately) to think of the last time they had a disagreement (in the last month) and to report whether they or their spouses exhibited certain behaviors during this disagreement. Spouses rated themselves and their partners on similar items, so we were able to derive measures of similarity, perceived similarity, and understanding of behaviors of self and spouse during conflict. (See Acitelli et al., 1993, for a more detailed explanation of the method of calculating such measures.) We then related these perceptual congruence variables to marital well-being.

In analyzing data, we related the perceptual congruence variables to the marital well-being of husbands and wives separately. In general the findings indicate that for a husband, the more he reports demonstrating constructive behaviors, the happier he is with his marriage; and the less he and his wife report using destructive tactics, the happier he is with his marriage. For a wife, with regard to the constructive behaviors, how the partners' perceptions are related to one another is more important than each of their separate reports. For example, the degree to which a wife understands her husband and the degree to which she sees them as similar are related to her marital well-being. A wife's marital well-being also relates to her reports of destructive behavior. As with the constructive behaviors, a wife's understanding of her husband's destructive behaviors is positively related to her marital well-being. Unexpectedly, actual similarity of destructive behaviors was negatively related to wives' marital well-being.

In this study (as in several other studies of interpersonal perception), "actual" similarity is an indication of the similarity between partners' responses to questionnaire or survey items. Whether they are "actually" similar is an issue about which these studies can only speculate. Furthermore the spouses in this study may not be aware of the possible similarity, and they may not even recognize that they perceive themselves as similar. But, as stated earlier in this chapter, one's recognition of something is not necessary for it to have influence on a person.

Caveats aside, the above study demonstrates the importance of looking at perception variables but also points to the fact that the perceptual referent and gender make a difference. Note that, overall, a wife's marital well-being is more connected to how her perceptions relate to her husband's, while a husband's marital well-being is more connected to what each spouse perceives they are doing individually.

In another study in progress (Acitelli & Antonucci, 1991), we are examining the relative effects of perceived similarity and actual similarity of response within older marital dyads on marital satisfaction, life satisfaction, and general well-being. We are looking again at perceptual congruence variables, but this time the referents of perceptions are social support that spouses are giving to and receiving from each other. Thus, in this study, perceived similarity is termed *perceived reciprocity* and actual similarity is *actual reciprocity.*

Data for this study were taken from the Social Supports of the Elderly project (Kahn & Antonucci, 1984). Respondents were married couples whose average age was 74 and length of marriage was 43 years. During interviews, spouses were asked to indicate who in their social network provided them with various kinds of social support and from whom in their network they received these same supports. Thus they indicated whom they could confide in; who provided them with reassurance, respect, and sick care; whom they would talk to when upset, nervous, or depressed; whom they would talk with about health; and to whom they gave these same kinds of support. By summing the number of times respondents identified their spouses on these items, aggregate scores of both giving and receiving social support were derived. We also were able to calculate the level of reciprocity reported by one spouse (perceived reciprocity) and a reciprocity score based on both spouses' separate reports (actual reciprocity). The indices of well-being were responses to questions on positive and negative affect, health, and marital and life satisfaction.

Preliminary analyses indicate that perceptions of giving, receiving, and reciprocity are related more consistently to wives' well-being than to husbands' well-being. These findings suggest that perceptions of social support within marriage are more important to the marital satisfaction of wives than of husbands. Such a result can be interpreted both methodologically and theoretically. Perhaps the measures of social support are assessing behaviors that are perceived as supportive to women but not to men. Note that most of the social support items are indicative of partners talking intimately to each other, a behavior often shown to vary by gender. For example, in a national survey by Veroff, Douvan, and Kulka (1981), women more than men reported that they wished their spouses talked more about their thoughts and feelings. Furthermore the support received from wives may match husbands' expectations of marriage so well that it has no effect on their marital satisfaction. Whereas for a wife in this data set, reciprocity of emotional social support with her husband is more unusual (she is more likely to give and receive from children and friends [Depner & Ingersoll-Dayton, 1985]) and therefore has more impact on her. Further analyses of these data can provide important insights concerning the often-reported sex differences in social support and social relationships.

Therefore we now have an indication that a wife's well-being is tied to relationally oriented perceptions (her understanding of him, her seeing her partner as similar to herself, her giving and receiving social support to and from her husband), while such perceptions are not related to a husband's well-being. This finding is consistent with findings from other studies showing that women, in general, are more relationship oriented than men (e.g., Gilligan, 1982; Markus & Oyserman, 1989). Thus even studies that focus on indirect assessments of relationship awareness show that it is important to distinguish between separate perceptions of self and partner and the relationship between these perceptions, not to mention perceptions of the relationship itself.

Awareness of Relationships

Turning to studies that are more relational in focus, this section describes studies that focus on thoughts about the relationship represented by the center circle in Figure 6.2. It is important to remember that studies of relationship awareness focus on a subset of the thinking and talking that goes on in relationships—namely, thinking and talking *about* relationships. To reiterate, such thoughts demonstrate relationship awareness and are about interaction patterns, comparisons, or contrasts between partners in a relationship. Thoughts about the couple or relationship as an entity are included. Talking about the relationship is considered to be a behavioral manifestation of relationship awareness.

Thinking About Relationships (2A, 2B)

To assess the association between relationship awareness and satisfaction in relationships, Acitelli (1992) developed a behavioral measure of relationship awareness from interviews with married couples. In these joint interviews, couples were asked to talk about their lives, not their relationships, so that if relationship talk were to occur, it could be said to occur more spontaneously than if couples were asked directly about relationships. Their responses were coded for relationship talk on the basis of the definition of *relationship awareness* stated above. Thus this study related a behavioral measure to written self-reports of marital quality. On the one hand, neither spouse's talking about the relationship had any relation to the husband's reports of marital satisfaction and life satisfaction. On the other hand, wives' reports of marital and life satisfaction were positively associated more with their husbands' relational talk and less with their own. The association between husbands' relational talk and wives' marital well-being was strongest for wives who talk very little about their relationship. Husbands' marital satisfaction was not related to either spouse's relationship talk. A similar pattern of results was found for contentment with life. Other gender differences were found. As predicted, wives tended to talk more about their marital relationships than did their husbands. Similarly, in questionnaires (adapted from Burnett, 1984), wives reported thinking more about their marital relationships than did their husbands (Acitelli, 1986).

In the above study, *relationship awareness* includes both the process of thinking about relationships and an orientation toward thinking in relational terms (a "we" orientation). These two components parallel the distinction that Wegner and Giuliano (1982, Chapter 2) make. Extending the reasoning of Polanyi (1966), the authors make the valuable distinction between focal awareness and tacit awareness, formalizing the difference between "topics of thought" and "perspectives on these topics" (Wegner & Giuliano, 1982). They apply this tacit-focal distinction to both self and group awareness. The next paragraph elaborates on this distinction by applying it to relationship awareness.

Distinguishing the targets of tacit and focal *self* awareness parallels the subject-object distinction McAdams (1992) makes between the "I" and the "me." Applying this tacit-focal (or subject-object) distinction to relationship awareness results in the "we" and the "us." The "we" becomes the lens through which one views the world, and the "us" becomes the object that one is viewing. Consider the following example: George attends a party where he is the only Republican, and he becomes self-conscious; in other words, the self ("me") becomes the object of George's focal awareness. One might argue that the object of tacit awareness is the group ("they") because George is thinking about himself the way he thinks the group would think about him. Mary, George's friend, who is also a Republican, arrives. Then George does not feel so alone. Now George and Mary begin to focus on the group activities. The group becomes the object of focal awareness ("them"), while the relationship between George and Mary ("we") becomes the perspective (tacit awareness) through which they are now looking at the group. Thus one may say to the other, "We don't agree with them that government programs can save our society, do we?" This statement demonstrates tacit relationship and focal group awareness—the speaker was looking at the group (object of focal awareness) through the eyes of the relationship (object of tacit awareness). If George and Mary were then to turn their attention to themselves as a unit ("us") noting how they felt much better because of their relationship, the relationship would be the target of both tacit and focal awareness.

Focal Relationship Awareness. In light of this distinction, studies by Cate and colleagues on relationship thinking (Cate, 1991; Cate, Koval, & Lloyd, 1989) can be construed as studies of *focal relationship awareness.* They define *relationship thinking* as "conscious thought processes that are focused on relationship patterns, aspects of the partner, and subjective conditions [like satisfaction] that are formed through interaction with a romantic partner" (Cate, 1991, p. 2). In relationship thinking, then, the relationship is the object of focal awareness. Wegner and Giuliano (1982) predicted that the more that targets are the objects of focal awareness, the more likely it is that these targets will be evaluated. Thus it is not surprising that when Cate examined people's thoughts about relationships, he discovered two broad categories of thought that may be seen as positive and negative thoughts about the relationship. Some thoughts seemed to be potentially detrimental to a relationship, and others were potentially enhancing to a relationship. In a factor analysis of his relational thinking measure, Cate (1991) found that the items consist of two broad factors that correspond to these negative and positive categories: (a) evaluative thinking (e.g., "I reflect on whether I am being treated fairly/unfairly in our relationship") and (b) reminiscent thinking (e.g., "I think about all the fun my partner and I have had together"). These two factors were examined in relationship to other variables ranging from individual characteristics to interactions with partners.

Cate and his colleagues hypothesized that relationship thinking would be related to relationship satisfaction. As expected, they found that relationship satisfaction related positively to reminiscent thinking and negatively to evaluative thinking. These findings held up even when accounting for the variance contributed by private self-consciousness, interpersonal orientation, romanticism, and attributional complexity. Cate and colleagues also looked for possible mediators between relationship satisfaction and relationship thinking. Ruling out self-disclosure, equity, and accommodation to the partner, they identified uncertainty reduction (Berger & Calabrese, 1975) as the possible link in the path from relationship thinking to relationship satisfaction (see also Parks & Adelman, 1983; Surra & Bohman, 1991). This finding implies that thinking about relationships leads to feeling more certain about the partner and relationship, and this certainty (or predictability) leads to satisfaction (Cate, 1991).

Tacit Relationship Awareness. Although the above studies by Cate and colleagues can be seen to highlight the characteristics and correlates of focal relationship awareness, the next study looks at another form of awareness: tacit relationship awareness. In this study, Acitelli and Veroff (1992) focus on the narrative technique introduced in the First Years of Marriage study (Veroff et al., 1985), in which couples were asked to tell the story of their relationship from the time they first met to what they think their future will be like. Various coding schemes were applied to the narratives, but for the purposes of this study, the coding of feelings was most relevant. Spontaneous expression of feelings or needs while telling a story was considered to be an expression of the couples' important concerns. Once a statement was coded as a statement of feeling or need, a measure was derived that represents the concept of *tacit relationship awareness.* It involves identifying when either spouse talks about the couple's feelings as relational (as opposed to reflecting an individual feeling or need). For example, a husband says, "We were very much in love at that point," or a wife says, "We wanted to get along better." Analyses indicate that this "we" orientation in telling the story leads to marital happiness and stability in the third year (Veroff, Sutherland, Chadiha, & Ortega, in press). Further analyses are being conducted on data from the first, second, and third years of marriage. These preliminary analyses suggest that relationship awareness may have an indirect effect on marital happiness and stability by creating a comfortable atmosphere characterized by understanding, a lack of tension and resentment, and an ease of adjustment to marriage.

Although the work on relationship awareness discussed thus far has assessed the frequency, content, and degree of relational thinking, additional work has begun that adds the dimension of complexity to the study of thinking about relationships. Martin (1991) has developed a measure that assesses the complexity or degree of elaboration of relational thoughts. Modeled after Crockett's (Crockett, 1965) Role Category Questionnaire, which elicits descriptions of persons, the Relational Cognition Complexity Instrument (RCCI) requires respondents to write descriptions of three of their relationships. Responses are coded by counting the number of times relational constructs (which are distinguished from personal constructs) occur in the descriptions. "Differentiation" or complexity scores are obtained by summing the number of different (or unique) relational constructs mentioned by the respondents. As expected, females scored higher on this scale than males. Scores on the RCCI also related to partners' patterns of interactions (more cooperative and flexible communication styles), suggesting that the way partners think about their relationship influences how they talk to each other about it (see also Martin, 1992). In the next section I turn to the factors that are expected to moderate the effects of relationship talk. In Figure 6.1 they are considered to be contextual factors and would be located within the square area enclosed by broken lines.

Talking About Relationships (2X)

In this chapter the term *relationship talk* (or *relational talk*) refers to talk *about* relationships only, not the more general talk *in* relationships. Although there are vast libraries of communication studies on talk in relationships, studies that focus on partners talking to each other about their relationships are rare. The notable exceptions are Acitelli (1986, 1988) Baxter (1987a), Baxter and

Bullis (1986), Bernal and Baker (1979), and Burnett (1986, 1987). Of those that look at relationship talk, only one was experimental and could with more certainty study the *effects* of relationship talk on the partners (Acitelli, 1988). What follows are the variables that are expected to condition the strength of the effects of the relationship talk (2X).

The Tone of the Interaction. Bernal and Baker (1979) discuss the beneficial effects of talking about the relationship during a conflictive situation. They describe a multilevel, metacommunicational framework to understand couple interactions that can be divided more generally into two basic levels. The lower level reflects the couple's focus on an issue or an individual partner; the higher level indicates that couples are focusing on the relationship and are acknowledging their own process. The research suggests that when in conflict, distressed couples get "locked" into the lower level, while nondistressed couples can shift from lower to higher levels when things get stuck and can examine partner differences in communication levels. Moreover, Baxter and her colleagues have discovered an association between relationship talk and changes in relationship commitment. Baxter and Bullis (1986) asked premarital partners to identify turning points in their relationships. Questioning partners about what had occurred at these turning points revealed that the points most likely to be associated with relationship talk involved initial passion (first kiss, first sex), making decisions about exclusivity and commitment, disengagement, and making up. Thus relationship talk can be seen as a way to define a relationship in its beginning stages and as a constructive attempt to fix a relationship that seems to be functioning poorly.

Thus there is a need to examine the full range of affective orientations in a relationship as a contextual factor influencing relationship awareness and its consequences. Few studies look at the effects of talking about one's relationship during both unpleasant and pleasant everyday situations (Acitelli, 1988; Duck, Rutt et al., 1991). In one of these, an experimental study, Acitelli (1988) examined the effects of talking about the relationship on perceptions of spouses' feelings of contentment. The experiment also was designed to determine whether talking about the relationship is seen to affect spouses differently in different situations. Married couples read stories about couples in which spouses either talk or do not talk about the relationship in pleasant or unpleasant situations. In a short questionnaire following each story, individual spouses rated the fictional spouses' feelings. Results of this study showed that talking about the relationship was perceived as making partners feel better than not talking about the relationship, regardless of the affective tone of the story (pleasant or unpleasant). Yet affective tone was shown to interact with gender such that relationship talk during good times had more of a positive impact on wives than on husbands. Men were seen to feel better about relationship talk in unpleasant situations than in pleasant ones. This gender difference may reflect that husbands view relationship talk as instrumental (used as a tool for "fixing" things, so it is especially valuable in conflictive situations), while wives feel equally as good about relationship talk in either setting. Scott et al. (1991) explain that, on the one hand, women may be more likely to view conversations with their partners as relationship relevant and thus store the conversation as a relationship memory. Men, on the other hand, are postulated to store conversations exclusively in terms of the issue discussed. Thus it is not surprising that men would see relationship talk as a means to an end, whereas women would see it as an end in itself or something to be valued for its own sake, and having consequences for relationship satisfaction (see Duck et al., 1991, or Wheeler & Nezlek, 1977, for further elaboration of this point).

Whether the Talk Is Descriptive or Analytic. It will be important to make the distinction between relationship talk that calls attention to and thus reinforces the status quo by describing it and that which is analytic (or attributional). For example, one might reinforce a pleasant situation by saying, "It's nice that we both enjoy playing tennis, isn't it?" A statement that is analytic might be, "Our problem does not seem to be merely one of disagreeing about which car to buy, but of understanding each other's point of view and being willing to compromise." Reinforcement theory and experience suggest the hypotheses that relationship talk is satisfying when it reinforces the pleasant interaction by stating how well things are going between the partners, whereas in a conflictive situation, relationship talk is beneficial when it is analytic with the goal of solving the problem. Conversely relationship talk may make people feel worse when it analyzes a positive situation ("Let's talk about why we are having fun!") and reinforces a negative one ("We can't see eye to eye on this, can we?"). The variable—type of talk—technically belongs in Box 2X, but because it is predicted to modify the effects of relationship talk in pleasant and unpleasant situations, it can be considered one of the contextual factors. Plans are underway to examine these hypotheses.

Which Partner Initiates the Talk. Although the initiation of talk may seem like an individual or interpersonal variable, the fact of one partner rather than the other initiating talk about the relationship creates part of the context for the conversation. One study (Acitelli, 1988) indicates that a husband talking about the relationship has a more positive impact on his wife in a pleasant situation than the wife's talk has on him. In an unpleasant situation, both husbands and wives were more satisfied with relationship talk when their partners initiated it. This finding in the unpleasant context is consistent with work by Fitness and Fletcher (1990) that showed that "partner-initiated, relationship-relevant behaviors (both positive and negative) elicited twice the number of self-reported emotions in an individual than did self-initiated, relationship relevant behaviors" (Fitness & Strongman, 1991, p. 193). Clearly more research is needed to find out whether there is a consistent pattern between partners regarding who initiates such talk and the way they respond to it.

The Degree of Similarity Between Partners. Is it the couple's overall degree of thinking and talking about the relationship that makes a difference, or is it the degree to which partners are *similar* in how much they value such thinking and talking? Similarity is a contextual factor in that it involves a comparison *between* individual variables that is predicted to effect the partners' interaction. In a study by Fletcher et al. (1987), respondents were given the task of describing (in writing) their relationship with their dating partners. These free-response descriptions were coded into four categories: actor, partner, interpersonal, and external. The researchers assumed that these descriptions represented how the respondents stored and retrieved relationship-related information. They found that when the *relationship* and the *interaction* between partners were the objects of cognitive focus, this was "generally associated with higher levels of happiness, commitment, and love" (p. 488). But because they studied 100 female and 31 male individuals (not couples) who were in heterosexual dating relationships, they could not assess how similar the partners were with regard to relational thinking.

On the other hand, Neimeyer's (1984) research design allowed him to test and support the hypothesis that "marital satisfaction should be related less to the overall *level*" of partners' cognitive complexity of personal constructs "than to their similarity in cognitive structure" (p. 259). For his study, 20 married couples took a modified version of Kelly's (1955) Role Construct Repertory Test. Measures of overall complexity were obtained by summing the husband's and wife's scores. Measures of structural similarity between partners were based on the absolute value of the discrepancy between the spouses' scores. Admittedly, cognitive complexity of personal constructs is not identical to relationship awareness, but his findings led him to recommend that marital therapy "be designed to assist partners in formulating *shared understandings* of their relationships" (p. 262). This recommendation suggests not only that relationship awareness may contribute to marital satisfaction but also that the similarity between partners may be more important than absolute levels of relationship awareness. Perhaps, as Duck (1991) points out, "the importance of similarity is not its existence, but the *recognition* of its existence by the persons concerned" (p. 21).

The recognition of similarities may be only part of the picture. Perhaps the recognition of the process of *mutuality* (Genero, Miller, Surrey, & Baldwin, 1992) is also crucial to relationship quality. *Mutuality* is defined as "the bidirectional movement of feelings, thoughts, and activity between persons in relationships . . . that transcends the immediate and reciprocal exchange of benefits" (pp. 36-37). The recognition of mutuality in a relationship may be the key to partners having a shared understanding of their relationship. Research is needed to distinguish the concepts of *perceived similarity* and *mutuality* and to explore their relative associations to relationship satisfaction.

The Degree of Commitment to the Relationship. At first glance, the few studies that do focus on talking about relationships seem contradictory. On the one hand, for example, Bernal and Baker (1979) have demonstrated that couples in conflict are less likely to remain in conflict if they are able to talk in relational terms. On other hand, in his studies of dating individuals, Cate (1991) found that evaluative relationship thinking was negatively related to relationship satisfaction. In addition, Baxter and colleagues (e.g., Baxter & Bullis, 1986; Baxter & Wilmot, 1984) have shown that talking about relationships is a "taboo topic" and is associated with conflict in the relationship. In their study of dating partners, Baxter and Wilmot (1984) had respondents indicate which topics they could and could not talk about with their partners. From this study they concluded that "the state of the relationship" is a "taboo topic" of conversation for dating partners (mentioned more often by females than males). They also found that partners gain access to information about the relationship through "secret tests" (such as flirting with another member of the opposite sex) designed to elicit some kind of reaction from the partner. Baxter purports that thinking about relational processes is valuable insofar as it allows partners to rely on indirect communication and that direct relationship talk is unnecessary and possibly harmful to a relationship.

Bernal and Baker, however, were studying married couples, while Baxter and Cate were studying dating couples. These seemingly contradictory findings point to the need for a comparison between dating and married couples to determine the extent to which the effects of relational talk is influenced by relationship status (public commitment) and the partners' private level of commitment to their relationship. In general it is expected that the more committed a partner is to a relationship, the more relationship talk will be valued. However, commitment probably will interact with length of relationship such that in the beginning stages of a committed relationship, talking about the relationship is valued as a way to define the relationship and would not be threatening if both partners are committed. But as time goes on and the relationship becomes more defined in the partners' minds, relationship talk will occur less as a means of defining the relationship and more as a problem-solving tool. I am planning work that explores the possibility that the level of commitment to a relationship is a mediating factor that determines the effects of relationship awareness.

Future Directions: Underlying Factors That Determine the Positive Effects of Thinking and Talking About One's Relationship

As stated earlier, the model depicted in Figure 6.1 is a general framework that organizes the literature on thinking and talking about relationships in valuable new ways. As such, the model can be a springboard for further research by pushing the field in new directions and by requiring distinctions that provoke new theoretical understandings of complex processes. In this section some avenues for future directions are mapped out. Here underlying factors that are individual (as opposed to interpersonal) are postulated to influence and be influenced by relational cognition.

Identity (1A, 1B). An adolescent girl's identity develops more through her relationships (talking with a same-sex intimate chum), whereas an adolescent boy's identity develops more through autonomy and achievement (Douvan & Adelson, 1966). Studies have demonstrated that women are more relationally oriented than men. In a national survey, women more than men reported that work satisfied their need for affiliation with others (Veroff et al., 1981). Gilligan (1982) has shown that when resolving moral dilemmas, females think more about how the consequences of their decisions affect others, while males think more in terms of abstract principles. In addition, Burnett's (1987) findings, based on free-responses to open-ended questions about the incidence and content of relationship reflections, as well as fixed responses to a more structured questionnaire, depict "men in general as less interested, thoughtful and communicative about relationships, placing less value on analysis and discussion about relationships" (p. 8), regardless of what kind of relationship they were thinking or talking about. However, her respondents were not couples but individuals reporting on the frequency and value of thinking and talking about their relationships (again pointing to the need for more data from both partners in a relationship). Using a similar questionnaire with married couples, Acitelli (1986) found comparable results.

The literature also suggests that husbands' intimacy maturity (White, Speisman, Jackson, Bartis, & Costos, 1986) and other interpersonal skills are positively related to couple satisfaction, while such characteristics in wives are not (Kalin & Lloyd, 1985; Murstein & Williams, 1985; Noller, 1980). Such findings support the idea that interpersonal skills and intimate relating are normative for women and, therefore, expected. Because these characteristics are more unusual and unexpected in men, they would have more of an impact on relational satisfaction. These studies were not, however, focusing on relationship talk. Although studies with married couples have indicated that a man talking about the relationship has more of a positive impact on a woman than her talking does on him (Acitelli, 1988, 1992), further work is needed that focuses more directly on how much relationship awareness in couples is associated with partners' individual identities.

Theorists (e.g., Jordan & Surrey, 1986; Markus & Oyserman, 1989) have proposed that a woman's self-concept is more relational than a man's self-concept; that is, instead of consisting of personality descriptors independent of others, the self-concepts of women are likely to include others with whom they have relationships. Males, in general, are not expected to be as relationally oriented as are females and thus will not be expected to think of themselves in relational terms as much as females do. Acitelli conducted a pilot study to develop a measure of relational identity similar to Markus's interpersonal self (Markus & Cross, 1990;

Markus & Kitayama, 1991). Respondents were asked to rate a list of characteristics and roles as descriptive or not descriptive of themselves. The terms used for characteristics were either relational (e.g., friendly) or nonrelational (e.g., decisive), as were the terms for roles (e.g., daughter/son or artist). Results supported the expectation that women would see themselves more in relational terms than men. Work is being planned that will examine the role of identity in relationship awareness and satisfaction to see whether having a relational identity enhances the value of thinking and talking about relationships.

The Perception of Uniqueness (2A, 2B). Very little has been written about partners perceiving their relationship to be unique. Rogers (1972) points out that self-disclosure serves to expose one's uniqueness to another. This divulgence could possibly be parallel to talking about one's relationship. If talking about the self exposes one's uniqueness, then talking about the relationship might serve to expose the uniqueness of the relationship to its partners and therefore to enhance its value. Moreover, Montgomery (1988) states that creating unique standards of communication is rewarding to couples and helps partners realize that their relationship is special. Thus it is expected that the more partners think and talk about their relationship, the more they will see their relationship as unique.

Work by Planalp (1987) has shown that people have general schemata for relationships and that either new information is assimilated into the existing schema or the existing schema is changed to accommodate to the new information. Surra and Bohman (1991), who present a developmental view of cognition in relationships, explain that people have different generalized schemata for various types of relationships (e.g., friends, lovers). They assert that as a specific relationship develops, these generalized schemata form the groundwork for a relationship-specific schema that develops for one particular relationship. (For a review of the social psychological literature relevant to relational schemata, see Baldwin, in press). In addition, Miller and Read (1991) have constructed an interesting theory of how partners form and develop models of themselves, others, and interactions,

providing a "moment-by-moment" account, from the initial encounter that activates related concepts already existing in a
partner's mind to the organization of these concepts into a
coherent model of the interaction. These theories set up the
argument that not only are there systematic differences between
schemata for different types of relationships but there also are
systematic differences between schemata of couples in the same
types of relationships. Thus it is postulated here that those
partners who think and talk about their relationship a great deal
will have much more differentiated (or unique) relationship-specific schemata than those who hardly think and talk about their
relationship at all. Martin's (1991) finding that women score
higher on the RCCI may be indicative of the fact that women
think more about relationships in general and are thus more
inclined to see their relationships as unique.

Understanding (2A, 2B). Married couples tend to assume that
they agree more than they actually do (e.g., Levinger &
Breedlove, 1966), and distressed couples are less likely to assume
agreement than are happy couples. Although assumed agreement may maintain the appearance of harmony, it can lead to
misunderstanding. Spouses can misunderstand one another by
assuming that they agree when they actually do not. And they
can assume that they disagree when they actually agree (Kenny
& Acitelli, 1989). One way to avoid such misunderstandings is
for partners to talk to one another about themselves or about
their relationship. Although literature on self-disclosure seems
to indicate that talking about the private aspects of oneself can
be beneficial to a relationship (Cozby, 1973; Derlega, 1984;
Franzoi, Davis, & Young, 1985; Gilbert, 1976), few studies focus
on talking about the relationship. Research is planned to fill this
gap by testing the hypotheses that talking about the relationship
leads to partners' greater understanding of each other and to a
shared understanding of the relationship; such understandings
can lead to greater satisfaction with the relationship. Whether
greater understanding leads to more or less relationship talk can
also be explored.

Conclusions

The growing interest in partners' perceptions of each other and their relationship comes from several sources. Relevant studies range from such topics as attributional processes, interpersonal perception, and interpersonal communication to personal relationships, marriage, and marital therapy. In sum, this chapter has outlined the research from these areas pertaining to thinking and talking about relationships and has identified directions that point to major questions that must be addressed more fully. Although several studies have begun to address the issues raised, they are only springboards for future work that will further explain (a) how relational cognitions are tied to individual and relational well-being, (b) how various contexts can modify the effects of relationship talk on partners and can increase or decrease the effects of gender differences in relationship awareness, (c) how the way individuals think of themselves can influence the way they behave in relationships, and (d) how relationship awareness relates to partners' understandings of each other and their relationships.

As stated earlier, research on relationship awareness thus far has focused on intimate heterosexual relationships, but one aim of this chapter is to encourage such research on other types of relationships as well. How important is relationship awareness in other types of relationships? Friends may be less inclined than spouses to think and talk about their relationships (Wiseman, 1990), and the effects of such thinking and talking on friends may differ from its effects on spouses. Would thinking and talking about relationships also function differently in homosexual relationships? Two alternative hypotheses could be tested: (a) Two partners of the same sex may make the gender differences in relationship awareness even stronger; that is, perhaps lesbians tend to talk a great deal more about their relationships with each other than would gay males, and (b) participation in a distinctive relationship might make thinking and talking about that relationship more commonplace regardless of gender; that is, would homosexuals think and talk more about their relationships than heterosexuals? Furthermore, relationship awareness could be explored in parent-child relationships. An imbalance in relationship awareness is expected to be great for parents and young children (with parents having more awareness than the child), and the imbalance is expected to decrease as the child matures. Moving from asymmetrical to symmetrical relationship awareness is expected in therapist-client relationships as well.

More longitudinal work needs to be done to help establish causal directions between cognition and well-being in relationships. For example, developmental studies could test the hypothesis that relationship awareness progresses in stages such that private self-consciousness and perspective taking (Franzoi et al., 1985) are necessary precursors. Such studies also could test the hypothesis that, over time, couples develop a shared reality. As such, differences in partners' perceptions of their relationships should decrease with length of the relationship (Berger & Kellner, 1964). This increase in similarity of perceptions of the relationship (or relationship-specific schemata) conceivably might lead to a decrease in relationship talk. Thus couples who have been married for a long time may talk less about their relationship than newlyweds. These suggestions are just straightforward examples of how longitudinal work may enrich the study of relationship awareness. As implied in the model in Figure 6.1, influences may not be so straightforward and can come from many directions. For instance, although a person's identity can influence whether and how one thinks about relationships, being in and thinking about relationships may also influence one's identity.

The research directions outlined in this chapter have the potential to fill out a more complete story of relationship awareness that earlier studies have begun to develop. These studies can set the stage, the mood, the script, and describe the characters. Work on underlying factors will go deeper into the partners' minds, looking at their identities, their understandings of each other, and the relationship. Studies of various contexts will help determine whether the story holds true for partners as they interact with each other in different scenes. Longitudinal studies can move the story into other chapters to see how relationship awareness changes over time. Work in this area has the potential to help researchers and couples alike think about relationships in new ways.

*Understanding
Relationship Processes:
Uncovering the
Human Search for Meaning*

Marcia Dixson

Steve Duck

> *[Humankind] is the symbol-using
> (symbol-making, symbol misusing)
> animal, inventor of the negative (or
> moralized by the negative), separated
> from [the] natural condition by
> instruments of his [or her] own making,
> goaded by the spirit of hierarchy (or
> moved by the sense of order), and rotten
> with perfection.*
>
> K. Burke, 1966, p. 16

AUTHORS' NOTE: We are grateful to Carlos Aleman, Michelle Fabian, Geoff
Leatham, and Julia T. Wood for their helpful comments on a previous draft of
this chapter.

There is a curiosity about relationships: They are composed of individuals, yet are more than the sum of their parts. In understanding relationship processes, one therefore is faced with understanding not only what it is that individuals think, know, and do in relationships but also what they share and how they come to share it. Our analysis of this curiosity focuses on symbols and meaning because both of these entities can be "owned" by individuals for themselves and also can be shared with others (Baxter, 1987b). Individuals can see symbolism and meaning in idiosyncratic ways that they have constructed for themselves. In relationships, partners also experience a commonality of meaning and symbolism between themselves on a variety of topics and concerns, and this experience "goes beyond" simple similarity in its effects.

We focus on this overlooked curiosity in a number of ways—sometimes looking at the ways two persons create, establish, and share meaning with one another as relaters, and sometimes looking at the ways researchers do exactly the same thing by developing terminologies and ways of experiencing the world that can be shared by colleagues. Threaded through this analysis is the notion that both examples are instances of a fundamental human tendency to use symbols, to seek, create, and develop meaning, and to analyze experience. Duck (1991) has developed the basis of this argument elsewhere, and here we go further and apply an analysis of this fundamental human tendency proposed by Kenneth Burke, a rhetorical theorist who focused on the human use of symbols and the ways this use structures thought and explanation—whether at the level of relationships or at the level of scholarly discourse. We also see connections with the work of personality psychologist George Kelly (1955, but especially, 1969), who also focused on the ways humans construct meanings as a way to deal with the "constantly unforeseen originality" (Shotter, 1987) of their lives.

It has been traditional to point to the fact that humans are able to live—actually cannot avoid living—simultaneously in reference to all three dimensions of time (past, present, and future). Thus our past, as we have accounted for it, echoes in the present and in the future; our present makes sense because of our images of the past and the future; and our anticipations of the future often recast the past and direct our behaviors of the moment. All three are always present, and all three are humanly, symbolically constructed. Use of symbols represents a parallel between social actors and researchers: All of us seek to describe (represent) and explain past and present happenings both for their own sake and to control and predict future events. Both Burke (1966) and Kelly (1955, 1969), however, retranslate these views into a future orientation; that is, they see humans as evaluating and interpreting the past in order to give it a meaning that helps one cope with it in the future if similar events happen again. Thus both theorists emphasize the importance, in understanding human behavior, of noting that humans are driven by a need to cope with the future that is unpredictable unless people develop categories of expectation ("constructs" for Kelly; "symbols" for Burke). Although meaning is often apparently retrospective, for Kelly constructs are personal creations developed and tested quasi-scientifically to deal with the future (Duck & Condra, 1989). Burke wrote of symbols as human devices and schemes for comprehending life as a whole; they are not inherent in the phenomena that humans experience. Kelly wrote of the "anticipation of events by construing of their replications"; Burke (1966, p. 16) wrote, more opaquely, that humans are "rotten with perfection," meaning that humans place order on the phenomena they encounter, so as to organize their experience. Such activity inevitably provokes a restless hunt for the best way to do this organizing and creates a search for perfection or completeness (a tendency to continually revise, update, and regard as unfinished the business of their application and extension). In one sense, then, "rotten with perfection" is yet another way of saying that more research needs to be done!

The theme of dealing with change and the future has been a part of human thought about human behavior since at least the early Greek philosophers (e.g., Heraclitus) and takes its modern form in the emphasis on prediction and control that is found in many recent models of relationships (e.g., Kelley et al., 1983). We share the view that it is an important channeler of human thinking but feel that more can be said about its implications for the study and conduct of relationships.

In this chapter, *symbols* and *meaning* are essentially motivating entities that exist in individual minds but about which two individual minds can (come to) agree. They are examples of important forms of cognitive overlap in relationships, in culture, and indeed in the professional terminologies that researchers develop and use among themselves. One important question, then, is how people come to *develop* such meaning systems (see Vol. 2 of this series). A second question is how such systems relate to cultural and social milieus (Vol. 3 of this series). A third question is how people come to share such symbols and meanings (an issue covered in Duck, in press), and a fourth is how people use and can develop them once they are shared—issues that we cover here.

This chapter draws parallels between the symbolic character of human cognitive and social life, on the one hand, and the symbol usage of social scientists, on the other. We argue that partners in relationships are using shared meaning systems or shared working models of the world to conduct the relational endeavor, just as scholars use shared specialized symbol systems or working models to conduct the collegial research endeavor. Indeed there are striking parallels between the theoretical activities of scholars in different disciplines once one focuses on that activity as examples of human "effort after meaning" (Bartlett, 1932).

One parallel that we note here would apply the same notion to the field of personal relationships research itself. This volume deals specifically with the individual minds that enter relationships between minds; later volumes take other perspectives emphasizing learning, social structure, transactional dynamics, and other aspects of relating. Just as two individuals bring their own individual systems of thinking into any relationship, so to researchers and scholars come to the study of relationships with their own patterns of thought, training, method, theory, perspective, and so on. Such patterns of thought, necessarily and ex hypothesi, influence the choice of phenomena selected for inquiry and inspection as the individual researchers take different perspectives on the phenomena. Sociologists will gravitate toward patterns of structure and power as issues to be explained. Social psychologists will focus on the individual or social cognitions that are evident to them in relationships and their participants. Communication scholars will look for the structures of messages or the construction of relationships that they imply. Developmentalists will ask how persons and their beliefs or skills change across time in relationships. In short, each discipline will take a perspective that focuses characteristically on those things that make most sense within its own frame of reference or terminological geography (agreed meaning systems). Although, for example, the differences between disciplines often are exaggerated at the expense of the similarities, such differences often are seen as little more than foibles caused by training, rather than as examples of human choices based on meaning systems. Nevertheless there is a deeper structural point about the human mind here, showing a common element that runs through most human action: that a fundamental structure of human minds is based on choice in the context of *meaning* and that this structure expresses itself in human behavior of all kinds, including the activities of scholars in various disciplines.

The reader already may be ahead of us in seeing that individuals who come to relationships are also examples of this same fact about the human mind. The anxious persons focus on likely evidence of rejection by others (Erickson, Sroufe, & Egeland, 1985; Raush, Barry, Hertel, & Swain, 1974); the extravert explores opportunities for social interaction, while the introvert seeks to avoid them in favor of quiet solitude; women typically notice the progress of intimate talk in relationships, while men are alerted to different aspects of social experience (Duck, Rutt et al., 1991).

The fundamental human commonality evident in all of these examples is that people choose to focus on things that make sense within their preexisting frames of reference, their system of meaning, about which deductions can be made on the basis of evident choices (Duck, 1991). Burke, a rhetorical theorist, put it thus:

> We can say that people interpret natural sequences in terms of cause and effect not because of something in the natural scene requiring this interpretation but because humans are the sort of

agents that see things in terms of necessary relations. In this view we do not derive our ideas of cause and effect from experience; all that we can derive from experience is the observation that certain happenings seem likely to follow certain other happenings. But our ideas of cause and effect are derived from the nature of the mind. (Burke, 1945/1969, p. 187)

Natural phenomena do not scream out at us to be interpreted in a particular way; they make rather subliminal whispers that different people choose to hear in slightly different ways, as make sense to them within their frames of reference of meaning.

Meaning and Sharing of Meaning in Talk

We believe that such a view connects easily with several lines of thinking in psychology (e.g., personality psychology), as well as in communication studies (e.g., study of rhetoric and persuasion) and sociology (e.g., symbolic interaction). It also demonstrates the relevance of choice in the human endeavor. Choice of discipline, of structure for a series, of topics for a volume, of methodology, of research problem, friends, affiliative strategies, and many others are all expressions of a general human tendency to make choices within a framework of meanings accepted by the chooser (who also may be "a researcher," "a partner," "an author," "an editor," or "a person").

The notion of *meaning* has proven difficult in the history of ideas. By focusing, as the rest of this volume does, on what an individual knows about relating, we are emphasizing the way the person organizes, for him- or herself, knowledge about relationships and partners; but this is only a part of the picture, even if it clearly ties in with work in this and other fields. In Volume 2, for example, several authors adopt Bowlby's (1988) term *working models* to refer to a similar concept. For us, *meaning* is an organizational concept too and refers to the way a person organizes knowledge about relationships in the context of what else he or she knows about the world. We believe that, having constructed organized knowledge about relationships in the ways discussed in other chapters in this volume, individuals represent that knowledge to other people by the language they use, as an invitation to those others to share and adopt that organization of knowledge. The formation of a dyadic relationship thus confronts the two partners with the organizational challenge of resolving any differences that exist between their respective working models or meaning systems. We follow Duck and Pond (1989) in seeing the formation, maintenance, and conduct of relationships as processes in which such organization and reconciliation of meaning systems is carried out, usually through talk—and everyday talk at that. But such talk is not to be dismissed as a trivial thing. One of our goals is to show that talk is not an idle medium in social (or scholarly) life: It represents, "constructs," and sustains (and perhaps helps develop and change) a person's system of meaning. It also represents the operation of cognition as choice, not just in the selection of terms and styles but also as reflected in the emphasis given to different terms in the presence of different audiences or for different purposes—or circumstances of human life not given the attention they truly deserve (cf. Billig, 1987). Finally it represents a *persuasive* activity with the effect of prodding other people into acceptance of the proffered organization of meaning.

Choice Between Alternatives

A recent development in the study of relationships has focused not so much on the choices that persons make of other people, as we used to do in the pioneering work on interpersonal attraction (Berscheid & Walster [Hatfield], 1969, 1978), but on the choices available to relational partners in the interpretation of events in their relationship. Olson (1977) describes a continuum of perspectives bounded by "insiders'" perspectives at one end and "outsiders'" at the other; Duck and Sants (1983) picked up on this as a critical feature of human experience of relationships. Recently the case has been developed by Duck (1988, 1990). Duck (1990) notes that two partners can disagree on relational events in the same relationship and states: "It is not that we cannot ask about the relationships between subjective reports and 'objective data'; rather we should be clear about what it means to make the comparison" (p. 14). He also argues that perspectives of the same individual in the same relationship can change meaningfully over time and that "we take perhaps too little notice of the temporal and perspectival fluctuations that probably affect our subjects" (p. 16). Noller and Guthrie (1992) recently reached the same conclusion.

This argument does not entail the conclusion that events in relationships are so chaotic that they cannot be studied; rather, it suggests that we need to explore variability of experience within the same subject with the same vigor with which we have studied stability and constancy over time—that is, that we explore the variance of relationships as carefully as we study the mean (Duck, 1991). Neither does it entail that events in relationships are so phenomenologically elusive that we should all give up social science, burn the instruments of our craft in despair, and become trainers of elephants; rather, it suggests that we need a framework for exploring the ways partners make choices between the alternative views of relationships that are available and how they come to share them with one another or argue about them. Our argument here is that Burke's approach to the use of symbols gives us a heuristic framework for exploring some of the system that lies beneath the apparent chaos that could otherwise afflict human choices. We argue that such a system is evident in the "deep structure" of human choices—which is itself evident in the language that people use in everyday life, once one sees it as "presentational and persuasive" (offering a view of the world for others to adopt) rather than as "representational" ("accurate" in some sense).

Such a view does not take us so far into the jungle of idiosyncratic phenomenalism as may at first be thought by traditional social scientists. Within psychology, Kelly (1969) argues that human beings create meaning systems that are best called "personalities" and that they do this by construing, making choices between alternative perspectives, and imposing order on the world, just as scientists do. Kelley (1979) theorizes about the ways humans make meaning through systematic choices and differentiations about causes in a quasi-scientific way, using the types of procedures and evidence that social scientists use. Humans, whether as persons or as scientists, select terms, use metaphors, or construct narratives in order to designate and encapsulate those construals and orders (Glucksberg, 1991; Weiner, 1991). When they are being human, we talk of "accounts" (Harvey et al., 1989) or "narratives"; when they are being scientists, we talk of "theories," though Antaki (1987) argues for the similarities between these two phenomena. Humans engage in narrative discourse with other humans about topics of mutual interest, whether at scholarly conferences or at home, using language that has meaning for all parties (Howard, 1991), meaning derived from encapsulations and interpretations shared within the relevant discourse community—popular, relational, or scientific (Duck, 1991).

Although enmeshed in past and present, humans' reflections on the past and present are influenced by the fact that humans are also future oriented and predictive, just as scientists are, both as they conduct relationships and as they move through life (Kelly, 1969). For example, many scientific accounts are first attempts to describe and explain before they predict and control, whereas much human relational activity is implicitly (or metaphorically) about the description, accounting for and then predicting of a possible future together, as Baxter's (1992) analysis of relational metaphors makes plain. Even the human activities apparently driven by past experiences (such as attachment styles or chronic loneliness) can be reinterpreted as essentially forward-looking. They encapsulate expectations and predictions of the general character of relationships with other people, on the basis of personal systems of meaning derived from past experience (Bowlby, 1988; Duck, Pond, & Leatham, 1992). Finally, although everyday human discourse focuses on topics and issues that have a common fascination for the interactors, on the basis of their significance, so also scholarly discourse selects and magnifies certain topics at the expense of others on the basis of common understanding of terms. In all of these cases, talk is a symbolic activity that sustains, constructs, and presents ("argues for") persons' ways of looking at the world and is not a simple expressive activity that just externalizes cognition (Duck, in press). It does more than that and can be an activity that transforms cognition as well as presents it.

All of the above enterprises involve the interaction of individual minds through communication and meaning. It is assumed, often naively, that communication is a simple matter that results from two people "having" similar meanings or ideas, but this notion is unsatisfactory in several ways (see Chapter 2, this volume, for an analysis). First, two individuals are really quite unlikely to start out thinking of everything in the same way but, through the interactions, debates, discussions, and arguments of everyday life, may develop a greater degree of similarity (Blankenship, Hnat, Hess, & Brown, 1984). Thus, although it makes perfect sense to learn what can be learned about cognition at the level of individual structure and function, it is not satisfactory to ignore the ways in which talk and discourse transform cognition. To explore the structure of individual schemata about relationships or to unravel the ways individuals think about being coupled with someone else is necessary and useful but does not entail the conclusion that the mere existence of such individual structures construct and create meaning between people on their own. The simple juxtaposition of two cognitive systems does not mean that they necessarily comprehend one another or give the same weights to phenomena; such comprehension has to be *established* through interaction and discourse. A crucial issue for the field is thus to show how individual minds carry their meaning systems into relationship with one another and construct a new system of shared meaning that constitutes a conflated whole.

Of course, the study of sociality has to assume some basic degree of underlying communicative and interpretative similarity between the participants, even if simply at the level of shared language and culture (Mead, 1934); zero overlap would negate the possibility of communication and relationship at every level. The importance of this notion for the understanding of relationships has been elaborated by Duck (in press). Most work to date, however, has looked at the fortuitous and adventitious similarities of background, understanding, or meaning systems (race, place, face, educational level, attitudes, socioeconomic status, background experiences, training, phenomenal experiences, etc., as amply documented in research literature compiled in, for example, Huston, 1974). It is true that the more of these similarities two people have, the more, by and large, they increase the communicative efficiency of a relationship. Nonetheless such things evidently do not determine the success of a relationship on their own. They are facilitative prerequisites for some other things that influence relationship development and satisfaction because they provide the very basis for discussion and development of relational forms, but it is the discussion or interaction that does the relational work, the sharing, and the *recognition* of sharing that has the relational consequences (Duck, in press).

Research on relationship development suggests quite strongly that one of the major occurrences in growth of affinity is the development and extension of conceptual frameworks by active discourse, although this is more often left implicit than explicated. For example, maps of each other are drawn and extended by partners through self-disclosure (Altman & Taylor, 1973), or growth and development of areas of similarity are pushed forward through certain kinds of conflict resolution (Lloyd & Cate, 1985), discussion, gossip, everyday talk, exchange, or uncertainty reduction (for example, Berger, 1988b; Neimeyer & Mitchell, 1988). Indeed the ideology of relationship development in most literature is that increases in commonality of meaning are the essence of relationship development, although the processes by which they are created are often taken for granted. Furthermore sociological research notes that part of the process of construction of relationships is based on development of relational organization: Like other organizations, relationships develop power structures, rules, rituals, and shared codes or language (McCall, 1988). These things can hardly develop without discussion and interactive debate or presentation of proposals and resolution of differences through dialogue and talk. Also necessary is construction of a shared approach to such activities as leisure management, everyday chores, personal idioms of language, reflective styles of behavior, and so on (Huston, Surra, Fitzgerald, & Cate, 1981; Suitor & Pillemer, in press). Again, although Huston et al. mention "negotiation" as a source for this construction, it is not the process of negotiation itself that is studied as part of their work, only its results.

Therefore Duck (1991) distinguishes between *similarity* and *sharing meaning* and argues:

> [The] importance of similarity is not its existence, but the *recognition* of its existence by the persons concerned . . . the most important thing that similarity indicates is the *sharing of meaning* not of attitudes or needs or roles or values. Each of these other things is a subtle and often disguised subset of meaning. (pp. 21-22)

Thus, although interpersonal relationships prerequire and presume the basic commonalities of meaning that make sociality possible, these are not enough. Active processes of communication based on symbols and meaning must occur to make them happen. Relationships do not require that the similarities merely exist to be discovered; rather, relationships require that individuals not only recognize and acknowledge such commonalities through their talk but also forge and create new ones by agreement and discussion. In other words, relationship development is a persuasive process involving the *active* construction of joint systems of meaning from the individual systems that enter into relationships.

A few implications of this view are perhaps not self-evident. First, for change to occur in a relationship (whether in the nature of the relationship through a direct proposal to increase intimacy, however it is made, or an affective change brought about by events), the two partners' perspectives on the relationship probably have to be different from each other initially such that one person takes the lead to change the other person. Second, and implied in the above, the two persons could have different views of the relationship or could have nonequivalent comprehensions of each other's psychological structures. Kelly (1955, 1969) proposes, in his sociality corollary, that the level and kind of relationship between two people are constrained and determined by the extent to which each comprehends the thought processes and psychological structure of the other person. This proposal means that two persons in "the same" physical relationship actually are able to be in different psychological relationships, in some sense, if they comprehend each other in different ways. An easy example is that parents usually understand their children's thought-worlds better than children understand parents', but the same point about nonequivalence of comprehension is true in relationships between adults. Indeed some analysts of power in relationships make this point in slightly different terms (e.g., Huston, 1983; Kelvin, 1977). Thus one not only is concerned with sharing of meaning as a simple creation of understanding but also could explore the effects on relationships of the two partners understanding each other to different degrees and extents. A mistake in past literature, we believe, has been to assume that understanding between two partners is always equivalent understanding. Rather, the need is to demonstrate the extent of understanding that exists in each of the two partners separately and to explore the effects of differences and similarities in the conduct of relationships—especially of the persuasive talk in relationships.

We believe that differences in perspective are a result of individual human cognitive activity and are not trivial errors wrought just to annoy investigators; rather, they are sources of motivation for partners to resolve differences and to develop new comprehension of both relational phenomena and each other. Nevertheless none of the above would be important if it were not for the fact that such differences mean something and represent choices initially made independently by the partners on their own as they thought about the world.

We thus assert that a choice of analytic framework for anything will be dependent on certain prior assumptions about the phenomenon, depending on the perspective that one takes on it initially, whether as researcher or as relational partner (Duck & Montgomery, 1991). Any perspective thus represents the fundamental activity of individual human choice among alternatives. Part of our point here is to show that many different choices can be taken with a legitimacy derived from one's initial purposes and prior cognizing; their resolution represents important processes of meaning making between people, whether these be relational scholars or relationship partners. We illustrate this point by noting some remarkable parallels between the dominant modes of thinking in rhetoric and some other modes of thinking in both personality psychology and the field of personal relationships. Thus this chapter draws parallels between the enterprise of understanding relationships at the "scientific level" and at the level of common human experience, as well as at the level of editorial choice. In essence, part of our purpose is to display an underlying human tendency that undergirds many different human activities: the individual construction of meaning and the persuasion of others to accept and share it. To complete our claims about human choice, one needs a framework within which to explore the decisions that are made to describe those choices in language, talk, and thought.

Relationships and Explanation

Even from a particular frame of reference, choices have to be made within it. Individuals do not capriciously pick out one alternative rather than another from those they see before them; rather, they orient themselves toward the issues within an individual conceptual framework. Dyads do not wildly pick one or another alternative from those perspectives brought to an issue by the two individual partners; rather, they discuss, negotiate, and resolve issues by creating new frameworks of meaning for the issues and for the couple. Likewise social scientists do not choose to gather just any "data" or to use just "a method"; rather, they define, for their purposes, the things that will count as data and the method that is to be credited above others. Other scientists may make other choices, and arguments about the nature or validity of the types of data or method are commonplace. Likewise individuals choose "partners" or take positions on a relational issue according to their own preferences, which may wax and wane at any given point in the life cycle or sets of circumstances and which are often different from choices made by others. Although the results are different, an assumption underlying all our scholarly work is that the principles of choice are the same.

Both in the conduct of relational choices and in the explanation of that conduct, an analysis of motives is readily seen to be a major element (Bradbury & Fincham, 1990; Harvey et al., 1989). Individuals talk of being attracted to others' characters and personalities, and scientists have looked at attributions of causality in relationships, as well as everywhere else (Fincham & Bradbury, 1987; Fletcher & Fitness, Chapter 5, this volume). The question that we raise here is whether (a) it is useful to look at such attempts to explain motives in only one way (e.g., by focusing on explaining the actor's acts) or (b) one can explore the description and attribution of motives in other complementary ways that will broaden our comprehension of what it is that humans are up to when they attempt to explain others' behavior. For example, one could look at the cultural style that prefers certain sorts of explanation over others ("She was angry" rather than "She was bitten by the god of anger"). Indeed the very understanding of behavior in terms of individual causes is a Western one, and in some cases Eastern views see causes as more holistic confluences of patterns of facilitating factors, such as karma. Thus the framework within which one moves, even at the cultural level, is essentially one that focuses one on certain ways of looking at the phenomena. In relationships, of course, one's starting point will be one's own individuality, one's own cognition, and one's own framework of personal meanings. So will one's partner's starting point on any issue also be selected from his or her framework of meaning or cognitive structure. The blending of these two frameworks, as joint relational meaning is constructed, will involve some sharing of frameworks and ways of comprehending others' "psychology."

Both in the approach to relationships and in the understanding of rhetorical principles, the comprehension of motives and other persons' thought patterns has great significance. Burke's (1945/1969) forbiddingly titled "dramatistic pentad" offers a systematic way of looking at motives and the ways humans attempt to comprehend them. It also shows us some interesting ways in which the arbitrary (but not capricious) choice of perspective influences fundamentally one's selection of interpretive weights.

Explaining Motives and Choosing
Frames of Reference

Burke's pentad consists of five terms: *act, scene, agent, agency,* and *purpose* (or the "what, where, who, how, why" pentad). The *act* is "any verb, no matter how specific or how general, that has connotations of consciousness or purpose" (p. 14, 1945/1969); the *agent* is the person or kind of person performing the act; the *scene* is the situation in which the act occurred; the *agency* is the instrument(s) used by the agent in performing the act; and the *purpose* is the reason for that act (Burke, 1945/1969). Burke employs this pentad as a way of attributing (and explaining the attribution of) motives to human actions in terms of "ratios" between (usually pairs of) the five terms. For example, as social scientists typically choose to do, we might latch on to a *scene:act ratio* and assume as a given that it is "only natural" to look for aspects in the scene that would influence the type of act performed there. "Using 'scene' in the sense of setting or background, and 'act' in the sense of action, one could say that 'the scene contains the act' " (Burke, 1945/1969, p. 3). In other words, certain scenes call for certain sorts of acts and almost presume them, so the adoption or acceptance of the scene as a given almost requires one to look for certain sorts of acts to occur in it. Indeed Burke goes further and claims that "one cannot separate the intrinsic properties of a character from the situation that enables him to be what he is" (Burke, 1966, p. 107). Burke's example is taken from Carlyle's *Heroes and Hero Worship,* which demonstrates the "correlation between the quality of the country and the quality of its inhabitants": "These Arabs Mohammed was born among are certainly a notable people. Their country itself is notable; the fit habitation for such a race. . . . Such a country is fit for a swift-handed, deep-hearted race of men" (Carlyle, quoted in Burke, 1945/1969, pp. 7-8).

In the realm of relationships, certain behaviors (acts) are expected to follow as a result of the definition of the relationship (scene), as has been interpreted in other terms by researchers of "the rules of relationships" (e.g., Argyle & Henderson, 1984). Thus we would expect two lovers to kiss each other good-bye (act) because that is consistent with the scene (romantic relationship), but we would not expect two business partners to do so. Thus we make the inference about the scene (relationship) on the basis of the acts (behaviors), or we predict the acts on the basis of our knowledge of the scene. Such assumptions run deep in relational literature, and, for instance, considerations of competence in relationships are inherently based on defining a "good match" between scene and act. As is occasionally noted by rules theorists of relationships, rules can be either prescriptive or descriptive, and, whenever such theorists refer to descriptive rules, they are essentially simply defining scenes in this sense, for which Burke thus offers a broader perspective than the above rules theorists.

Burke expounds the ways in which choice of different emphasis on the terms of the ratios can force us to follow through in particular ways and expect particular outcomes:

> By the act-agent ratio, a "democratic people" would continue to perform "democratic acts"; and to do so they would even, if necessary, go to the extent of restoring former conditions most favorable to democracy. By the scene:act ratio, if the "situation" itself is no longer a "democratic" one, even an "essentially democratic" people will abandon democratic ways. (Burke, 1945/1969, pp. 17-18)

Thus, by initial choice of the ratio on which to place emphasis, we as human beings or as scholars influence the ways we examine the nature of relationships. On the basis of such implicit choices, we are constrained in respect of what we include in the analysis or discussion as worthy of study and, just as important, what we choose to exclude or implicitly to ignore. Thus to some extent our explanatory efforts are guided by the frameworks that are selected initially, such as a scene:act ratio, within which to begin our explanatory work. If we set the scene as a scientific one, we will do acts that are "scientific"; for example, we will follow present-day canons of science and look for aspects of the scene or situation that modify acts or behavior. Burke's point, however, is that such initial suppositions are choices and that these choices have subtle effects not only on

our subsequent choices of what to study but also on our interpretations of what we find. He is saying something interesting
not only about relationships but also about our understanding of
relationships. As people who choose a social scientific framework for our activities, for example, we tend to use a meaning
system that organizes things in terms of a preference for scene:act
analysis. As a relational partner, one may tend to have an explanatory style that is initially different from one's partner's; and part
of one's need in relationships is to comprehend not only the
other person's behavior but also the other person's mind and the
framework for his or her choices and explanations.

If used reflexively, the pentad can become a way of looking
both at modes of description or investigation and at influences
on human action. For example, Duck and Pond (1989) discuss
the grammatical ratios of the various aspects of the pentad that
can be used as a framework for looking at relationships. In their
application of the scene:act ratio to relationships between friends,
they discuss the scene as the relationship's current state that
renders "certain actions by the speaker as *determined,* and so
logical, predictable, normative, reasonable, understandable, or
absolved of blame" (p. 31). When a "friend" acts in a way
consistent with the scene, the relationship seems stable, but
otherwise may not. For example, in discussing the origins of
their relationship breakup, persons habitually identify an act by
a partner that was inconsistent with the scene (Harvey et al.,
1989): The partner failed to act like a friend. The ratios can be
employed thus by researchers as a general implicit framework or
theory of motivation about behavior occurring in the context of
the relationship. From the subject's viewpoint, however, it also
provides a context for making attributions about the behavior of
the partner and explaining that behavior. In this way the pentad
provides a description of a naive epistemology of elements considered when making attributions about *acts.* It also makes
claims about the ways humans (whether as scientists or as
themselves) tend to think about causes. We believe that it offers
a way to make researchers more aware of their own frames of
reference and the ways a change of such frames can expand
explanatory power. Also, and in parallel, we believe that it tells

us something about the frameworks that individuals use in resolving, discussing, and negotiating in dyadic relationship processes and also shows the deep structure human framework in which one can come to reassess or reframe one's knowledge of a partner's meaning system.

Choice of Framework and Choice of Explanation

Burke's pentad is itself situated within the larger framework of his theory of dramatism, which discusses the nature of explanation. First, *dramatism* is defined by Burke as "a method of analysis and corresponding critique of terminology designed to show that the most direct route to the study of human relations and human motives is via a methodical inquiry into cycles or clusters of terms and their functions" (1968, p. 445). The "terms" he refers to are the terms of the pentad. This definition locates dramatism as an epistemological method—a way of knowing—in this instance, a way of "knowing about" or studying human social interaction. In 1985, however, Burke argued that dramatism is also an ontological system offering "a general definition about the nature of the human being under any condition or in any stage of history. We are symbol using animals" (p. 24). Whether dramatism is a view of human motivation or a way of studying human behavior has not, as far as we could ascertain, been decided in any consensual fashion. Certainly both sides have solid arguments (see *Communication Quarterly*, Vol. 33, 1985, for a symposium on the subject). Either way, dramatism provides relational researchers with a systematic approach to relationship processes at both the level of understanding of relational activity and at the level of understanding research activity focused on those relationships.

It also has some other important attributes. For instance, Burke does not posit the ratios as deterministic or dictated by the phenomena. He also argues that the terms of the pentad are essentially interactive and that, although one can focus on one term or set of terms for analytic purposes, the influence of other elements is always latent. Although we may, for given research purposes, look only at agent:act or agent:agent or act:act ratios, we should not overlook the fact that these ratios occur in a scene that affects the acts and the agents and the choices that are made about agency or the attributions that are made about purpose. Thus the ratios chosen by observers (whether these are relating human beings or researching scholars) themselves reflect a preference for certain styles of explanation while also influencing the choice of items *included* in the analysis and thought worthy of explanation, as well as those *excluded.* It also may be that, at certain stages of relational development, a preference for some kinds of ratios would prevail over others and that such prevalences can change as a part of the natural course of relational change.

By becoming aware of what they are doing as human beings in operating with ratios and reorganizing meaning by subtle shifting of emphasis on the ratios, therefore, investigators can learn new things about relationships; on the other hand, relational partners can learn new ways of comprehending each other. For example, although norms of reciprocity of self-disclosure would normally be treated as scenes for acts of self-disclosure, Miell (1984) cleverly tested subjects' use of their *knowledge* of such norms and showed that subjects often provoked self-disclosure in others by doing it themselves (Miell shifted emphasis from scene:act to act:agency). We believe that researchers can increase their explanatory abilities by considering phenomena in terms of more that just scene:act ratios. We also suggest that individuals shift their focus from scene:act ratios at the start of relationships (a classic focus for observers, based on just understanding the other person's behavior) to agent:act or scene:agent explanations as they gain a greater understanding of the partner's psychology or meaning systems in different situations and circumstances.

Another important feature of the pentad is that, although Burke often discusses the terms in ratios of two (e.g., scene:act or scene:agent, as illustrated above), he also states that "when a philosopher would feature one of the terms, recreating the others in its image, the original claims of these other terms are nonetheless still in the offing" (Burke, 1945/1969, p. 136) and should you "reduce the terms to any one of them, you will find them branching out again; for no one of them is enough" (Burke,

1945/1969, p. xxi). It is an important suggestion that we can focus on the interaction of a certain amount of terms but must acknowledge the influence of the others. In selecting terms to explain relationships (such as *situation* [scene] vs. *person* [agent]), one can never entirely remove the possibility of their interaction or entirely eliminate other terms' effects.

Although not a complete answer, this interlocking of terms at least acknowledges Montgomery's (1984) case for not trying to break down a situation too simplistically. She maintains that "the complexity associated with multiple dimensions of communication context is compounded because the various dimensions have not been organized into a coherent structure for investigation" (pp. 322-323). We posit that the pentad offers such a structure without losing sight of the complexity associated with any study of social interaction or knowledge of the other person's mental frameworks. The pentad offers the ability to increase the incisiveness of analysis by systematically adding more terms to the investigators' initial ratios and, subsequently, to the focus of the particular study (the pentad can illustrate how we select what to study and how we then explain it). To benefit from the pentad's insights about human symbolic activity, researchers need occasionally to reframe their work and to explore phenomena in terms of other ratios and other terms.

For instance, Shaw and Emery (1987) looked at the effects of family structure (a scene) and marital conflict (which could be argued as an act or a scene, dependent on the study, but is here taken to be a scene) on the child's (agent) adjustment to the scene. So this scene:scene:agent ratio reflects a particular way of conceptualizing the possible interactions and influences that these variables might have on each other: The two scenes influence the agent to act, and that is the causal direction investigated. Thus the researcher who has conceptualized the problem this way will want to look at how family structure and marital conflict affect the child. However, because the ratios are not deterministic, they offer the possibility of also studying how family structure affects marital conflict or how marital conflict affects family structure; this choice would fundamentally alter the sorts of research questions the investigator studies. As another instance, Dunn

(1992) argues that our comprehension of children's development of relational skills would be increased greatly by exploration of the family context (scene) and the ways a child observes and interprets the conversations of parents with the child's sibling(s). The child's knowledge of this scene can become, in our terms, a purpose in the child's behavior (e.g., to restore equality of parental attention), or can affect the child's beliefs about his or her own status as agent.

In parallel with this way of reframing research questions, the pentad also offers us a way to see how an individual could use the terms of the pentad to comprehend a partner's psychological framework and to develop shared meaning with that person. For instance, it appears that the early information that two partners can gather about one another is necessarily scene:act dependent until the point where they know enough about each other to develop a differentiated concept of the other person as agent. Part of getting to know another person well is the development of more complex views of his or her inner psychology as agent. In exploring the development of relationships, one thus would derive the hypothesis that the kinds of knowledge developed by people as they come to share meaning will tend to be less evidently scene:act information and more like agent:act information. Some evidence supports this hypothesis (Berger, 1988b). The general point, however, is that the process of getting to know another person involves movement from reliance on particular ways of describing the other's behavior and reframing explanations in broader terms by using some of the other ratios in the pentad than just scene:act.

This point leads to another aspect of Burke's dramatism: paradox. Paradox is central to dramatism. A paradox discussed by Burke offering rich soil for relational researchers is his definition of *reality*. He has described a reality that is shaped by "human symbolizing based upon how one responds to and labels a situation. Reality in this sense is paradoxical because it is both internal (symbolic) and external (situations)" (Burke, 1985, p. 97). Based on this definition, the "reality" of a relationship for an individual becomes a product, so to speak, of the interaction between the act and the agent. This interaction conceivably could explain the fact, discussed earlier, that reports of two partners in a relationship often differ and lead to claims of them really "being in different relationships" (Acitelli, Chapter 6, this volume; Duck, 1990; Duck & Sants, 1983; Surra & Ridley, 1991). Although the external situation (scene or act) may be the same for both participants, their internal (agent) representations of these acts or scenes may be vastly different. These can be seen, for instance, in studies dealing with how communications and interactions are "punctuated" differently by different partici-pants, each seeing different things as important or "causes" of reaction (Duck, Pond, & Leatham, 1991; Gottman, 1979).

Burke does not see the direction of influence moving in only one direction. He strongly emphasizes the importance of recip-rocal influence and the interactive nature of the various terms on each other, as noted earlier. The agent can be affected by the scene (for instance, siblings can dislike or be envious of one another because of the way the other sibling is treated by parents), but Burke also maintains that there may be reciprocity of influence and that the scene may be affected by the agent (for example, a child may attempt to influence the parents' treatment of siblings by claiming that the other has received favored treatment and that the balance should be redressed). Such reciprocity of influence can be discussed in ways that can alter the emphasis of our research questions in understanding personal relationships. In essence the driving force is the organizing meaning that the researcher attri-butes to the phenomena. It is here, then, that Burke's schema can open new ways of attributing meaning in research.

If we choose to consider the relationship as a scene acting on agents, as well as on acts, we then create numerous possibilities for interaction of the relationship on the participants and, of course, the influence of the participants on the relationship. If we consider the relationship as an entity arising between, but different from, the partners in that relationship, we can see it as an agent. The choice of direction of influence is, to some extent, arbitrary (but not capricious) and represents the same sorts of choices as often are made by different disciplines, as well as by different relational partners, in deciding "who or what is to blame" for relational dissolution (Orbuch, 1992).

The importance of the notion of reciprocal influence in this context relates to our points about disciplinary differences in choice of perspective and implicitly establishes the relativity of such choices and the benefits of their combination in "the big picture." Those who see personal relationships as a scene but place most explanatory emphasis on agency (such as psychology) are likely to seek the effects of persons (agents) on that scene; those who emphasize the influence of scenes (such as sociologists) are likely to look for the effects of scenes on agents. It is a matter of choice. However, recognition of reciprocity of influence is also important and has proven to be a major growth area in the study of parent-child relationships. Recognition of reciprocity of influence has led to work demonstrating that the child's behavior has the potential to influence the parents, as well as vice versa (see Baumrind, 1980, for an extensive discussion, or Glass, Bengston, & Dunham, 1986). That parents influence their children is a commonly accepted concept and one that dominated the literature for several decades, until researchers began to see—as Burke would have suggested—a reciprocal relationship between the two agents in the scene.

Such reciprocity of influence between parents and their children is demonstrated in a study by Dixson (1991), which looked at talk in relationships through transcripts of conversations between parents and their children. In looking at ways parents and their children "do" positive and negative affect, Dixson found that positive affect is demonstrated in conversations through the acceptance by one partner of an invitation to engage in a certain type of communicative behavior from the other partner. So we might characterize these interactions as agent:agent (parent affects child, and child affects parent; cf. Mills & Grusec, 1988), if considering long-term interactions of people's personalities or, within an interaction or conversation, as act:act. In essence such work can be seen to show that focus on only one direction of influence more or less forces us to accept the naive model that meaning is simply transmitted by one person to another (cf. Berger, Chapter 2, this volume). By contrast, later work acknowledging reciprocity of influence suggests instead that this is only a part of the picture; in actuality, meaning is jointly constructed from reciprocal influence (Ross, Cheyne, & Lollis, 1988) and that communication is more than the simple delivery of "messages" from A to B. The act of communication itself is a scene, and the act of communicating transforms meanings and conveys information about relationships over and above the message's literal content (Watzlawick et al., 1967).

Now we come to another key possibility arising from consideration of the pentad and Burke's notions of reciprocal influence: the idea that an agent's acts can affect not only another person's acts but also the agent's own future acts and, ultimately, the agent. Along these lines, Burke talks about the possibilities inherent in the agent:act ratio. Agents perform act, but acts can also influence agents. Burke (1945/1969, p. 16) remarks that acts "can make or remake [the agents] in accordance with their nature," by which he means that individuals continue their individuality by performing acts consistent with it and can change by performing transforming acts. As an example in other terminology, reflected appraisal of the self-concept derives from an agent:agent analysis.

In essence this claim can be developed to argue that a person also is guided by surrounding ideology or relational culture (Wood, 1982) and that even relationships between individuals occur in a social and relational setting that is influential. Thus communication (talk) functions to create and re-create structure in relationships rather than merely to transmit thought from one agent to another. Such a view is consistent with recent work on everyday, routine communication patterns on relationships and relational partners (Duck, Rutt et al., 1991), which suggests that relationships are embodied in talk rather than merely affected by it. Talk and routine behaviors cause changes within the relational partners and/or the relationship itself. In other contexts this sort of argument was made by Hendrick (1988) in his claim that relationships are processes within structures. He states that "each relationship reproduces and transforms the rules that govern it" (p. 435). We would take this one step further and say that relationships are processes *and* structures. Interaction is the relational process for creating, reproducing, and transforming the relational structures (cf. the findings of Duck,

Rutt et al., 1991, that friendship is realized and sustained by everyday talk even when the content of talk is of no relational significance).

Other examples of the ways awareness of one's implicit ratios can influence approaches to a relational research topic or explanation and comprehension within a relationship are provided in several other areas of research. One example is that much of the literature on children and divorce presently looks for "causes" and "influences," especially of divorce on a child's behavior. Recognition of the ways humans use terms, via the pentad, can help clarify and develop this search by helping point out the ways studies could be done slightly differently to manifest the role of talk in meaning construction and sharing of meaning. For instance, in the terms of the pentad, some researchers use divorce as an act, others as a scene. This is an important distinction. Divorce as an act causes a new scene to be constructed: the single-parent family. Thus researchers considering divorce as an act are more likely to concentrate on the ensuing scene:agent or scene:act ratio when looking for causes or influences. Much research has shown that it is not the divorce itself but the ensuing changes that make a difference in a child's adjustment (Hetherington, Stanley-Hagan, & Anderson, 1989). If researchers consider divorce itself as a scene, then these researchers may be incorrectly attributing child adjustment (or other variables) to the act of divorce rather than to the ensuing scene. A child does not *adjust* or *not adjust* to the act of divorce but to the scene of his or her parents *being* divorced, to being the child of divorced parents, and/or to living in a single-parent family. Researchers considering divorce as a scene should be concentrating on how the child adjusts *during the process of* divorce. This distinction may seem trivial, but research that does not discriminate between divorce as an act and divorce as a scene or ensuing process has caused contradictory results to be attributed to divorce (Duck, 1982), and the different results have very different practical implications. Research that attributes children's problems to divorce as an act may influence people to stay married "because of the children" because, according to such research, the act of divorce itself dooms children.

More recently, however, researchers have redefined divorce as an act leading to a new scene and have concentrated on looking at the effects of this new scene (e.g., single-parent family). Such researchers have found that variations in this scene (not in divorce itself), such as quality of parent-child relationships and changes in life-style, account for variations in child adjustment (Amato, 1986; Hetherington et al., 1989; Peterson & Zill, 1986). This approach redirects our thinking to allow for the possibility that children of divorced parents can adjust and grow up "normally." Thus, by recognition of the elements of the pentad, researchers can clarify for themselves and others new emphases in the exploration of the phenomena they are studying.

Applications to Future Research

We have argued that researchers should recognize fully the ways human usage of symbols affects the other activities they engage in. We have claimed also that Burke's pentad, being an analysis of human symbol usage, offers us a way of understanding such activity in relationships. We also now develop the further claim that application of the pentad to the research endeavor produces some exciting new ways of reconceptualizing phenomena and research questions, as well as elucidating differences in the approaches of different researchers. Application produces these effects by focusing research away from reliance on only the scene:act ratio (which is not to argue that this focus should be abandoned and makes no contribution to knowledge; merely it is to argue that it can be supplemented usefully by other foci derived from the pentad).

The above analysis can be applied to several issues that are central to the development of the field of research into personal relationships. For instance, we have alluded to the need to understand how emphasis on different elements of the pentad can change the ways researchers view topics in relationship research. We have emphasized other choices in the context of discussions of meaning. We believe there are many examples of ways the above analysis can help redirect research by making researchers more reflective about how their research questions are framed. Essentially our task is to reinterpret old concepts by using "effort after personal meaning" and "sharing of meaning" as the central themes and to propose hypotheses applicable to each area in this new light by shifting emphasis to other parts of the pentad (e.g., from act to scene or to agency). Because we already have given several examples from the developmental and the divorce literatures, we now focus on social psychological topics.

Adult Attachment Styles (Hazan & Shaver, 1987). The central attachment concept of working models readily translates into the above analysis because working models arise from the same source that we claim for everything else—namely, effort after meaning. For the child as for the adult, the *meaning* of others' treatment of oneself is what gives it formative significance, not the behavior per se (cf. Dunn, 1992). Infants react, accordingly, to the meanings that they attach to behavior, not to the behavior per se, which is why infants react differently to the same behavior at different ages as they develop "better" frames of reference for understanding it and as they elaborate the language concepts to interpret it and generalize it to other situations. They then develop a working model or attachment style that reflects the meaning that they think they have to other people and that other people have to the child. Thus an *attachment style* is a reification of a meaning system focused on others and the infant's beliefs about its meaning to others. In situations where subjects' meaning to others can be manipulated (where the scene can be manipulated), we predict that the least stable styles (anxious) would be most likely to change and give variable readings. Rather as Perlman and Serbin (1984) showed that loneliness increases after self-esteem or self-worth (which here is reinterpreted to embody one's meaning to oneself and to others) is diminished (e.g., after a defeat at racquetball), so too we predict that anxious people would become more anxious when authority figures denigrate them and less anxious when authority figures praise them, while secure people will not. It is not a matter of definition of style, but an instructive case of where symbol and meaning influence reactions within a style, if one changes the notion of style from agent to scene.

Love Styles (Hendrick & Hendrick, 1988). Love styles also are cases in which individuals essentially are attaching different meanings and weight to different symbolic forms. For those who show predominance of one given style element, the characteristics associated with that style of love have a particularly strong meaning, in the circumstances when they are measured. We believe that the patterns of such profiles could be shown to change as a relationship (scene) changes in form if one sees the relationships as a scene. In line with rhetorical principles, persons reporting on love to one audience or in one situation may not do it in precisely the same manner each time because the scene is thereby altered. Thus, in situations of passionate excitement, an investigator who interrupts the activity is likely to find more erotic items checked than is one who overhears a discussion of a proposal of marriage where pragma will rule the day. Attention to scene would lead us to predict that speakers and lovers can adjust their message to the rhetorical situation just as humans do everywhere else. Beyond this, the pentad offers other ways to explore the phenomenon. For instance, with the agent:act ratio, we would predict that persons (agents) with a ludic style would produce behaviors (acts) different from persons with a manic style when the scene is held constant. Leading from this and focusing on the notion of reciprocal influence, we also might explore the possibility of an agent changing his or her love style if the scene (relationship) consistently calls for a type of behavior (act) inconsistent with the previous love style. As discussed above, the scene would take precedence here over the agents' usual habits and might "cause" a change in the agents (so that the acts "remake the agents in the accordance with their nature," as Burke (1945/1969, p. 16) puts it). Thus one could move from a scene:act interpretation to an act:agent interaction.

Self-Disclosure (Derlega & Winstead, 1986). The importance of the act of intimate disclosure is not *of itself* but what it means in terms of relational value to the other and interpretation of other within the scene or context (social, cultural, relational, personal) where it occurs. For example, reciprocity of disclosure would be predicted to occur in cases where individuals are constrained by the scene to use cultural generalities (e.g., when they are meeting a stranger). However, one would predict from our position that such reciprocity would be less obvious in cases of developed relationships where the meaning of the relationship to the participants (scene, agency) would be of a different hue. This is hardly a new proposal, but the pentad could be used to derive it and the further prediction that manipulation of the scene of the relationship (e.g., by emphasizing the importance of the *display* of friendship) would likewise affect the agency by which subjects convey their feelings. Because most laboratory work on self-disclosure adopts a standard scene (the laboratory and the "audience" of researchers), it is likely that some of the findings on self-disclosure can be explained as due to that. In other scenes (e.g., daily life) self-disclosure is provoked by other agencies and, in fact, occurs far less frequently than most laboratory research would lead one to expect (some 2% of talk in two separate studies into this issue: Dindia, Fitzpatrick, & Kenny, 1989; and Duck, Rutt et al., 1991).

We believe that we could give a similar sort of analysis of such important constructs in this field as *investment, communal relationships,* and *exchange.* The basic point would be the same: that such items are not important for what their commonly held meaning is, but for the personal meaning it has to the subject in the relevant scene at the time of measurement (with which common meaning will necessarily interact and overlap on occasion). In broad terms we argue that these items do not matter only as agents in relationships but also as scenes. Indeed CL and CL$_{ALT}$ are both disguised assessments of personal meanings about scenes. Although much work on exchange theory, for instance, has focused on the extraction of the common and culturally shared understanding of the value of exchanges out of other contexts, the work of Mills and Clark (1982) on communal relationships essentially focuses researchers on the nature of a different scene and its effects on agency, for example. Interestingly the research produces findings about the nature of exchange and the power of exchange variables that are quite different from the findings previously observed in work on exchange.

Discrepancies in the social support literature are equally accountable in terms of personal meanings. Albrecht and Halsey (in press) recently explored a notion of "perceptual congruence" in social support that has many similarities to the present idea. *Social support* conveys a message that one is personally valued, and this meaning constitutes a scene for subsequent relational activity. Studies telling us that different meanings are attributed to social support by different individuals (Lehman, Ellard, & Wortman, 1986) essentially are indicating that individuals attribute different scenic meanings to types and forms of support, just as they do to personal crises requiring support. Thus they show us that the personal perception of the scene of support is the determinant of action for the person concerned, and so it becomes an agent.

Conclusion

Brain surgeons face an interesting dilemma: Brain tumors can be destroyed by a given amount of radiation, but the amount required can also fry all of the healthy brain cells in its track from the skull to the tumor. A recent advance has come from the introduction of laser treatment that allows four or five different tracks of radiation of intermediate strength to pass harmlessly through the healthy cells and converge on the tumor where their combined effect is sufficient to destroy the tumor without destroying the healthy cells on the way. In a sense, interdisciplinary work on relationships (or awareness of possible ratios for conceptualizing problems) is like this, in that it is the intersection of the work that is more valuable than a large dose of only one discipline's contribution (or ratio) on its own. The activities of relational partners in creating new meaning from the intersection of two individual and personal meaning systems are also somewhat like this.

Disciplines, authors, editors, and scholars are alike in one key respect: They have many different ways of looking at "the same" phenomenon, just as do persons in relationships. Our question should not be which perspective is best or should rule the others imperialistically (because any decisions about that matter would depend on the types of problem that we think we "should" be trying to answer and that very precisely begs the question). Nor should we be looking to see which partner's view is "correct." Rather our emphasis should be on how a greater knowledge of each discipline contributes information that better develops our work and on the ways the perspectives of relational partners intersect as they continually comprehend one another. We believe that the concepts offered in Burke's pentad actually help us understand some general principles that the several disciplines have each been uncovering in different ways and also cast light on the frameworks within which partners comprehend one another.

This volume initiates a series that makes some choices about the ways we should look at relationships. The series emphasizes that elements of relationship processes can be crystallized into various groups (volumes) for some useful, but not exhaustive, purposes or that they can be explored and understood in other crystallized clumps (disciplines). Such clumps are the results of human choices, not of natural order, we contend. Thus this volume and the series that it initiates together offer one style for interpreting major themes in this growing field in a way that, we believe, emphasizes the similarities of human style rather than the differences of dogma.

References

Abbey, A. (1982). Sex differences in attributions for friendly behavior: Do males misperceive females' friendliness? *Journal of Personality and Social Psychology, 42,* 830-838.

Abbott, E. A. (1884). *Flatland: A romance of many dimensions.* London: Seeley.

Abbott, V., & Black, J. B. (1986). Goal-related inferences in comprehension. In J. A. Galambos, R. P. Abelson, & J. B. Black (Eds.), *Knowledge structures* (pp. 123-142). Hillsdale, NJ: Lawrence Erlbaum.

Abelson, R. P. (1981). Psychological status of the script concept. *American Psychologist, 36,* 715-729.

Acitelli, L. K. (1986). The influence of relationship awareness on perceived marital satisfaction and stability. *Dissertation Abstracts International, 47,* (10-B), 4340. University Microfilms Inc.

Acitelli, L. K. (1988). When spouses talk to each other about their relationship. *Journal of Social and Personal Relationships, 5,* 185-199.

Acitelli, L. K. (1992). Gender differences in relationship awareness and marital satisfaction among young married couples. *Personality and Social Psychology Bulletin, 18,* 102-110.

Acitelli, L. K., & Antonucci, T. C. (1991, May). *Perceptions of social support in older married couples.* Paper presented at the Third International Conference on Personal Relationships, Normal, IL.

Acitelli, L. K., Douvan, E., & Veroff, J. (1993). Perceptions of conflict in the first year of marriage: How important are similarity and understanding? *Journal of Social and Personal Relationships, 10,* 5-19.

Acitelli, L. K., & Duck, S. W. (1987). Intimacy as the proverbial elephant. In D. Perlman & S. W. Duck (Eds.), *Intimate relationships: Development, dynamics and deterioration* (pp. 297-308). Beverly Hills, CA: Sage.

Acitelli, L. K., & Holmberg, D. (1993). Reflecting on relationships: The role of thoughts and memories. In W. Jones & D. Perlman (Eds.), *Advances in personal relationships* (pp. 71-100). London: Jessica Kingsley.

Acitelli, L. K., & Veroff, J. (1992, October). *Does taking a relationship perspective increase marital well-being?* Paper presented at the Seventh Annual Preconference on Close Relationships, Society of Experimental Social Psychologists, San Antonio, TX.

Albrecht, T. L., & Halsey, J. (in press). Mutual support in mixed status relationships. *Journal of Social and Personal Relationships.*

Allen, J. L., & Perrault, C. R. (1980). Analyzing intention in utterances. *Artificial Intelligence, 15,* 143-178.

Altman, I., & Taylor, D. S. (1973). *Social penetration: The development of interpersonal relationships.* New York: Holt, Rinehart & Winston.

Altman, I., Vinsel, A., & Brown, B. (1981). Dialectic conceptions in social psychology: An application to social penetration and privacy regulation. In L. Berkowitz (Ed.), *Advances in experimental social psychology* (Vol. 14, pp. 76-100). New York: Academic Press.

Amato, P. R. (1986). Marital conflict, the parent-child relationship and child self-esteem. *Family Relations, 35,* 403-410.

Andersen, J. F., Andersen, P. A., & Lustig, M. W. (1987). Opposite sex touch avoidance: A national replication and extension. *Journal of Nonverbal Behavior, 11,* 89-109.

Andersen, K., & Clevenger, T., Jr. (1963). A summary of experimental research in ethos. *Speech Monographs, 30,* 59-78.

Andersen, P. A. (1984, April). *An arousal-valence model of nonverbal immediacy exchange.* Paper presented at the Annual Meeting of the Central States Speech Association, Chicago, IL.

Andersen, P. A. (1985). Nonverbal immediacy in interpersonal communication. In A. W. Siegman & S. Feldstein (Eds.), *Multichannel integrations of nonverbal behavior* (pp. 1-36). Hillsdale, NJ: Lawrence Erlbaum.

Andersen, P. A. (1986). Consciousness, cognition, and communication. *Western Journal of Speech Communication, 50,* 87-101.

Andersen, P. A. (1987). The trait debate: A critical examination of the individual differences paradigm in interpersonal communication. In B. Dervin & M. J. Voigt (Eds.), *Progress in communication sciences* (Vol. 8, pp. 47-82). Norwood, NJ: Ablex.

Andersen, P. A. (1988). Explaining intercultural differences in nonverbal communication. In L. A. Samovar & R. E. Porter (Eds.), *Intercultural communication: A reader* (pp. 272-281). Belmont, CA: Wadsworth.

Andersen, P. A. (1989, May). *A cognitive valence theory of intimate communication.* Paper presented at the Second Conference of the International Network on Personal Relationship, University of Iowa, Iowa City, IA.

Andersen, P. A. (1992, July). *Excessive intimacy: An account analysis of behaviors, cognitive schemata, affect, and rational outcomes.* Paper presented at the 6th International Conference on Personal Relationships, Orono, Maine.

Andersen, P. A. (in press). *Beside language: Nonverbal communication in interpersonal interaction.* Newbury Park, CA: Sage.

Andersen, P. A., & Coussoule, A. R. (1980). The perceptual world of the communication apprehensive: The effect of communication on interpersonal perception. *Communication Quarterly, 28,* 44-54.

Andersen, P. A., & Leibowitz, K. (1978). The development and nature of the construct touch avoidance. *Environmental Psychology and Nonverbal Behavior, 3,* 89-106.

Andersen, P. A., Lustig, M. W., & Andersen, J. F. (1987). Regional patterns of communication in the United States: A theoretical perspective. *Communication Monographs, 54,* 128-144.

Andersen, P. A., Lustig, M. W., & Andersen, J. F. (1990). Changes in latitude, changes in attitude: The relationship between climate and interpersonal communication predispositions. *Communication Quarterly, 38,* 291-311.

Andersen, P. A., & Sull, K. K. (1985). Out of touch, out of reach: Tactile predispositions as predictors of interpersonal distance. *Western Journal of Speech Communication, 49,* 57-72.

Anderson, J. R. (1983). *The architecture of cognition.* Cambridge, MA: Harvard University Press.

Antaki, C. (1987). Performed and unperformable: A guide to accounts of relationships. In R. Burnett, P. McGee, & D. Clarke (Eds.), *Accounting for relationships* (pp. 97-113). New York: Methuen.

Argyle, M., & Dean, J. (1966). Eye contact, distance, and affiliation. *Sociometry, 28,* 289-304.

Argyle, M., & Henderson, M. (1984). The rules of friendship. *Journal of Social and Personal Relationships, 1,* 211-237.

Argyle, M., & Henderson, M. (1985). The rules of relationships. In S. W. Duck & D. Perlman (Eds.), *Understanding personal relationships: An interdisciplinary approach* (pp. 63-84). Beverly Hills, CA: Sage.

Aron, A., & Westbay, L. (1991). *Latent structure of love-prototype features and its relation to Erikson's intimacy stage.* Unpublished manuscript, University of California, Santa Cruz.

Askham, J. (1981). Telling stories. *Sociological Review, 30,* 555-573.

Baars, B. J. (1983). Conscious contents provide the nervous system with coherent, global information. In R. J. Davidson, G. E. Schwartz, & D. Shapiro (Eds.), *Consciousness and self-regulation: Advances in research* (Vol. 3, pp. 41-79). New York: Plenum.

Badzinski, D. M. (1986, November). *Towards understanding the effects of mood on interaction processes.* Paper presented to the Speech Communication Association, Chicago, IL.

Baldwin, M. W. (in press). Relational schemas and the processing of social information. *Psychological Bulletin.*

Bargh, J. A. (1989). Conditional automaticity: Varieties of automatic influence in social perception and cognition. In J. S. Uleman & J. A. Bargh (Eds.), *Unintended thought* (pp. 3-51). New York: Guilford.

Bargh, J. A., & Tota, M. E. (1988). Context-dependent automatic processing in depression: Accessibility of negative constructs with regard to self but not to others. *Journal of Personality and Social Psychology, 54,* 925-939.

Bartlett, F. (1932). *Remembering.* Cambridge, UK: Cambridge University Press.

Bateson, G. (1972). *Steps to an ecology of mind.* New York: Ballantine.

Baucom, D. H., Epstein, N., Sayers, S., & Sher, T. G. (1989). The role of cognitions in marital relationships: Definitional, methodological, and conceptual issues. *Journal of Consulting and Clinical Psychology, 57,* 31-38.

Baumrind, D. (1980). New directions in socialization research. *American Psychologist, 35*(7), 639-652.

Bavelas, J. B., Black, A., Chavel, N., & Mullett, J. (1990). *Equivocal communication.* Newbury Park, CA: Sage.

Baxter, L. A. (1982). Strategies for ending relationships: Two studies. *Western Journal of Speech Communication, 46,* 223-241.

Baxter, L. A. (1985). Accomplishing relationship disengagement. In S. W. Duck & D. Perlman (Eds.), *Understanding personal relationship: An interdisciplinary approach* (pp. 243-265). Beverly Hills, CA: Sage.

Baxter, L. A. (1986). Gender differences in the heterosexual relationship rules embedded in break-up accounts. *Journal of Social and Personal Relationships, 3,* 289-306.

Baxter, L. A. (1987a). Communication and cognition in the relationship process. In R. Burnett, P. McGhee, & D. D. Clarke (Eds.), *Accounting for relationships: Explanation, representation and knowledge* (pp. 192-212). New York: Methuen.

Baxter, L. A. (1987b). Symbols of relationship identity in relationship cultures. *Journal of Social and Personal Relationships, 4,* 261-279.

Baxter, L. A. (1988). A dialectical perspective on communication strategies in relationship development. In S. W. Duck (Ed.), with D. F. Hay, S. E. Hobfoll, W. Ickes, & B. Montgomery, *Handbook of personal relationships* (pp. 257-273). New York: John Wiley.

Baxter, L. A. (1990). Dialectical contradictions in relationship development. *Journal of Social and Personal Relationships, 7,* 69-88.

Baxter, L. A. (1992). Root metaphors in accounts of developing romantic relationships. *Journal of Social and Personal Relationships, 9,* 253-275.

Baxter, L. A. (in press). Thinking dialogically about communication in personal relationships. In R. L. Conville (Ed.), *Structures of interpretation.* Norwood, NJ: Ablex.

Baxter, L. A., & Bullis, C. (1986). Turning points in developing romantic relationships. *Human Communications Research, 12,* 469-493.

Baxter, L. A., & Wilmot, W. W. (1984). Secret tests: Social strategies for acquiring information about the state of the relationship. *Human Communication Research, 11,* 171-201.

Bell, R. A., Buerkel-Rothfuss, N. L., & Gore, K. E. (1987). "Did you bring the yarmulke for the cabbage patch kid?": The idiomatic communication of young lovers. *Human Communication Research, 14,* 47-67.

Bell, R. A., & Daly, J. A. (1984). The affinity-seeking function of communication. *Communication Monographs, 51,* 91-115.

Bell, R. A., & Healy, J. G. (1992). Idiomatic communication and interpersonal solidarity in friends' relational culture. *Human Communication Research, 18,* 307-335.

Bem, D. J. (1972). Self-perception theory. In L. Berkowitz (Ed.), *Advances in experimental social psychology* (Vol. 6, pp. 1-62). New York: Academic Press.

Berg, J. H. (1984). The development of friendship between roommates. *Journal of Personality and Social Psychology, 46,* 346-356.

Berger, C. R. (1979). Beyond initial interaction: Uncertainty, understanding, and the development of interpersonal relationships. In H. Giles & R. St. Clair (Eds.), *Language and social psychology* (pp. 122-144). Oxford, UK: Basil Blackwell.

Berger, C. R. (1987). Communicating under uncertainty. In M. E. Roloff & G. R. Miller (Eds.), *Interpersonal processes: New directions in communication research* (pp. 39-62). Newbury Park, CA: Sage.

Berger, C. R. (1988a). Planning, affect, and social action generation. In L. Donohew, H. E. Sypher, & E. T. Higgins (Eds.), *Communication, social cognition, and affect* (pp. 93-116). Hillsdale, NJ: Lawrence Erlbaum.

Berger, C. R. (1988b). Uncertainty and information exchange in developing relationships. In S. W. Duck (Ed.), *Handbook of personal relationships* (pp. 239-255). New York: John Wiley.

Berger, C. R. (in press). A plan-based approach to strategic communication. In D. E. Hewes (Ed.), *Cognitive bases of interpersonal communication.* Hillsdale, NJ: Lawrence Erlbaum.

Berger, C. R., & Bell, R. A. (1988). Plans and the initiation of social relationships. *Human Communication Research, 15,* 217-235.

Berger, C. R., & Bradac, J. J. (1982). *Language and social knowledge: Uncertainty in interpersonal relations.* London: E. E. Arnold.

Berger, C. R., & Calabrese, R. J. (1975). Some explorations in initial interaction and beyond: Toward a developmental theory of interpersonal communication. *Human Communication Research, 1,* 99-112.

Berger, C. R., & diBattista, P. (1992). Information-seeking and plan elaboration: What do you need to know to know what to do? *Communication Monographs, 59,* 368-387.

Berger, C. R., & Jordan, J. M. (1992). Planning sources, planning difficulty, and verbal fluency. *Communication Monographs, 59, 130-149.*

Berger, C. R., Karol, S. H., & Jordan, J. M. (1989). When a lot of knowledge is a dangerous thing: The debilitating effects of plan complexity on verbal fluency. *Human Communication Research, 16,* 91-119.

Berger, C. R., & Kellermann, K. (1983). To ask or not to ask: Is that a question? In R. N. Bostrom (Ed.), *Communication yearbook 7* (pp. 342-368). Beverly Hills, CA: Sage.

Berger, C. R., & Kellermann, K. (1986, May). *Goal incompatibility and social action: The best laid plans of mice and men often go astray.* Paper presented at the Annual Convention of the International Communication Association, San Francisco, CA.

Berger, C. R., & Kellermann, K. (1989). Personal opacity and social information gathering: Explorations in strategic communication. *Communication Research, 16,* 314-351.

Berger, C. R., & Kellermann, K. (in press). Acquiring social information. In J. Daly & J. Wiemann (Eds.), *Communicating strategically.* Hillsdale, NJ: Lawrence Erlbaum.

Berger, C. R., & Roloff, M. E. (1982). Thinking about friends and lovers: Social cognition and relational trajectories. In M. E. Roloff & C. R. Berger (Eds.), *Social cognition and communication* (pp. 151-192). Beverly Hills, CA: Sage.

Berger, P., & Kellner, H. (1964). Marriage and the construction of social reality. *Diogenes, 46,* 1-24.

Bernal, G., & Baker, J. (1979). Toward a metacommunicational framework of couple interaction. *Family Process, 18,* 293-302.

Bernard, J. (1972). *The future of marriage.* New York: World.

Berscheid, E. (1983). Emotion. In H. H. Kelley, E. Berscheid, A. Christensen, J. Harvey, T. Huston, G. Levinger, E. McClintock, A. Peplau, & D. Peterson (Eds.), *Close relationships* (pp. 110-168). San Francisco: Freeman.

Berscheid, E., & Walster [Hatfield], E. (1969). *Interpersonal attraction.* Reading, MA: Addison-Wesley.

Berscheid, E., & Walster [Hatfield], E. (1978). *Interpersonal attraction* (2nd ed.) Reading, MA: Addison-Wesley.

Billig, M. (1987). *Arguing and thinking: A rhetorical approach to social psychology.* Cambridge, UK: Cambridge University Press.

Black, J. B., & Bower, G. H. (1979). Episodes as chunks in narrative memory. *Journal of Verbal Learning and Verbal Behavior, 18,* 309-318.

Black, J. B., & Bower, G. H. (1980). Story understanding as problem solving. *Poetics, 9,* 223-250.

Blankenship, V., Hnat, S., Hess, T., & Brown, D. R. (1984). Reciprocal interaction and similarity of personality attributes. *Journal of Social and Personal Relationships, 1,* 415-432.

Bochner, A. (1984). The functions of human communication in interpersonal bonding. In C. Arnold & J. Bowers (Eds.), *Handbook of rhetorical and communication theory* (pp. 544-621). Boston: Allyn & Bacon.

Boster, F., & Stiff, J. B. (1984). Compliance-gaining message selection behavior. *Human Communication Research, 10,* 539-556.

Bower, G. H., Black, J. B., & Turner, T. J. (1979). Scripts in memory for text. *Cognitive Psychology, 11,* 177-200.

Bowlby, J. (1988). *A secure base: Parent-child attachment and healthy human development.* New York: Basic Books.

Bradbury, T. N., & Fincham, F. D. (1988). Individual difference variables in close relationships: A contextual model of marriage as an integrative framework. *Journal of Personality and Social Psychology, 54,* 713-721.

Bradbury, T. N., & Fincham, F. D. (1989). Behavior and satisfaction in marriage: Prospective meditating processes. In C. Hendrick (Ed.), *Review of personality and social psychology, Vol 10: Close relationships* (pp. 119-143). Newbury Park, CA: Sage.

Bradbury, T. N., & Fincham, F. D. (1990). Attributions in marriage: Review and critique. *Psychological Bulletin, 107,* 3-33.

Brand, M. (1984). *Intending and acting: Toward a naturalized theory of action.* Cambridge: MIT Press.

Bratman, M. E. (1987). *Intention, plans, and practical reason.* Cambridge, MA: Harvard University Press.

Bratman, M. E. (1990). What is intention? In P. R. Cohen, J. Morgan, & M. E. Pollack (Eds.), *Intentions in communication* (pp. 15-31). Cambridge: MIT Press.

Brown, P., & Levinson, S. C. (1978). Universals in language usage: Politeness phenomena. In E. E. Goody (Ed.), *Questions and politeness* (pp. 56-289). Cambridge, UK: Cambridge University Press.

Bruce, B., & Newman, D. (1978). Interacting plans. *Cognitive Science, 2,* 195-233.

Burgoon, J. K. (1983). Nonverbal violations of expectations. In J. M. Wiemann & R. P. Harrison (Eds.), *Nonverbal interaction* (pp. 77-111). Beverly Hills, CA: Sage.

Burgoon, J. K., Buller, D. B., & Woodall, W. G. (1989). *Nonverbal communication: The unspoken dialogue.* New York: Harper & Row.

Burgoon, J. K., & Jones, S. B. (1976). Toward a theory of personal space expectations and their violations. *Human Communication Research, 2,* 131-146.

Burgoon, J. K., & Koper, R. J. (1984). Nonverbal and relational communication associated with reticence. *Human Communication Research, 10,* 601-626.

Burgoon, J. K., Parrott, R., LePoire, B. A., Kelley, D., Walther, J. B., & Penny, D. (1989). Maintaining and restoring privacy through communication in different types of relationships. *Journal of Social and Personal Relationships, 6,* 131-158.

Burke, K. (1945/1969). *A grammar of motives.* Berkeley: University of California Press.

Burke, K. (1962). *A grammar of motives and a rhetoric of motives.* Cleveland: World.

Burke, K. (1966). *Language as symbolic action: Essays on life, literature and method.* Berkeley: University of California Press.

Burke, K. (1968). Dramatism. In D. L. Suis (Ed.), *International encyclopedia of the social sciences.* New York: Free Press.

Burke, K. (1985). Commentary. In Brock, B. L., Burke, K. L., Burgess, P. G., & Simons, H. W. (1985). Dramatism as ontology or epistemology: A symposium. *Communication Quarterly, 33,* 17-33.

Burleson, B. R. (1984). Age, social-cognitive development, and the use of comforting strategies. *Communication Monographs, 51,* 140-153.

Burleson, B. R., & Samter, W. (1985). Consistencies in theoretical and naive evaluations of comforting messages. *Communication Monographs, 52,* 103-123.

Burnett, R. (1984, July). *Thinking and communicating about personal relationships: Some sex differences.* Paper presented at the Second International Conference on Personal Relationships, Madison, WI.

Burnett, R. (1986). *Conceptualisations of personal relationships.* Unpublished doctoral dissertation, Oxford University.

Burnett, R. (1987). Reflection in personal relationships. In R. Burnett, P. McGhee, & D. C. Clarke (Eds.), *Accounting for relationships: Explanation, representation and knowledge* (pp. 74-93). New York: Methuen.

Buss, D. M. (1988). The evolutionary biology of love. In R. J. Sternberg & M. L. Barnes (Eds.), *The psychology of love* (pp. 100-118). New Haven, CT: Yale University Press.

Button, C. M., & Collier, D. R. (1991, June). *A comparison of people's concepts of love and romantic love.* Paper presented at the Canadian Psychological Association Conference, Calgary, Alberta.

Byrne, D., & Blaylock, B. (1963). Similarity and assumed similarity of attitudes between husbands and wives. *Journal of Abnormal and Social Psychology, 6,* 636-640.

Cahill, A., & Mitchell, D. C. (1987). Plans and goals in story comprehension. In R. G. Reilly (Ed.), *Communication failure in dialogue and discourse: Detection and repair processes* (pp. 257-268). New York: Elsevier.

Cappella, J. N. (1988). Personal relationships, soical relationships, and patterns of interaction. In S. W. Duck (Ed.), with D. F. Hay, S. E. Hobfoll, W. Ickes, & B. Montgomery, *Handbook of personal relationships* (pp. 323-342). New York: John Wiley.

Cappella, J. N., & Greene, J. O. (1982). A discrepancy-arousal explanation of mutual influence in expressive behavior for adult and infant-adult interaction. *Communication Monographs, 49,* 89-114.

Carberry, S. (1990). *Plan recognition in natural language dialogue.* Cambridge: MIT Press.

Carbonell, J. G. (1981). Counterplanning: A strategy-based model of adversary planning in real-world situations. *Artificial Intelligence, 16,* 295-329.

Card, O. S. (1991). A sepulchre of songs. In *Maps in a mirror: The short fiction of Orson Scott Card.* New York: Tom Doherty.

Carlston, D. E. (1980). Events, inferences and impression formation. In R. Hastie, T. M. Ostrom, E. B. Ebbesen, R. S. Wyer Jr., D. L. Hamilton, & D. E. Carlston (Eds.), *Person memory: The cognitive bias of social perception* (pp. 84-119). Hillsdale, NJ: Lawrence Erlbaum.

Cate, R. M. (1991, May). *Relationship thinking: A measure and some initial studies.* Paper presented at the Third International Network Conference on Personal Relationships, Normal, IL.

Cate, R. M., Koval, J. E., & Lloyd, S. A. (1989). *The measurement of relationship consciousness.* Unpublished manuscript.

Cheek, J. M., & Buss, A. H. (1981). Shyness and sociability. *Journal of Personality and Social Psychology, 41,* 330-339.

Chelune, G. J., Robison, J. T., & Kammar, M. J. (1984). A cognitive interactional model of intimate relationships. In V. Derlega (Ed.), *Communication, intimacy, and close relationships* (pp. 11-40). New York: Academic Press.

Cline, R. J. W. (1989). The politics of intimacy: Costs and benefits determining disclosure intimacy in male-female dyads. *Journal of Social and Personal Relationships, 6,* 5-20.

Cloven, D. H., & Roloff, M. E. (1991). Sense-making activities and interpersonal conflict: Communicative cures for the mulling blues. *Western Journal of Speech Communication, 55,* 134-158.

Cody, M. (1982). A typology of disengagement strategies and an examination of the role intimacy, reactions to inequity, and behavioral problems play in strategy selection. *Communication Monographs, 49,* 148-170.

Cody, M. J., & McLaughlin, M. L. (1985). The situation as a construct in communication research. In M. L. Knapp & G. R. Miller (Eds.), *Handbook of interpersonal communication* (pp. 263-312). Beverly Hills, CA: Sage.

Cody, M. J., McLaughlin, M. L., & Jordan, W. J. (1980). A multidimensional scaling of three sets of compliance-gaining strategies. *Communication Quarterly, 28,* 34-46.

Cody, M. J., McLaughlin, M. L., & Schneider, M. J. (1981). The impact of relational consequences and intimacy on the selection of interpersonal persuasion tactics: A reanalysis. *Communication Quarterly, 29,* 91-106.

Cohen, P. R., Morgan, J., & Pollack, M. E. (1990). *Intentions in communication.* Cambridge: MIT Press.

Cohen, P. R., & Perrault, C. R. (1979). Elements of a plan-based theory of speech acts. *Cognitive Science, 3,* 177-212.

Coleman, S. (1977). A developmental stage hypothesis for non-marital dyadic relationships. *Journal of Marriage and the Family, 3,* 71-76.

Contarello, A., & Volpato, C. (1991). Images of friendship: Literary depictions through the ages. *Journal of Social and Personal Relationships, 8,* 49-75.

Cozby, P. C. (1973). Self-disclosure: A literature review. *Psychological Bulletin, 79,* 73-91.

Crockett, W. H. (1965). Cognitive complexity and impression formation. In B. A. Maher (Ed.), *Progress in experimental personality research* (2nd ed., pp. 47-90). New York: Academic Press.

Cronen, V. E., Pearce, W. B., & Snavely, L. M. (1979). A theory of rule structure and types of episodes and a study of perceived enmeshments in undesired repetitive patterns (URPS). In D. Nimmo (Ed.), *Communication yearbook* (Vol. 3, pp. 225-240). New Brunswick, NJ: Transaction Books.

Cupach, W. R., & Metts, S. (1986). Dating and marital accounts of why a relationship ended. *Communication Monographs, 53,* 311-334.

Davis, K. E., & Todd, M. J. (1982). Friendship and love relationships. In K. E. Davis (Ed.), *Advances in descriptive psychology* (Vol. 2, pp. 79-122). Greenwich, CT: JAI.

deCharm, R. (1968). *Personal causation: The internal affective determinants of behavior.* New York: Academic Press.

Delia, J. (1980). Some tentative thoughts concerning the study of interpersonal relationships and their development. *Western Journal of Speech Communication, 44,* 97-103.

Depner, C. E., & Ingersoll-Dayton, B. (1985). Conjugal social support: Patterns in later life. *Journal of Gerontology, 40,* 761-766.

Derlega, V. J. (1984). Self-disclosure and intimate relationships. In V. J. Derlega (Ed.), *Communication, intimacy and close relationships* (pp. 1-9). New York: Academic Press.

Derlega, V. J., Wilson, M., & Chaiken, D. L. (1976). Friendship and disclosure reciprocity. *Journal of Personality and Social Psychology, 34,* 578-582.

Derlega, V. J., & Winstead, B. A. (1986). *Friendship and social interaction.* New York: Springer Verlag.

deTurck, M. A. (1985). A transactional analysis of compliance-gaining behavior: Effects of noncompliance, relational contexts, and actors' gender. *Human Communication Research, 12,* 54-78.

Dillard, J. P. (1990). The nature and substance of goals in tactical communication. In M. J. Cody & M. L. McLaughlin (Eds.), *The psychology of tactical communication* (pp. 70-90). Clevedon: Multilingual Matters.

Dillard, J. P., & Burgoon, M. (1985). Situational influences on the selection of compliance-gaining messages: Two tests of the Cody-McLaughlin typology. *Communication Monographs, 52,* 289-304.

Dindia, K., Fitzpatrick, M. A., & Kenny, D. A. (1989, May). *Self disclosure in spouse and stranger interaction: A social relations analysis.* Paper presented at the International Communication Association, New Orleans, LA.

Dion, K. K., & Dion, K. L. (1985). Personality, gender, and the phenomenology of romantic love. In P. Shaver (Ed.), *Review of personality and social psychology* (Vol. 6, pp. 209-239). Beverly Hills, CA: Sage.

Dixson, M. D. (1991, May). *Mothers and their sons: Everyday communication as an indicator and correlate of relationship satisfaction.* Paper presented at the Annual Convention of the International Communication Association, Chicago, IL.

Dornbusch, S. M., Hastorf, A. H., Richardson, S. A., Muzzy, R. E., & Vreeland, R. S. (1965). The perceiver and the perceived: Their relative influence on the categories of interpersonal perception. *Journal of Personality and Social Psychology, 1,* 434-440.

Douglas, W. (1987). Affinity-testing in initial interactions. *Journal of Social and Personal Relationships, 4,* 3-15.

Douvan, E., & Adelson, J. (1966). *The adolescent experience.* New York: John Wiley.

Duck, S. W. (1973). *Personal relationships and personal constructs: A study of friendship formation.* New York: John Wiley.

Duck, S. W. (1980). Personal relationships research in the 1980s: Towards an understanding of complex human sociality. *Western Journal of Speech Communication, 44,* 114-119.

Duck, S. W. (1982). A topography of relationship disengagement and dissolution. In S. W. Duck (Ed.), *Personal relationships 4: Dissolving personal relationships* (pp. 1-30). New York: Academic Press.

Duck, S. W. (1985). Social and personal relationships. In M. L. Knapp & G. R. Miller (Eds.), *Handbook of interpersonal communication* (pp. 655-686). Beverly Hills, CA: Sage.

Duck, S. W. (1988). *Relating to others.* Belmont, CA: Dorsey Press.

Duck, S. W. (1990). Relationships as unfinished business: Out of the frying pan and into the 1990s. *Journal of Social and Personal Relationships, 7,* 5-28.

Duck, S. W. (1991, May). *New lamps for old: A new theory of relationships and a fresh look at some old research.* Paper presented at the Third Conference of the International Network on Personal Relationships, Normal/Bloomington, IL.

Duck, S. W. (1992). *Human relationships* (2nd ed.). Newbury Park, CA: Sage.

Duck, S. W. (in press). *Meaningful relationships: Metaphor and intimacy.* Newbury Park, CA: Sage.

Duck, S. W., & Condra, M. B. (1989). To be or not to be: Anticipation, persuasion and retrospection in personal relationships. In R. Neimeyer & G. Neimeyer (Eds.), *Review of personal construct theory* (pp. 187-202). Greenwich, CT: JAI.

Duck, S. W., & Craig, C. (1978). Personality similarity and the development of friendship: A longitudinal study. *British Journal of Social and Clinical Psychology, 17,* 237-242.

Duck, S. W., & Miell, D. E. (1986). Charting the development of personal relationships. In R. Gilmore & S. W. Duck (Eds.), *The emerging field of personal relationships* (pp. 133-141). Hillsdale, NJ: Lawrence Erlbaum.

Duck, S. W., & Montgomery, B. M. (1991). The interdependence among interaction substance, theory, and methods. In B. M. Montgomery & S. W. Duck (Eds.), *Studying interpersonal interaction* (pp. 3-15). New York: Guilford.

Duck, S. W., & Pond, K. (1989). Friends, Romans, countrymen, lend me your retrospections: Rhetoric and reality in personal relationships. In C. Hendrick (Ed.), *Close relationships* (pp. 17-38). Newbury Park, CA: Sage.

Duck, S. W., Pond, K., & Leatham, G. (1991, May). *Remembering as a context for being in relationships: Different perspectives on the same interaction.* Paper presented at the Third Conference of International Network on Personal Relationships, Normal/Bloomington, IL.

Duck, S. W., Pond. K., & Leatham, G. B. (1992, November). *Trick or trait? Loneliness and the recall of relational events.* Paper presented at the Annual Convention of the Speech Communication Association, Chicago, IL.

Duck, S. W., Rutt, D. J., Hurst, M. H., & Strejc, H. (1991). Some evident truths about conversations in everyday relationships: All communications are not created equal. *Human Communication Research, 18,* 228-267.

Duck, S. W., & Sants, H. K. A. (1983). On the origin of the specious: Are personal relationships really interpersonal states? *Journal of Social and Clinical Psychology, 1,* 27-41.

Dunn, J. (1992). Siblings and development. *Current Directions in Psychological Science, 1,* 6-9.

Eidelson, R. J., & Epstein, N. (1982). Cognition and relationship maladjustment: Development of a measure of dysfunctional relationship beliefs. *Journal of Consulting and Clinical Psychology, 50,* 715-720.

Eloy, S. V., Guerrero, L. K., Andersen, P. A., & Spitzberg, B. H. (1992, May). *Coping with the green-eyed monster: Relational satisfaction and communicative reactions to jealousy.* Paper presented at the Annual Meeting of the International Communication Association, Miami, FL.

Epstein, N., Pretzer, J. L., & Fleming, B. (1987). The role of cognitive appraisal in self-reports of marital communication. *Behavior Therapy, 18,* 51-69.

Erickson, M. F., Sroufe, L. A., & Egeland, B. (1985). The relationship between quality of attachment and behavior problems in preschool in a high-risk sample. In I. Bretherton & E. Waters (Eds.), *Growing points of attachment theory and research* (Monographs of the Society for Research in Child Development, 50[Serial No. 209]) (pp. 147-166). Chicago: University of Chicago Press.

Eysenck, H. J. (1967). *The biological basis of personality.* Springfield, IL: Charles C. Thomas.

Eysenck, H. J. (1982). *Personality, genetics and behavior.* New York: Praeger.

Falbo, T. (1977). Multidimensional scaling of power strategies. *Journal of Personality and Social Psychology, 35,* 537-547.

Falbo, T., & Peplau, L. A. (1980). Power strategies in intimate relationships. *Journal of Personality and Social Psychology, 38,* 618-628.

Fehr, B. (1986). *Prototype analysis of the concepts of love and commitment.* Unpublished doctoral dissertation, University of British Columbia, Vancouver.

Fehr, B. (1988a, May). *Dating partners' views of love: How important is similarity?* Paper presented at the Nags Head Conference on Interaction and Close Relationships, Nags Head, NC.

Fehr, B. (1988b). Prototype analysis of the concepts of love and commitment. *Journal of Personality and Social Psychology, 55,* 557-579.

Fehr, B., & Broughton, R. (1991). *Individual differences in views of love.* Unpublished manuscript, University of Winnipeg, Manitoba, Canada.

Fehr, B., & Russell, J. A. (1984). Concept of emotion viewed from a prototype perspective. *Journal of Experimental Psychology: General, 113,* 464-486.

Fehr, B., & Russell, J. A. (1991). Concept of love viewed from a prototype perspective. *Journal of Personality and Social Psychology, 60,* 425-438.

Festinger, L. (1954). A theory of social comparison processes. *Human Relations, 7,* 117-140.

Fincham, F. D. (1985). Attribution processes in distressed and nondistressed couples: 2. Responsibility for marital problems. *Journal of Abnormal Psychology, 94,* 183-190.

Fincham, F. D., & Bradbury, T. N. (1987). The impact of attributions in marriage: A longitudinal analysis. *Journal of Personality and Social Psychology, 53,* 510-517.

Fiske, S. T. (1982). Schema-triggered affect: Applications to social perception. In M. S. Clark & S. T. Fiske (Eds.), *Affect and cognition* (pp. 55-78). Hillsdale, NJ: Lawrence Erlbaum.

Fiske, S. T., & Taylor, S. E. (1991). *Social cognition* (2nd ed.). New York: McGraw-Hill.

Fitness, J., & Fletcher, G. J. O. (1990). Emotion labeling in close relationships. *New Zealand Journal of Psychology, 19,* 63-69.

Fitness, J., & Fletcher, G. J. O. (in press). Love, hate, anger, and jealousy in close relationships: A prototype and cognitive appraisal analysis. *Journal of Personality and Social Psychology.*

Fitness, J., & Strongman, K. (1991). Affect in close relationships. In G. J. O. Fletcher & F. D. Fincham (Eds.), *Cognition in close relationships* (pp. 175-202). Hillsdale, NJ: Lawrence Erlbaum.

Fitzpatrick, M. A. (1987). Marital interaction. In C. R. Berger & S. H. Chaffee (Eds.), *Handbook of communication science* (pp. 564-618). Newbury Park, CA: Sage.

Fletcher, G. J. O., & Fincham, F. D. (1991a). Attribution in close relationships. In G. J. O. Fletcher & F. D. Fincham (Eds.), *Cognition in close relationships* (pp. 7-35). Hillsdale, NJ: Lawrence Erlbaum.

Fletcher, G. J. O., & Fincham, F. D. (1991b). *Cognition in close relationships.* Hillsdale, NJ: Lawrence Erlbaum.

Fletcher, G. J. O., Fincham, F. D., Cramer, L., & Heron, N. (1987). The role of attributions in close relationships. *Journal of Personality and Social Psychology, 51,* 875-884.

Fletcher, G. J. O., & Fitness, J. (1990). Occurrent social cognition in close relationship interaction: The role of proximal and distal variables. *Journal of Personality and Social Psychology, 59,* 464-474.

Fletcher, G. J. O., Fitness, J., & Blampied, N. M. (1990). The link between attributions and happiness in close relationships: The roles of depression and explanatory style. *Journal of Social and Clinical Psychology, 9,* 243-255.

Fletcher, G. J. O., & Kininmonth, L. (1991). Interaction in close relationships and social cognition. In G. J. O. Fletcher & F. D. Fincham (Eds.), *Cognition in close relationships* (pp. 235-256). Hillsdale, NJ: Lawrence Erlbaum.

Fletcher, G. J. O., & Kininmonth, L. (in press). Measuring relationship beliefs: An individual differences scale. *Journal of Research in Personality.*

Fletcher, G. J. O., Rosanowski, J., & Fitness, J. (1992). *Automatic processing in intimate settings: The role of relationship beliefs.* Manuscript submitted for publication.

Frank, C., Anderson, O. N., & Rubenstein, D. (1980). Marital role ideas and perceptions of marital role behavior in distressed and nondistressed couples. *Journal of Marital and Family Therapy, 6,* 55-64.

Franzoi, S., Davis, M. H., & Young, R. D. (1985). The effects of private self-consciousness and perspective taking on satisfaction in close relationships. *Journal of Personality and Social Psychology, 48,* 1584-1594.

Gaelick, L., Bodenhausen, G. V., & Wyer, R. S. (1985). Emotional communication in close relationships. *Journal of Personality and Social Psychology, 49,* 1246-1265.

Galambos, J. A., Abelson, R. P., & Black, J. B. (1986). Goals and plans. In J. A. Galambos, R. P. Abelson, & J. B. Black (Eds.), *Knowledge structures* (pp. 101-102). Hillsdale, NJ: Lawrence Erlbaum.

Garrison, J. P., Sullivan, D. L., & Pate, L. E. (1976, December). *Interpersonal valance dimensions as discriminators of communication contexts: An empirical assessment of dyadic linkages.* Paper presented at the Speech Communication Association Convention, San Francisco, CA.

Genero, N. P., Miller, J. B., Surrey, J., & Baldwin, L. M. (1992). Measuring perceived mutuality in close relationships: Validation of the Mutual Psychological Development Questionnaire. *Journal of Family Psychology, 6,* 36-48.

Gerbner, G., Gross, L., Morgan, M., & Signorielli, N. (1980, April). *Media and the family: Images and impact.* Paper presented at the National Research Forum on Family Issues, White House Conference on Families, Washington, DC.

Gergen, K. J., & Gergen, M. M. (1983). Narratives of the self. In T. R. Sarbin & K. E. Scheibe (Eds.), *Studies in social identity* (pp. 254-272). New York: Praeger.

Gergen, K. J., & Gergen, M. M. (1984). The social construction of narrative accounts. In K. Gergen & M. Gergen (Eds.), *Historical social psychology* (pp. 173-189). Hillsdale, NJ: Lawrence Erlbaum.

Gergen, K. J., & Gergen, M. M. (1987). Narratives of relationship. In R. Burnett, P. McGhee, & D. D. Clarke (Eds.), *Accounting for relationships* (pp. 269-315). New York: Methuen.

Gibran, K. (1923). *The prophet.* New York: Knopf.

Gilbert, S. J. (1976). Self disclosure, intimacy and communication in families. *Family Coordinator, 25,* 221-231.

Gilligan, C. (1982). *In a different voice: Psychological theory and women's development.* Cambridge, MA: Harvard University Press.

Ginsburg, G. P. (1988). Rules, scripts and prototypes in personal relationships. In S. W. Duck (Ed.), *Handbook of personal relationships* (pp. 23-40). New York: John Wiley.

Glass, J., Bengtson, V. L., & Dunham, C. C. (1986). Attitude similarity in three-generation families: Socialization, status inheritance, or reciprocal influence? *American Sociological Review, 51,* 685-698.

Glucksberg, S. (1991). Beyond literal meanings: The psychology of allusion. *Psychological Science, 2,* 146-152.

Goffman, J. (1959). *The presentation of self in everyday life.* Garden City, NY: Doubleday.

Goodwin, C. (1981). *Conversational organization: Interaction between speakers and hearers.* New York: Academic Press.

Gottman, J. M. (1979). *Marital interaction: Experimental investigations.* New York: Academic Press.

Gottman, J. M., & Krokoff, L. J. (1989). Marital interaction and satisfaction: A longitudinal view. *Journal of Consulting and Clinical Psychology, 57*, 47-52.

Green, G. M. (1989). *Pragmatics and natural language understanding.* Hillsdale, NJ: Lawrence Erlbaum.

Greene, J. O. (1984). A cognitive approach to human communication: An action assembly theory. *Communication Monographs, 51,* 289-306.

Greene, J. O. (1990). Tactical social action: Towards some strategies for theory. In M. J. Cody & M. L. McLaughlin (Eds.), *The psychology of tactical communication* (pp. 31-47). Clevedon: Multilingual Matters.

Grice, H. P. (1975). Logic and conversation. In P. Cole & J. L. Morgan (Eds.), *Syntax and semantics: Vol. 3. Speech acts* (pp. 41-58). New York: Seminar.

Grigg, F., Fletcher, G. J. O., & Fitness, J. (1989). Spontaneous attributions in happy and unhappy dating relationships. *Journal of Social and Personal Relationships, 6,* 61-68.

Gudykunst, W. B., & Kim, Y. Y. (1984). *Communicating with strangers: An approach to intercultural communication.* New York: Random House.

Guerrero, L. K., & Andersen, P. A. (1991). The waxing and waning of relational intimacy: Touch as a function of relational stage, gender and touch avoidance. *Journal of Social and Personal Relationships, 8,* 147-165.

Gumperz, J. J., & Tannen, D. (1979). Individual and social differences in language use. In J. Fillmore, D. Kempler, & S. Y. Wang (Eds.), *Individual differences in language ability and language behavior* (pp. 306-326). New York: Academic Press.

Gurwitsch, A. (1974). *Phenomenology and the theory of science.* Evanston, IL: Northwestern University Press.

Hammond, K. J. (1989). *Case-based planning: Viewing planning as a memory task.* New York: Academic Press.

Hample, D. (1984, November). *Argumentation and the unconscious.* Paper presented at the Annual Meeting of the Speech Communication Association, Chicago, IL.

Harvey, J. H., Agostinelli, G., & Weber, A. L. (1989). Account-making and the formation of expectations about close relationships. In C. Hendrick (Ed.), *Review of personality and social psychology: Vol. 10. Close relationships* (pp. 39-62). Newbury Park, CA: Sage.

Harvey, J. H., Weber, A. L., & Orbuch, T. L. (1990). *Interpersonal accounts: A social psychological perspective.* Oxford, UK: Basil Blackwell.

Hastie, R., & Park, B. (1986). The relationship between memory and judgment depends on whether the judgment task is memory-based or on-line. *Psychological Review, 93,* 258-268.

Hastie, R., & Pennington, N. (1989). Notes on the distinction between memory-based versus on-line judgments. In J. N. Bessili (Ed.), *On-line cognition in person perception* (pp. 1-17). Hillsdale, NJ: Lawrence Erlbaum.

Hatfield, E. (1982). Passionate love, companionate love, and intimacy. In M. Fisher & G. Stricker (Eds.), *Intimacy* (pp. 267-292). New York: Plenum.

Hatfield, E., & Walster, G. W. (1978). *A new look at love.* Lanham, MD: University Press of America.

Hays, R. B. (1985). A longitudinal study of friendship development. *Journal of Personality and Social Psychology, 48,* 909-924.

Hays, R. B. (1988). Friendship. In S. W. Duck (Ed.), *Handbook of personal relationships* (pp. 391-408). New York: John Wiley.

Hazan, C., & Shaver, P. R. (1987). Romantic love conceptualised as an attachment process. *Journal of Personality and Social Psychology, 52,* 511-524.

Heider, F. (1958). *The psychology of interpersonal relations.* New York: John Wiley.

Hendrick, C. (1988). Roles and gender in relationships. In S. W. Duck (Ed.), with D. F. Hay, S. E. Hobfoll, W. Ickes, & B. Montgomery, *Handbook of personal relationships* (pp. 429-447). New York: John Wiley.

Hendrick, C., & Hendrick, S. S. (1986). A theory and a method of love. *Journal of Personality and Social Psychology, 50,* 392-402.

Hendrick, C., & Hendrick, S. S. (1988). Lovers wear rose colored glasses. *Journal of Social and Personal Relationships, 5,* 161-183.

Hetherington, M., Stanley-Hagan, M., & Anderson, E. R. (1989). Marital transitions: A child's perspective. *American Psychologist, 44,* 303-312.

Hewes, D. E. (1986). A socio-egocentric model of group decision-making. In R. Y. Hirokawa & M. S. Poole (Eds.), *Communication and group decision-making* (pp. 265-291). Beverly Hills, CA: Sage.

Hewes, D. E., Graham, M. L., Doelger, J., & Pavitt, C. (1985). "Second guessing": Message interpretation in social networks. *Human Communication Research, 11,* 299-334.

Hewes, D. E., & Planalp, S. (1982). There is nothing as useful as a good theory . . . The influence of social knowledge on interpersonal communication. In M. E. Roloff & C. R. Berger (Eds.), *Social cognition and communication* (pp. 107-150). Beverly Hills, CA: Sage.

Hewes, D. E., & Planalp, S. (1987). The individual's place in communication science. In C. R. Berger & S. H. Chaffee (Eds.), *Handbook of communication science* (pp. 146-183). Newbury Park, CA: Sage.

Hill, C. T., Rubin, C., & Peplau, L. A. (1976). Breakups before marriage: The end of 103 affairs. *Journal of Social Issues, 32,* 147-168.

Hinde, R. A. (1979). *Towards understanding relationships.* New York: Academic Press.

Hjelmquist, E. (in press). Planning and execution of discourse in conversation. *Communication and Cognition.*

Hjelmquist, E., & Gidlund, A. (1984). Planned ideas versus expressed ideas in conversation. *Journal of Pragmatics, 8,* 329-344.

Hobbs, J. R., & Evans, D. A. (1980). Conversation as planned behavior. *Cognitive Science, 4,* 349-377.

Holmes, J. G., & Rempel, J. K. (1989). Trust in close relationships. In C. Hendrick (Ed.), *Close relationships* (pp. 187-220). Newbury Park, CA: Sage.

Holtzworth-Munroe, A., & Jacobson, N. S. (1985). Causal attributions of married couples: When do they search for causes? What do they conclude when they do? *Journal of Personality and Social Psychology, 48,* 1398-1412.

Honeycutt, J. M. (1989). A functional analysis of imagined interaction activity in everyday life. In J. E. Shorr, P. Robin, J. A. Connelia, & M. Wolpin (Eds.), *Imagery: Current perspectives* (pp. 13-25). New York: Plenum.

Honeycutt, J. M. (1991a). Imagined interactions, imagery and mindfulness/mindlessness. In R. Kunzendorf (Ed.), *Mental imagery* (pp. 121-128). New York: Plenum.

Honeycutt, J. M. (1991b). The role of nonverbal behaviors in modifying expectancies during initial encounters. *Southern Communication Journal, 56,* 161-177.

Honeycutt, J. M., & Cantrill, J. G. (1991). Using expectations of relational actions to predict number of intimate relationships: Don Juan and Romeo unmasked. *Communication Reports, 4,* 14-21.

Honeycutt, J. M., Cantrill, J. G., & Allen, T. (1992). Memory structures for relational decay: A cognitive test of the sequencing of actions and stages. *Human Communication Research, 18,* 528-562.

Honeycutt, J. M., Cantrill, J. G., & Greene, R. W. (1989). Memory structures for relational escalation: A cognitive test of the sequencing of relational actions and stages. *Human Communication Research, 16,* 62-90.

Honeycutt, J. M., Zagacki, K. S., & Edwards, R. (1989). Intrapersonal communication and imagined interactions. In C. Roberts & K. Watson (Eds.), *Readings in intrapersonal communication* (pp. 167-184). Scottsdale, AZ: Gorsuch Scarisbrick.

Hopper, R., Knapp, M. L., & Scott, L. (1981). Couples' personal idioms: Exploring intimate talk. *Journal of Communication, 31,* 23-33.

Howard, G. S. (1991). Culture tales: A narrative approach to thinking, cross-cultural psychology and psychotherapy. *American Psychologist, 46,* 187-197.

Huston, T. L. (1974). *Foundations of interpersonal attraction.* New York: Academic Press.

Huston, T. L. (1983). Power. In H. H. Kelley, E. Berscheid, A. Christensen, J. Harvey, T. L. Huston, G. Levinger, D. McClintock, L. A. Peplau, & D. Peterson (Eds.), *Close relationships* (pp. 169-219). San Francisco: Freeman.

Huston, T. L., Surra, C. A., Fitzgerald, N. M., & Cate, R. M. (1981). From courtship to marriage: Mate selection as an interpersonal process. In S. W. Duck & R. Gilmour (Eds.), *Personal relationships 2: Developing personal relationships* (pp. 53-88). New York: Academic Press.

Ickes, W., Robertson, E., Took, W., & Teng, G. (1986). Naturalistic social cognition: Methodology, assessment and validation. *Journal of Personality and Social Psychology, 51,* 66-82.

Jones, E. E. (1964). *Ingratiation: A social psychological analysis.* New York: Meredith.

Jones, E. E., & Davis, K. E. (1965). From acts to dispositions: The attribution process in person perception. In L. Berkowitz (Ed.), *Advances in experimental social psychology* (pp. 219-266). New York: Academic Press.

Jones, E. E., & Nisbett, R. E. (1971). The actor and the observer: Divergent perceptions on the causes of behavior. In E. E. Jones et al. (Eds.), *Attribution: Perceiving the causes of behavior* (pp. 79-94). Morristown, NJ: General Learning.

Jones, E. E., & Wortman, C. (1971). *Ingratiation: An attributional approach.* Morristown, NJ: General Learning.

Jordan, J. V., & Surrey, J. L. (1986). The self-in-relation: Empathy in the mother-daughter relationship. In T. Bernay & D. W. Cantor (Eds.), *The psychology of today's woman: New psychoanalytic visions* (pp. 81-104). Cambridge, MA: Harvard University Press.

Kahn, R. L., & Antonucci, T. C. (1984). *Supports of the elderly: Family/friends/professionals.* (Final report to the National Institute on Aging). Washington, DC: Government Printing Office.

Kalin, R., & Lloyd, C. A. (1985). Sex role identity, sex role ideology and marital adjustment. Special issue: Feminist psychology: Single life and married life and women's sexuality. *International Journal of Women's Studies, 8,* 32-39.

Kellermann, K. A., & Berger, C. R. (1984). Affect and the acquisition of social information: Sit back, relax, and tell me about yourself. In R. N. Bostrom (Ed.), *Communication yearbook 8* (pp. 412-445). Beverly Hills, CA: Sage.

Kellermann, K., Broetzmann, S., Lim, T. S., & Kitao, K. (1989). The conversation MOP: Scenes in the stream of discourse. *Discourse Processes, 12,* 27-61.

Kelley, H. H. (1967). Attribution theory in social psychology. In D. Levine (Ed.), *Nebraska Symposium on Motivation* (Vol. 15, pp. 192-238). Lincoln: University of Nebraska Press.

Kelley, H. H. (1979). *Personal relationships: Their structures and processes.* Hillsdale, NJ: Lawrence Erlbaum.

Kelley, H. H. (1983). Love and commitment. In H. H. Kelley, E. Berscheid, A. Christensen, J. H. Harvey, T. L. Huston, G. Levinger, E. McClintock, L. A. Peplau, & D. R. Peterson (Eds.), *Close relationships* (pp. 265-314). San Francisco: Freeman.

Kelley, H. H., Berscheid, E., Christensen, A., Harvey, J. H., Huston, T. L., Levinger, G., McClintock, E., Peplau, L. A., & Peterson, D. R. (1983). Analyzing close relationships. In H. H. Kelley, E. Berscheid, A. Christensen, J. H. Harvey, T. L. Huston, G. Levinger, E. McClintock, L. A. Peplau, & D. R. Peterson (Eds.), *Close relationships* (pp. 20-67). San Francisco: Freeman.

Kelly, G. A. (1955). *The psychology of personal constructs.* New York: Norton.

Kelly, G. A. (1969). Ontological acceleration. In B. Maher (Ed.), *Clinical psychology and personality: The collected papers of George Kelly* (pp. 7-45). New York: John Wiley.

Kelvin, P. (1977). Predictability, power and vulnerability in interpersonal attraction. In S. W. Duck (Ed.), *Theory and practice in interpersonal attraction* (pp. 355-378). New York: Academic Press.

Kenny, D. A., & Acitelli, L. K. (1989). The role of the relationship in marital decision-making. In D. Brinberg & J. J. Jaccard (Eds.), *Dyadic decision making* (pp. 51-62). New York: Springer Verlag.

King, S. W., & Sereno, K. K. (1984). Conversational appropriateness as a conversational imperative. *Quarterly Journal of Speech, 70,* 264-273.

Kintsch, W., & vanDijk, T. A. (1978). Toward a model of text comprehension and production. *Psychological Review, 85,* 363-394.

Knapp, M. L. (1984). *Interpersonal communication and human relationships.* Boston: Allyn & Bacon.

Knapp, M. L., & Vangelisti, A. (1992). *Interpersonal communication and human relationships* (2nd ed.). Boston: Allyn & Bacon.

Kreitler, S., & Kreitler, H. (1987). Plans and planning: Their motivational and cognitive antecedents. In S. L. Friedman, E. K. Scholnick, & R. R. Cocking (Eds.), *Blueprints for thinking: The role of planning in cognitive development* (pp. 110-178). New York: Cambridge University Press.

Laing, R. D., Phillipson, H., & Lee, C. (1966). *Interpersonal perception.* New York: Harper & Row.

Lannaman, J. W. (1991). Interpersonal communication research as ideological practice. *Communication Theory, 1,* 179-203.

Lee, L. (1984). Sequences in separation: A framework for investigating endings of the personal (romantic) relationship. *Journal of Social and Personal Relationships, 1,* 49-73.

Lehman, D. R., Ellard, J. H., & Wortman, C. B. (1986). Social support for the bereaved: Recipients' and providers' perspectives on what is helpful. *Journal of Consulting and Clinical Psychology, 54,* 438-446.

Leone, C., & Ensley, E. (1985). Self-generated attitude change: Another look at the effects of thought and cognitive schemata. *Representative Research in Social Psychology, 15,* 2-9.

Levelt, W. J. M. (1989). *Speaking: From intention to articulation.* Cambridge: MIT Press.

Levinger, G. (1974). A three-level approach to attraction: Toward an understanding of pair relatedness. In T. L. Huston (Ed.), *Foundations of interpersonal attraction* (pp. 100-120). New York: Academic Press.

Levinger, G., & Breedlove, J. (1966). Interpersonal attraction and agreement: A study of marriage partners. *Journal of Personality and Social Psychology, 3,* 367-372.

Lewin, K. (1935). *A dynamic theory of personality.* New York: McGraw-Hill.

Lewis, R. A. (1973). A longitudinal test of a developmental framework for premarital dyadic formation. *Journal of Marriage and the Family, 35,* 16-25.

Lichtenstein, E. H., & Brewer, W. F. (1980). Memory for goal directed events. *Cognitive Psychology, 12,* 412-445.

Livingston, K. R. (1980). Love as a process of uncertainty reduction—cognitive theory. In K. S. Pope et al. (Eds.), *On love and loving* (pp. 133-151). San Francisco: Jossey-Bass.

Lloyd, S. A., & Cate, R. M. (1985). The developmental course of conflict in dissolution of premarital relationships. *Journal of Social and Personal Relationships, 2,* 179-194.

Locke, H. H., & Wallace, K. M. (1959). Short marital adjustment and prediction tests: Their reliability and validity. *Marriage and Family Living, 21,* 251-255.

Luby, V., & Aron, A. (1990, July). *A prototype structuring of love, like, and being in-love.* Paper presented at the Fifth International Conference on Personal Relationships, Oxford, UK.

Lustig, M. W., & Andersen, P. A. (1990, February). *The influence of individualism on interpersonal communication behavior and research: A synoptic view from the United States.* Paper presented at the Western Speech Communication Association Convention, Sacramento, CA.

Lustig, M. W., & Andersen, P. A. (1991). Generalizing about communication apprehension and avoidance: Multiple replications and meta-analyses. In J. W. Neuliep (Ed.), *Replication research in the social sciences* (pp. 297-328). Newbury Park, CA: Sage.

Mabe, F. A., & West, S. G. (1982). Validity of self-evaluation of ability: A review and meta-analysis. *Journal of Applied Psychology, 67,* 280-296.

Mandler, G. (1982). The structure of value: Accounting for taste. In M. S. Clark & S. T. Fiske (Eds.), *Affect and cognition* (pp. 3-36). Hillsdale, NJ: Lawrence Erlbaum.

Mandler, J. M., & Johnson, N. S. (1977). Remembrance of things parsed: Story structure and recall. *Cognitive Psychology, 9,* 111-151.

Markus, H. (1983). Self-knowledge: An expanded view. *Journal of Personality, 51,* 543-565.

Markus, H. R., & Cross, S. E. (1990). The interpersonal self. In L. Pervin (Ed.), *Handbook of personality theory and research* (pp. 576-608). New York: John Wiley.

Markus, H. R., & Kitayama, S. (1991). Culture and the self: Implications for cognition, emotion, and motivation. *Psychological Review, 98,* 224-253.

Markus, H. R., & Oyserman, D. (1989). Gender and thought: The role of the self concept. In M. Crawford & M. Hamilton (Eds.), *Gender and thought* (pp. 100-127). New York: Springer Verlag.

Marston, P. J., Hecht, M. L., & Robers, T. (1987). "True love ways": The subjective experience and communication of romantic love. *Journal of Social and Personal Relationships, 4,* 387-407.

Martin, P., Hagestad, G. O., & Diedrick, P. (1988). Family stories: Events (temporarily) remembered. *Journal of Marriage and the Family, 50,* 533-541.

Martin, R. W. (1991). Examining personal relationship thinking: The Relational Cognition Complexity Instrument. *Journal of Social and Personal Relationships, 8,* 467-480.

Martin, R. W. (1992). Relational cognition complexity and relational communication. *Communication Monographs, 59,* 150-163.

McAdams, D. (1992, July). *How the I and the me came to be: Attachment vs. intimacy.* Paper presented to the Sixth International Conference on Close Relationships, Orono, Maine.

McAdams, D. P. (1988). Personal needs and personal relationships. In S. W. Duck (Ed.), *Handbook of personal relationships* (pp. 7-22). New York: John Wiley.

McCall, G. J. (1988). The organizational life cycle of relationships. In S. W. Duck (Ed.), *Handbook of personal relationships* (pp. 467-484). New York: John Wiley.

McCroskey, J. C., & McCain, T. A. (1974). The measurement of interpersonal attraction. *Speech Monographs, 41,* 261-266.

McKoon, G., & Ratcliff, R. (1986). Inferences about predictable events. *Journal of Experimental Psychology: Learning, Memory, and Cognition, 12,* 82-91.

McLaughlin, M. L. (1984). *Conversation: How talk is organized.* Beverly Hills, CA: Sage.

McLaughlin, M. L., Cody, M. J., & Robey, C. S. (1980). Situational influences on the selection of strategies to resist compliance-gaining attempts. *Human Communication Research, 7,* 14-36.

McLeod, J. M., & Chaffee, S. H. (1972). The construction of social reality. In J. T. Tedeschi (Ed.), *The social influence processes* (pp. 50-99). Hawthorne, NY: Aldine.

Mead, G. H. (1934). *Mind, self, and society.* Chicago: University of Chicago Press.

Mehrabian, A. (1971). *Silent messages.* Belmont, CA: Wadsworth.

Mervis, C. B., & Rosch, E. (1981). Categorization of natural objects. *Annual Review of Psychology, 35,* 113-138.

Metts, S., Sprecher, S., & Cupach, W. R. (1991). Retrospective self-reports. In B. M. Montgomery & S. W. Duck (Eds.), *Studying interpersonal interaction* (pp. 162-178). New York: Guilford.

Miell, D. E. (1984). *Cognitive and communicative strategies in developing relationships: Converging and diverging social environments.* Unpublished doctoral dissertation, University of Lancaster, UK.

Miller, G. A., Galanter, E., & Pribram, K. H. (1960). *Plans and the structure of behavior.* New York: Holt, Rinehart & Winston.

Miller, G. R. (1987). Persuasion. In C. R. Berger & S. H. Chaffee (Eds.), *Handbook of communication science* (pp. 446-483). Newbury Park, CA: Sage.

Miller, G. R., Boster, F. J., Roloff, M. E., & Seibold, D. R. (1977). Compliance-gaining message strategies: A typology and some findings concerning the effects of situational differences. *Communication Monographs, 44,* 37-51.

Miller, G. R., Boster, F. J., Roloff, M. E., & Seibold, D. R. (1987). MBRS rekindled: Some thoughts on compliance gaining in interpersonal settings. In M. E. Roloff & G. R. Miller (Eds.), *Interpersonal processes: New directions in communication research* (pp. 89-116). Newbury Park, CA: Sage.

Miller, L., Berg, J. H., & Archer, R. L. (1983). Openers: Individuals who elicit intimate self-disclosure. *Journal of Personality and Social Psychology, 44,* 1234-1244.

Miller, L., & Read, S. J. (1991). On the coherence of mental models of persons and relationships: A knowledge structure approach. In G. J. O. Fletcher & F. Fincham (Eds.), *Cognition in close relationships* (pp. 69-99). Hillsdale, NJ: Lawrence Erlbaum.

Mills, J., & Clark, M. S. (1982). Communal and exchange relationships. In L. Wheeler (Ed.), *Review of personality and social psychology* (Vol. 3, pp. 121-144). Beverly Hills, CA: Sage.

Mills, R. S. L., & Grusec, J. E. (1988). Socialization from the perspective of the parent-child relationship. In S. W. Duck (Ed.), with D. F. Hay, S. E. Hobfoll, W. Ickes, & B. Montgomery, *Handbook of personal relationships* (pp. 177-191). New York: John Wiley.

Montgomery, B. M. (1984). Communication in intimate relationships: A research challenge. *Communication Quarterly, 32*(4), 318-325.

Montgomery, B. M. (1988). Quality communication in personal relationships. In S. W. Duck (Ed.), *Handbook of personal relationships* (pp. 343-359). New York: John Wiley.

Murstein, B. I. (1986). *Paths to marriage.* Beverly Hills, CA: Sage.

Murstein, B. I. (1987). A clarification and extension of the SVR theory of dyadic pairing. *Journal of Marriage and the Family, 49,* 929-933.

Murstein, B. I., & Williams, P. D. (1985). Assortative matching for sex-role and marriage adjustment. *Personality and Individual Differences, 6,* 195-201.

Neimeyer, G. J. (1984). Cognitive complexity and marital satisfaction. *Journal of Clinical and Social Psychology, 2,* 258-263.

Neimeyer, R. A., & Mitchell, K. A. (1988). Similarity and attraction: A longitudinal study. *Journal of Social and Personal Relationships, 5,* 131-148.

Newman, H. (1981). Communication within ongoing intimate relationships: An attributional perspective. *Personality and Social Psychology Bulletin, 7,* 59-70.

Nisbett, R., & Ross, L. (1980). *Human inference: Strategies and shortcomings of social judgment.* Englewood Cliffs, NJ: Prentice-Hall.

Noller, P. (1980). Misunderstandings in married communication: A study of couples' nonverbal communication. *Journal of Personality and Social Psychology, 39,* 1135-1148.

Noller, P., & Guthrie, D. (1992). Studying communication in marriage: An integration and critical evaluation. In W. H. Jones & D. Perlman (Eds.), *Advances in personal relationships* (Vol. 3, pp. 37-74). London: Jessica Kingsley.

Nye, F. I. (1982). The basic theory. In F. I. Nye (Ed.), *Family relationships: Rewards and costs* (pp. 13-31). Beverly Hills, CA: Sage.

Olson, D. H. (1977). Insiders' and outsiders' views of relationships: Research studies. In G. Levinger & H. Raush (Eds.), *Close relationships: Perspectives on the meaning of intimacy* (pp. 115-135). Amherst: University of Massachusetts Press.

Omanson, R. C. (1982). The relation between centrality and story category variation. *Journal of Verbal Learning and Verbal Behavior, 21*, 326-337.

Orbuch, T. L. (Ed.). (1992). *Relationship loss*. New York: Springer Verlag.

Owen, W. F. (1984). Interpretive themes in relational communication. *Quarterly Journal of Speech, 70*, 274-287.

Park, K. A., & Waters, E. (1988). Trait and relationships in developmental perspective. In S. W. Duck (Ed.), *Handbook of personal relationships* (pp. 161-176). New York: John Wiley.

Parks, M. R., & Adelman, M. B. (1983). Communication networks and the development of romantic relationships: An expansion of uncertainty reduction theory. *Human Communications Research, 10*, 55-79.

Pavitt, C. (1991). An analysis of artificial intelligence based models for describing communicative choice. *Communication Theory, 1*, 204-224.

Perlman, D. & Serbin, R. (1984, July). *A sports report: The effects of racquetball matches on loneliness*. Paper presented at the International Conference on Personal Relationships, Madison, WI.

Perlmutter, M. S., & Hatfield, E. (1980). Intimacy, intentional metacommunication and second order change. *American Journal of Family Therapy, 8*, 17-23.

Peterson, J. L., & Zill, N. (1986). Marital disruption, parent-child relationships and behavior problems in children. *Journal of Marriage and Family, 48*, 295-307.

Planalp, S. (1985). Relational schemata: A test of alternative forms of relational knowledge as guides to communication. *Human Communication Research, 12*, 3-29.

Planalp, S. (1987). Interplay between relational knowledge and events. In R. Burnett, P. McGhee, & D. Clarke (Eds.), *Accounting for relationships* (pp. 175-191). New York: Methuen.

Planalp, S., & Honeycutt, J. M. (1985). Events that increase uncertainty in personal relationships. *Human Communication Research, 11*, 593-604.

Planalp, S., Rutherford, D. K., & Honeycutt, J. M. (1988). Events that increase uncertainty in personal relationships II: Replication and extension. *Human Communication Research, 14*, 516-547.

Planalp, S., & Surra, C. A. (in press). The role of account-making in the growth and deterioration of close relationships. In J. Harvey, T. Orbuch, & A. Weber (Eds.), *Attributions, accounts, and close relationships* (pp. 71-92). New York: Springer Verlag.

Polanyi, M. (1966). *The tacit dimension*. Garden City, NY: Doubleday.

Pryor, J. B., & Merluzzi, T. V. (1985). The role of expertise in processing social interaction scripts. *Journal of Experimental Social Psychology, 21*, 362-379.

Raush, H. L., Barry, W. A., Hertel, R. K., & Swain, M. A. (1974). *Communication, conflict, and marriage*. San Francisco: Jossey-Bass.

Rawlins, W. K. (1983). Negotiating close friendship: The dialectic of conjunctive freedoms. *Human Communication Research, 9*, 255-266.

Rawlins, W. K. (1989). A dialectical analysis of the tensions, functions and strategic challenges of communication in young adult friendships. In J. A. Anderson (Ed.), *Communication yearbook 12* (pp. 157-189). Newbury Park, CA: Sage.

Reddy, M. J. (1979). The conduit metaphor—A case of frame conflict in our language about language. In A. Ortony (Ed.), *Metaphor and thought* (pp. 284-324). New York: Cambridge University Press.

Reeves, B., & Lometti, G. E. (1979). The dimensional structure of children's perceptions of television characters: A replication. *Human Communication Research, 5,* 247-256.

Reis, H. T., & Shaver, P. (1988). Intimacy as an interpersonal process. In S. W. Duck (Ed.), *Handbook of personal relationships* (pp. 367-389). New York: John Wiley.

Riesbeck, C. K., & Schank, R. C. (1989). *Inside case-based reasoning.* Hillsdale, NJ: Lawrence Erlbaum.

Roberts, D. F., & Bacher, C. M. (1982). Mass communication effects. In D. C. Whitney & E. Wartella (Eds.), *Mass communication review yearbook* (Vol. 3, pp. 29-78). Beverly Hills, CA: Sage.

Rogers, C. (1972). *Becoming partners: Marriage and its alternatives.* New York: Dell.

Rogers, E. M., & Shoemaker, F. F. (1971). *Communication of innovations.* New York: Free Press.

Roloff, M. E. (1981). *Interpersonal communication: The social exchange approach.* Beverly Hills, CA: Sage.

Rosch, E. (1973). Natural categories. *Cognitive Psychology, 4,* 328-350.

Rosenthal, R., Hall, J. A., DiMatteo, M. R., Rogers, P. L., & Archer, D. (1979). *Sensitivity to nonverbal communication: The Pons Test.* Baltimore, MD: Johns Hopkins University Press.

Ross, H. S., Cheyne, J. A., & Lollis, S. P. (1988). Defining and studying reciprocity in young children. In S. W. Duck (Ed.), with D. F. Hay, S. E. Hobfoll, W. Ickes, & B. Montgomery, *Handbook of personal relationships* (pp. 143-159). New York: John Wiley.

Ross, L. (1977). The intuitive psychologist and his shortcomings: Distortions in the attribution process. In L. Berkowitz (Ed.), *Advances in experimental social psychology* (Vol. 10, pp. 173-220). New York: Academic Press.

Rotter, J. B. (1965). Generalized expectancies for internal versus external control of reinforcement. *Psychological Monographs, 80,* entire issue.

Rousar, E. E. III, & Aron, A. (1990, July). *Valuing, altruism, and the concept of love.* Paper presented at the Fifth International Conference on Personal Relationships, Oxford, UK.

Rule, B. G., & Bisanz, G. L. (1987). Goals and strategies of persuasion: A cognitive schema for understanding social events. In M. P. Zanna, J. M. Olson, & C. P. Herman (Eds.), *Social influence: The Ontario symposium* (Vol. 5, pp. 185-206). Hillsdale, NJ: Lawrence Erlbaum.

Rule, B. G., Bisanz, G. L., & Kohn, M. (1985). Anatomy of a persuasion schema: Targets, goals, and strategies. *Journal of Personality and Social Psychology, 48,* 1127-1140.

Sabatelli, R. M. (1988). Exploring relationship satisfaction: A social exchange perspective on the interdependence between theory, research, and practice. *Family Relations, 37,* 217-222.

Sacerdoti, E. D. (1977). *A structure for plans and behavior.* New York: Elsevier.

Schank, R. C. (1982). *Dynamic memory: A theory of reminding and learning in computers and people.* Cambridge, UK: Cambridge University Press.

Schank, R. C., & Abelson, R. P. (1977). *Scripts, plans, goals, and understanding.* Hillsdale, NJ: Lawrence Erlbaum.

Schenk-Hamlin, W. J., Wiseman, R. L., & Georgacarakos, G. N. (1982). A model of properties of compliance-gaining strategies. *Communication Quarterly, 30,* 92-99.

Schmidt, C. F. (1976). Understanding human action: Recognizing the plans and motives of other persons. In J. S. Carroll & J. W. Payne (Eds.), *Cognition and social behavior* (pp. 47-67). Hillsdale, NJ: Lawrence Erlbaum.

Schmidt, C. F., Sridharan, N. S., & Goodson, J. L. (1978). The plan recognition problem: An intersection of psychology and artificial intelligence. *Artificial Intelligence, 11,* 45-83.

Schutz, A. (1967). *The phenomenology of the social world.* Evanston, IL: Northwestern University Press.

Schutz, A., & Luckman, T. (1973). *The structures of the life-world.* Evanston, IL: Northwestern University Press.

Scott, C. K., Fuhrman, R. W., & Wyer, R. S. (1991). Information processing in close relationships. In G. J. O. Fletcher & F. D. Fincham (Eds.), *Cognition in close relationships* (pp. 37-67). Hillsdale, NJ: Lawrence Erlbaum.

Seifert, C. M., Robertson, S. P., & Black, J. B. (1985). Types of inferences generated during reading. *Journal of Memory and Language, 24,* 405-422.

Seligman, M. E. P. (1975). *Helplessness.* San Francisco: Freeman.

Shaver, P., Schwartz, J., Kirson, D., & O'Connor, C. (1987). Emotion knowledge: Further explorations of a prototype approach. *Journal of Personality and Social Psychology, 52,* 1061-1086.

Shaw, D. S., & Emery, R. E. (1987). Parental conflict and other correlates of the adjustment of school-age children whose parents have separated. *Journal of Abnormal Child Psychology, 15*(2), 269-281.

Shotter, J. (1984). *Social accountability and selfhood.* Oxford, UK: Basil Blackwell.

Shotter, J. (1987). The social construction of an "us": Problems of accountability and narratology. In R. Burnett, P. McGhee, & D. D. Clarke (Eds.), *Accounting for relationships* (pp. 225-247). New York: Methuen.

Sidner, C. L. (1985). Plan parsing for intended response recognition in discourse. *Computational Intelligence, 1,* 1-10.

Sillars, A. L. (1981). Attributions and interpersonal conflict resolution. In J. H. Harvey, W. Ickes, & R. F. Kidd (Eds.), *New directions in attribution research* (Vol. 3, pp. 279-305). Hillsdale, NJ: Lawrence Erlbaum.

Sillars, A. L. (1982). Attribution and communication: Are people "naive scientists" or just naive? In M. E. Roloff & C. R. Berger (Eds.), *Social cognition and communication* (pp. 73-106). Beverly Hills, CA: Sage.

Sillars, A. L. (1985). Interpersonal perception in relationships. In W. Ickes (Ed.), *Compatible and incompatible relationships* (pp. 277-305). New York: Springer Verlag.

Sillars, A. L., Burgraff, C. S., Yost, S., & Zietlow, P. H. (in press). Conversational themes and marital relationship definitions. *Human Communication Research.*

Sillars, A. L., Pike, G. R., Jones, T. S., & Murphy, M. A. (1984). Communication and understanding in marriage. *Human Communication Research, 10,* 317-350.

Sillars, A. L., & Scott, M. D. (1983). Interpersonal perception between intimates: An integrative review. *Human Communication Research, 10,* 153-176.

Smith, M. J. (1982). Cognitive schema theory and the perseverance and attenuation of unwanted empirical beliefs. *Communication Monographs, 49,* 115-126.

Smith, S. W. (1987, May). *Input processes in reception of nonverbal messages.* Paper presented at the Annual International Communication Association Conference, Montreal.

Snell, W. (1988, April). *The Relationship Awareness Scale: Measuring relationship consciousness, relationship-monitoring, and relationship anxiety..* Paper presented at the 34th Annual Meeting of the Southwestern Psychological Association, Tulsa, OK.

Solomon, R. C. (1988). *About love.* New York: Simon & Schuster.

Sorensen, G. A. (1979, May). *The effects of touch on interpersonal perceptions.* Paper presented at the Annual Meeting of the Eastern Communication Association, Philadelphia, PA.

Spanier, G. D. (1976). Measuring dyadic adjustment: New scales for assessing the quality of marriage and similar dyads. *Journal of Marriage and the Family, 38,* 15-28.

Spitzberg, B. H., & Cupach, W. R. (1984). *Interpersonal communication competence.* Beverly Hills, CA: Sage.

Spitzberg, B. H., & Cupach, W. R. (1989). *Handbook of communication competence.* Beverly Hills, CA: Sage.

Stacks, D. W., & Andersen, P. A. (1989). The modular mind: Implications for intrapersonal communication. *Southern Communication Journal, 54,* 273-293.

Stein, N. L., & Glenn, C. G. (1979). An analysis of story comprehension in elementary school children. In R. Freedle (Ed.), *New directions in discourse processing* (pp. 53-120). Norwood, NJ: Ablex.

Stephen, T. D. (1985). Fixed-sequence and circular-causal models of relationship development: Divergent views on the role of communication in intimacy. *Journal of Marriage and the Family, 47,* 955-963.

Stern, D. T. (1980). *A first relationship: Mother and infant.* Cambridge, MA: Harvard University Press.

Sternberg, R. J. (1986). A triangular theory of love. *Psychological Review, 93,* 119-135.

Sternberg, R. J. (1987). *The triangle of love: Intimacy, passion, commitment.* New York: Boston Books.

Suitor, J. J., & Pillemer, K. (in press). Status transitions and marital satisfaction: The case of adult children caring for elderly parents suffering from dementia. *Journal of Social and Personal Relationships.*

Surra, C. A. (1990). Mate selection and premarital relationships. *Journal of Marriage and the Family, 52,* 844-861.

Surra, C. A., & Bohman, T. (1991). The development of close relationships: A cognitive perspective. In G. J. O. Fletcher & F. D. Fincham (Eds.), *Cognition in close relationships* (pp. 281-306). Hillsdale, NJ: Lawrence Erlbaum.

Surra, C. A., & Ridley, C. (1991). Multiple perspectives on interaction: Participants, peers and observers. In B. M. Montgomery & S. W. Duck (Eds.), *Studying interpersonal interaction* (pp. 35-55). New York: Guilford.

Swerdlow, A., Bridenthal, R., Kelly, J., & Vine, P. (1981). *Household and kin.* New York: McGraw-Hill.

Taylor, D. A., & Altman, I. (1987). Communication in interpersonal relationships: Social penetration processes. In M. E. Roloff & G. R. Miller (Eds.), *Interpersonal processes: New directions in communication research* (pp. 257-277). Newbury Park, CA: Sage.

Tesser, A. (1978). Self-generated attitude change. In L. Berkowitz (Ed.), *Advances in experimental social psychology* (Vol. 11, pp. 289-338). New York: Academic Press.

Tesser, A., & Leone, C. (1977). Cognitive schemas and thought as determiners of attitude change. *Journal of Experimental Social Psychology, 13,* 340-356.

Thibaut, J. W., & Kelley, H. H. (1959). *The social psychology of groups.* New York: John Wiley.

Trabasso, T., & van den Broek, P. (1985). Causal thinking and the representation of narrative events. *Journal of Memory and Language, 24,* 612-630.

Tracy, K., Craig, R. T., Smith, M., & Spisak, F. (1984). The discourse of requests: Assessment of a compliance-gaining approach. *Human Communication Research, 10,* 513-538.

Trimble, B. (1976). *The Star Trek concordance.* New York: Ballantine.

Uleman, J. S., & Bargh, J. A. (Eds.). (1989). *Unintended thought.* New York: Guilford.

Vallacher, R. R., & Wegner, D. M. (1985). *A theory of action identification.* Hillsdale, NJ: Lawrence Erlbaum.

Vallacher, R. R., & Wegner, D. M. (1987). What do people think they're doing? Action identification and human behavior. *Psychological Review, 94,* 3-15.

Vallacher, R. R., Wegner, D. M., & Somoza, M. (1989). That's easy for you to say: Action identification and speech fluency. *Journal of Personality and Social Psychology, 56,* 199-208.

vanDijk, T. A., & Kintsch, W. (1983). *Strategies of discourse comprehension.* New York: Academic Press.

Van Lear, C. A. (1992). Testing a cyclical model of communicative openness in relationship development: Two longitudinal studies. *Communication Monographs, 58,* 337-361.

Veroff, J., Douvan, E., & Hatchett, S. (1985). *The early stages of marriage.* NIMH Grant Proposal, MH 41253-01.

Veroff, J., Douvan, E., & Kulka, K. (1981). *The inner American.* New York: Basic Books.

Veroff, J., Sutherland, L., Chadiha, L., & Ortega, R. (in press). Newlyweds tell their stories: A narrative about a method for assessing marital experiences. *Journal of Social and Personal Relationships.*

Waldron, V. R. (1990). Constrained rationality: Situational influences on information acquisition plans and tactics. *Communication Monographs, 57,* 184-201.

Watzlawick, P., Beavin, J., & Jackson, D. D. (1967). *Pragmatics of human communication: A study of interactional patterns, pathologies and paradoxes.* New York: Norton.

Wegner, D. M., & Giuliano, T. (1982). The forms of social awareness. In W. J. Ickes (Ed.), *Personality, roles, and social behavior* (pp. 165-198). New York: Springer Verlag.

Wegner, D. M., & Vallacher, R. R. (1977). *Implicit psychology: An introduction to social cognition.* New York: Oxford University Press.

Weiner, B. (1986). *An attributional theory of motivation and emotion.* New York: Springer Verlag.

Weiner, B. (1991). Metaphors in motivation and attribution. *American Psychologist, 46,* 921-930.

Weiner, B., Frieze, I., Kukla, A., Reed, L., Rest, S., & Rosenbaum, R. M. (1972). Perceiving the causes of success and failure. In E. E. Jones et al. (Eds.), *Attribution: Perceiving the causes of behavior.* Morristown, NJ: General Learning.

Wheeler, L., & Nezlek, J. (1977). Sex differences in social participation. *Journal of Personality and Social Psychology, 35,* 742-754.

Wheeless, L. R. (1978). A follow-up study of the relationships among trust, disclosure, and interpersonal solidarity. *Human Communication Research, 4,* 143-157.

Wheeless, L. R., Barraclough, R., & Stewart, R. (1983). Compliance-gaining and power in persuasion. In R. N. Bostrom (Ed.), *Communication yearbook 7* (pp. 105-145). Beverly Hills, CA: Sage.

White, J. M. (1985). Perceived similarity and understanding in married couples. *Journal of Social and Personal Relationships, 2,* 45-57.

White, K. M., Speisman, J. C., Jackson, D., Bartis, S., & Costos, D. (1986). Intimacy maturity and its correlates in young married couples. *Journal of Personality and Social Psychology, 50,* 152-162.

White, R. W. (1959). Motivation reconsidered: The concept of competence. *Psychological Review, 66,* 297-333.

Wiggins, J. S. (1979). A psychological taxonomy of trait-descriptive terms: The interpersonal domain. *Journal of Personality and Social Psychology, 37,* 395-412.

Wilensky, R. (1983). *Planning and understanding: A computational approach to human reasoning.* Reading, MA: Addison-Wesley.

Wilmot, W. W., & Baxter, L. A. (1983). Relationship definitions and episodic interaction. *Western Journal of Speech Communication, 47,* 205-217.

Wilmot, W. W., & Baxter, L. A. (1984, February). *Defining relationships: The interplay of cognitive schemata and communication.* Paper presented at the Annual Convention of the Western Speech Communication Association, Seattle, WA.

Wiseman, J. P. (1990, July). *The mechanics of "making up": Friendship as contrasted with marriage.* Paper presented at the 5th International Conference on Personal Relationships, Oxford, UK.

Wood, J. T. (1982). Communication and relational culture: Bases for the study of human relationships. *Communication Quarterly, 30,* 75-83.

Wyer, R. S., & Srull, T. K. (Eds.). (1984). *Handbook of social cognition* (Vols. 1-3). Hillsdale, NJ: Lawrence Erlbaum.

Zietlow, P. H. (1986). *An analysis of the communication behaviors, understanding, self-disclosure, sex roles, and marital satisfaction of elderly couples and couples in earlier life stages.* Unpublished doctoral dissertation, Ohio State University, Columbus.

Author Index

Subject Index

About the Contributors

Linda K. Acitelli is a Research Psychologist at the Institute for Social Research at the University of Michigan, Ann Arbor. She is the Principal Investigator of a 5-year research project funded by the National Institute of Mental Health. The goal of her project is to examine the effects of thinking and talking about relationships on married and unmarried partners.

Peter A. Andersen is a Professor of Speech Communication at San Diego State University and editor of the *Western Journal of Communication*. He has published more than 50 journal articles and 20 book chapters on a wide range of topics, including interpersonal communication, nonverbal communication, philosophy of science, neurophysiology, intercultural communication, persuasion, and political communication. His current interests are in the process of intimacy exchange, nonverbal behavior in close relationships, and excessive intimacy, jealousy, and ideology.

Charles R. Berger is a Professor in the Department of Rhetoric and Communication at the University of California, Davis. He is a former editor of *Human Communication Research* and, with Sandra Ball-Rokeach, is co-editor of *Communication Research*. He co-edited, with Steven H. Chaffee, *Handbook of Communication*

Science. He is a Fellow of the International Communication Association. He currently is researching plan alterations that individuals make in response to communication failure.

Marcia Dixson is a graduate student in Communication Research at the University of Iowa, Iowa City. She received her MA and BSE in English Education at Northeast Missouri State University, Kirksville, and taught in the Department of Language and Literature at Northeast Missouri State University. She is interested primarily in studying family communication, especially the role of everyday talk in the parent-child relationship.

Steve Duck is the founding editor of the *Journal of Social and Personal Relationship,* the editor of *Wiley Handbook of Personal Relationships,* and the editor or author of 25 other books on personal relationships. He also founded the International Network on Personal Relationships, the professional organization for the field, and two series of international conferences on relationships. He is presently the Daniel and Amy Starch Research Professor at the University of Iowa, Iowa City.

Beverley Fehr is an Associate Professor of Psychology at the University of Winnipeg, Manitoba. She has published several articles on lay conceptions of emotion, with an emphasis on the relationship-relevant emotions of love and anger. Her current research on lay conceptions of commitment is funded by the Social Sciences and Humanities Research Council of Canada. She is co-authoring a book on friendship with D. Perlman and serves as an associate editor for the *Journal of Social and Personal Relationships.*

Julie Fitness is a Lecturer in Social Psychology at Macquarie University, Sydney, Australia. She received her PhD at Canterbury University, Christchurch, New Zealand, in 1991. Her research interests include emotion and cognition in close relationships, and she currently is studying the links between cognitive appraisals and emotions in laboratory-based couple interactions.

Garth J. O. Fletcher received his PhD from the University of Waikato in 1981. He completed postdoctoral work at the University of California, Los Angeles, and was Assistant Professor at Illinois State University, Normal, until 1985. He returned to New Zealand and took a position in the Psychology Department at the University of Canterbury in Christchurch, where he now lives. His research interests have included work in social cognition and close relationships and have concentrated on the interface between these two areas from a social psychological perspective.

James M. Honeycutt is an Associate Professor of Speech Communication at Louisiana State University, Baton Rouge. He received his PhD from the University of Illinois in 1987 and since has published numerous articles on developmental models of communication, marital functioning, and information processing. He has developed a continuing research program involving social cognition, memory, and intrapersonal communication processes on "imagined interactions," internal dialogues we have with significant others that help frame our expectancies for behavior and interpret past actions.